Conscript Heroes

by
Peter Scott Janes

First published in 2004

PUBLISHED BY
PAUL MOULD PUBLISHERS

Copyright © Keith Janes 2004

ISBN 0 9528708 7 8

Printed in Great Britain by
CLE Print Limited

Dedication

Passeurs and *helpers* only feature in part of this story, but this publication is dedicated to them. They are the largely unknown, forgotten or ignored men and women of France and Belgium. They are represented here by the Bodlet, Françoise and MacLeod families who risked their lives and liberty daily to shelter and protect men like my father. Their only request was that they not be forgotten. The shameful truth is that despite the best efforts of organisations like ELMS and RAFES, many, like their bretheren in other occupied countries, too often have been.

Our motto should continue to be

"Nous ne vous oublions pas"

Because we owe them a debt that we can never repay

Editor's Note

On the 13 November 1939 Peter Scott Janes was a twenty-one year old grocers assistant working at the International Tea Stores in Esher, Surrey. His main interests up until that time had been girls, one in particular - Miss Gladys Doreen Cooper - with whom he recently fallen out. Of more immediate concern to him that day though was receipt of his Military Service Registration papers - Peter Janes was about to become a soldier.

There is no evidence that my father was ever a hero to anyone except possibly my mother and myself but I have called this story *Conscript Heroes* because that was the name of the book my father intended to write as a result of his experience in France but never completed. My father died unexpectedly on 3 March 1998 aged eighty-one.

On going through his things I found a diary that he had written during the latter part of the war covering his time in Italy. In it were mentioned other diaries that he had written during his time in France but which had been left behind there. I told my uncle Donald, Dad's youngest brother about it and he casually told me that Dad had always kept a diary, but after seeing the warning *'You who read this book have no right to'* had never read any. He then said that Dad had come to his house about a year earlier and, Donald believed, taken his diaries away, probably to be destroyed. Donald died the following year and almost the first things I found at his home were my father's diaries, safely tucked away in a leather case in the bottom drawer of his old dresser. Not only was there a short résumé written in Gibraltar and starting with his last few days at Miranda but also a full resume of his time in France, with his subsequent escape through Spain and return home continued back in England. Then, amazingly, there were the three diaries actually written at the time, that had been left behind and subsequently posted back from Marseille in 1945, still in their original envelope. In addition to all

Editor's Note

that was his earlier diary written on foolscap pages and dating back to January 1934 which I have used the last few pages of in order to set the scene for subsequent events.

As well as the diaries I also found various supporting documents, including the letters he sent to his mother from Miranda together with her reply, and a collection of photographs taken in France in 1940 and 1941.

In editing I have combined the diaries and resumes to make a more coherent storyline - all the words are my father's and nothing has been added to the main text apart from the foot-notes and other obvious comments in square brackets. Further details that my father could not have known at the time may be found in the historic notes at the end.

Keith Janes

Somerset

April 2004

Acknowledgements

John Redfern (Major) sent me copies of Alec Thomson's diaries, together with situation maps of the areas concerned, and resumes of his and Alec Thomson's subsequent military careers. He also put me in touch with Tom Thomson.

Alex 'Alec' Thomson (Major) died on 4 June 2000. His son Tom also sent me copies of his father's diaries and the information from them has been used with his kind permission. Despite any impressions my father's diaries might give to the contrary, it was obvious to me that he remembered Alec with some affection. Of the few war stories my father told, most were amusingly apocryphal and many included Alec in some undignified position. Whilst he was recovering from his wounds Alec wrote several times to Vale Road, updating them with his efforts to discover my father's fate and Alec was one of the first people they contacted in September 1940 when the first news came from France that my dad was alive and well.

Arthur Fraser was a particular friend of my father's in France and so I was delighted to find him and his wife Hélène mentioned in a recently published book about the 51st Highland Division. Using contact numbers from John Redfern, I phoned several people in Scotland before finding George Burns who had had lunch with Arthur just two hours earlier. Having finally found Arthur, I introduced myself by saying I had a photograph of him in the snow with my dad and Hélène taken in 1941. He immediately said that he remembered Peter well and told me that the picture had been taken behind Hélène's house in the rue Wagner. I was invited to visit their home at any time and so was with them on the sixtieth anniversary of the surrender at St Valery. I am very grateful to both of them for being able to add notes from Arthur's own account and their joint memories of that terrible time.

Alfred Bodlet-Martin is the son of the family that first took my father into their home at 200 rue d'Alsace Lorraine. Now living in nearby Marles-les-Mines, he was the first person I found on my initial visit to France. He was able to show me the spot in Divion where my dad was rescued from the line of march, allowing me to return the next day on the exact sixtieth anniversary of that event. Having introduced me to all his friends and relations in the area he then drove me to Leforest to meet his surviving sister Solange.

Jean Paul Hermant is the Maire at Sains-les-Pernes and son-in-law of Bernadette. I also met Jean Paul on my first visit by simply knocking on the door of the Mairie. Having looked through my photograph collection he was able to tell me that sadly both Gilberte and Bernadette had passed away. However he drove me to meet two of Bernadette's sisters and one of Gilberte's. He also gave me Louisa's address at a nursing home in Bethune so I was able to visit her as well.

Unfortunately my knowledge of the French language was limited and as the only two people I met who spoke any English were the waiter at my hotel and Zenon Bartkowiak (died 2003) a Polish fighter pilot shot down in May 1944, I am afraid that many interesting details were missed. I later discovered that Zenon had listed Hélène Macleod amongst his helpers.

Subsequent visits to Jean Paul resulted in meeting another of Gilberte's sisters and more contact names and addresses including Marie-Hélène Gournay, daughter of Berthe and niece of Marcelle Cruppe, who wrote to me and with help from her aunt was able to add captions to the photographs taken at her family's farm at Locon.

Christopher Long and his web-site provided the first link in the chain that led to Sherri Ottis and "Safe Houses" and all the other contacts I subsequently made in my research of escape line details for this book. He has become a good friend with whom I regularly correspond and occasionally visit in France.

Sherri Ottis had recently completed a thesis on WWII escape and evasion lines. Having found her via the internet I offered her details of my dad's escape along what I then only suspected to be the 'Pat Line'. In exchange she gave me all kinds of leads and extra information as well as an extensive reading list. She also sent me relevant chapters of her book "Silent Heroes" in advance of publication for which I am particularly grateful. In September 2000 we met in person for the inaugural Freedom Trail crossing of the western Pyrenees to commemorate the Belgian *Réseau Comète* escape line.

Roger Stanton is secretary of the Escape Lines Memorial Society (ELMS) and it was through him that I was able to take part in the Freedom Trail crossings and make so many new friends and contacts amongst the escape line community, especially Al Day who put me in touch with Larry Robillard, and Squadron Leader Chris Goss who supplied details from the 222 Squadron and Northolt Combat Wing Diaries.

Helen Long wrote "Safe House are Dangerous" in 1985. It was the first book I read about escape lines and was an inspiration for my research as it suddenly gave perspective and authenticity to my father's diary - especially since my father's name appears in it. Helen also agreed to write the historic note on her uncle and aunt the Rodocanachis shortly before her death in July 2001.

Derek Richardson was completing research for his own book about "Detachment W" when I was first introduced to him by Sir Brooks Richards. His searching of the PRO files was much more extensive than my own at the time and he was able to provide detail for the some of the historic notes that I might never have have found.

In June 2001 I returned to France once again to see Alfred Bodlet and Jean Paul Hernant and to meet Marie-Hélène Gournay and her aunt as well as visiting the two St Valerys. I also took the opportunity to pay my respects to the memory of the Abbé Pierre Carpentier at Abbeville, see the demarcation line crossing-point near St Martin-le-Beau and to walk from Banyuls across the mountains in much the same way as my father's party had so many years earlier. Although I crossed in daylight without the threat of arrest I still experienced at first hand the difficulty of the journey and gained similar scars to legs and arms. A few days later I joined the annual four day "Chemin de la Liberte" Freedom Trail crossing of the central Pyrenees from St Girons to commemorate the Pat Line by following one of the toughest routes they ever used. Two years later I also walked across from Laroque-des-Alberes by what I now believe to have been the route my father's party actually used.

Diary

50 Vale Road, Claygate, Surrey

Monday 18th December Got my papers calling me up for a medical examination on the last day of the year, so they are going to give me Christmas after all, I shall not be sorry to go. Had our turkeys in on Saturday. Today one of Germany's new Pocket Battleships, the *Graf von Spee*, was blown up by her own commander in the harbour of Montevideo. The man, Captain Langsdorf shot himself through the right temple with a service revolver, which is an action that has led to very many explanations of it, all given by people with an axe to grind. As far as I can understand it he was ordered to scuttle her and did so, but one can understand how he felt her loss, especially as she was hailed as the best in the world. She had over a hundred of our men on board, prisoners from boats that she had sunk during her career as a commerce raider. A day later one of our submarines blew up another German cruiser and damaged another one by firing six torpedoes at them as they steamed past. Just a gentle reminder that two can play at that game. Bought a very big pineapple at Finches for Uncle Arthur for Xmas, cost me five bob.

Wednesday 20th December Did most of the rounds for the rest of the week and weighed off the turkeys that came in. The poultry was very easy to do as I had plenty of time to do it and also a very sharp knife of my own. Bought all sorts of crazy presents for various people, an underset and stockings for Babe [Doreen Cooper] chocolates for Flo [ex-girl friend Miss Ruby Lee of Beaconsfield Road, Malden] a pineapple for Arthur [Uncle Arthur Scott who lived in nearby Telegraph Lane] slippers for both Mum and Mrs Simmonds, two knives and a chopper for Donald [his younger brother then aged fourteen] gloves for Dad, toffees for Roland [his middle brother who was serving in the Royal Marines] and six bob's worth of post cards, including one that cost 1/6 for Kitten [Miss

Diary

Wynne Eggleton, the platonic love of his life who lived a few doors down in Vale Road]. Also bought myself a butcher's knife and a bottle of port. I managed to get a bit of mistletoe from Finches, it has been very hard to even see any this year, but the only one whom I managed to get under it was poor little Pet. She just said 'all right' and closed her eyes and I don't think I ever saw anyone look so pathetic. She is not a very good kisser unless she was not trying this time as she has very small lips and mouth, in fact she is very small altogether (as far as we can see). Never mind, she did show willing which is more than any of the others were. Went home with her, also bought a lot of whisky for me and Bob [Bob Foster was Kitten's boyfriend]. Poor old Bob is called up for medical examination at the same time as I am but he wants to go in the RASC.

Monday 15th January 1940 Received my calling up papers at last. No particular emotion or elation at all, just a job done at last. Dad and Mother did not seem pleased and on the whole other people are much more concerned about it than I am. Told the manager down the shop and learned that Bob had got his too. Had to finish the round in two days instead of five. The customers all said much the same 'Hope to see you again soon' and 'Look me up when you get back on leave'. Said goodbye to all and shook hands with more people than the King ever has in one day. What struck me most of all was the spontaneity of their adieus. Put all my stuff at home away as best I could and tried to arrange for the disposal of most of it in the event of my demise. Cleaned my guns and greased them down, also unloaded all except my .45 revolver. Went to bed rather excited.

Tuesday 16th February Last day of freedom. Finished my rounds, having to do Oxshott in the afternoon. Just as I finished it, it started to snow hard. Bought Pet, that is Miss Gilbert, a long woollen scarf for a farewell present, she protested that she could not take it but did so in the end. Went in to see Beige Bud [yet another alias for Babe

Diary

Cooper] and kissed her 'Goodbye', a very trying emotional moment for us both and promised to write to her. Also collected a bad debt for her firm up in Clarehill. Bought a bottle of port for the shop and had to buy ten glasses for them to drink it out of. We all drank it as soon as the shop was closed. And so home. Finished off everything including making my will. And so to bed again. The last time I shall sleep with the comforting thought of having a loaded gun within reach.

Wednesday 17th February Got up at the usual time and said goodbye at home, including Mr Potts [Leodride Knight alias 'Jeep' the family's pet bulldog]. Met Kitten just outside the gate and had the pleasure of walking down with her. She was nicer to me than I have ever known her before, not 'Goodbye Peter, I hope to see you again soon'. Ordered a rabbit from the Mac Fisheries for Mr Potts and caught the 8.29 train to Horsley. Got mixed up in the trains and so was nearly a hour late in getting to Horsham, Sussex. But I need not have worried at all, when we got there we only mucked about until gone four in the afternoon. Had our first Army dinner at Horsham in a firing range. Then they took us all by lorry and we did not know where we were going. At first we thought that we were going to Kingston but that went on past and we arrived at Richmond where we had a meal at the Barracks. Our sleeping quarters however turned out to be a large and draughty church, St Pauls of Raleigh Road, Richmond. We were given a mattress and three big blankets. We then spent a thoroughly uncomfortable night, especially as some mug woke up at intervals of an hour and called out 'Anybody want to buy a Bren gun' or a battleship or a submarine or some such silly thing. Another stunt is to wake up some poor chump and say 'Hey chum, do you want to piss', and so on.

Thursday 18th February Marched down to Barracks for each meal in very irregular fashion, so much so that many remarks were passed about 'Fred Karno's Army' and some wag remarked 'Thank God we have a Navy'. Also learned for the first time of the respect that the officers of the service hold for the Royal Marines. When showing us various drills they said 'Wait until you see the Marines do it, then you will see something'. We also had physical exercises by a most likeable bloke, namely a Sergeant Instructor. Also met our future Sergeant Major – Platoon Sergeant-Major Broad. Also learned that we were going to Chatham for our training and received many warnings about the type of place that Chatham is – namely full of prostitutes and venereal disease and other unpleasant things. The food at the Barracks is superlatively good and there seems to be no end to it. Slept better this time but still not perfectly. Handled for the first time the Short Lee Enfield Service rifle. A beautiful weapon, beautifully made but I do not approve of the way that it is handled according to regulations, all the slamming and banging of the bolt and so forth. Learned also that the magazine can hold ten rounds at a pinch and not as I supposed only five. Wrote home to Mother.

Friday 8th March I have now been in the Army for seven weeks and I believe that I am not deluding myself when I say that I have enjoyed every minute if it. The work has been mainly hard and mainly automatic but wholly interesting to anyone with intelligence. I have come to the conclusion that I shall make a good soldier and also have thrown overboard some queer ideas that I had before. I have had only one half pint of beer since I joined and have not felt the need for it. I have seen Doreen three times and still do not know where we stand in regards to each other. Although we have only fired 15 rounds I have come to the conclusion that I am not such a wonderful shot as I thought that I was although I am above average (as I ought to be). The Sergeant (Cassells) of our lot believes that I shall make a good killer with rifle and bayonet and I hope that he is right. That subject is still mixed with me, I do not know whether to pity the Germans or hate them, the realisation of what they have

Diary

done makes me intend to bayonet every one I meet through the
stomach and the realisation that the men I shall really bayonet have
probably never hurt a louse makes me wonder if I am not just being
silly. When I see the lads around me I wonder if victory is so certain
as we are led to believe, some of them will never make soldiers and
do not try. We have had the terrors of gas and chemical warfare
impressed upon us and they are bad enough in all conscience. We
have had our own planes sweep over us and have realised how
helpless an infantry regiment is to aircraft. We have yet to see our
weapons in action, the only one we have seen has been a Bren Gun
Carrier, a light armoured vehicle which moves at a terrific speed
across impossible country. We have seen the only anti-tank rifle in
the world, a weapon weighing 42lbs which fires a .550 bullet that
can penetrate through pretty near any armour that tanks can carry.
Then I have met Flo again after three years. I wrote to her from
Chattenden and when I got to Richmond I arranged to meet her. I
did this last Sunday on the 2nd of March and kissed her in the Bus
Station at Kingston. Then I found that she had left her young man on
the other side of the road while she came over to meet me. Can you
beat it? We went to tea afterwards, all through we were only
together for about an hour, then she went off to see the other boy's
mother at Twickenham. I have had a parcel from Mrs Brett of
Simmil Road, one of my customers and have gone three days
without a red cent in my pocket, a unique experience. I have bought
a chopper from Woolworth's and have had a fire for every night
whereas no one else has in the whole building. The building is Wick
House in Richmond Hill and is an old hotel. We have what I believe
to be the best room in the place with a wash basin, a wardrobe and a
cupboard as well as innumerable nails knocked into the wall by
well-meaning Pioneers who occupied the place before we did. The
food here is sumptuous compared with the other place that we were
at, that is Chattenden, and also we have plenty of it which is a

change at any rate. I have found myself the job of waiting at tables, it means getting your dinner last but it also means you get as much as you can eat. What we have been mainly occupied with however has been field training and route marches, we have not had much physical training this last fortnight. On Wednesday I saw Queen Elizabeth at the Star and Garter home for wounded men of the last war. I saw her twice, once from a distance of only about two feet. She is still a remarkably handsome woman of about medium height and dark. Her eyes are perhaps her best feature and her smile is charming but I noticed that her teeth were the colour of milk, a perfect dull white but no sparkle or glisten about them. She looked very tired and her wave was purely automatic.

Sunday 10th March We have been hearing for the last three days that we are going to have embarkation leave and going to France with the Regiment. We do not know how true it is but it seems to be pretty well certain. I came home this Sunday although I had no pass and had a lot of trouble getting back in at night. We have been told to wear our big green belts when we go out now and I think that they look very smart. On Saturday I was asked to play football for B team and I accepted because I was told 'Sergeant asked you because you never refused to try anything'. We had to play in canvas trousers and ammunition boots because we had no sports gear and worse than that we had to walk over two miles through the town before we played, the result being that we were, in the popular parlance 'sold out' when we got there. The transport beat us 6-3 which was not surprising. On the way back we passed a very brave or very foolish young man, I do not know which nomenclature he belongs to, a bloke with two sandwich boards entreating people to join the conscientious objectors society. And this in a town that is full of troops. Truly it has to be said that a true canvasser only canvasses where he can make the most trouble and meet the most antagonism.

Diary

Still as I said, he's got more guts than I have in one way at least, I should not have the courage to do it.

Monday 11th March 1940 Had our leave at last, after a Battalion Parade in which we were told that we were going to France and that the news was both secret and confidential and must only be imparted to close relatives. Less than six hours later a German announcer speaking from Bremen in English told the world about it. We did not have a lot of time about getting ready to get off but we had a lot of trouble packing away our kits and storing our rifles and getting passes and eventually we had to stay for tea. Got home about half past seven.

Tuesday 12th March Had a special shave and haircut and shampoo at Deniz's, that is Gashew's cousin and then went over to Esher after dinner and saw Doreen. She was not particularly enthusiastic about things as I have written her a very beautifully phrased and intensely bitter letter in reply to one of hers that hit me pretty hard. At last however she agreed to meet me on Wednesday. Went along and saw all the people at the shop especially the girls, Kitten especially for she is still the only perfect thing that I have never lost faith in, Pet who was a revelation in how a girl can change from an angel to a virago in a short time, Little Flowering Wilderness, that is Olive Catchpole, who is going to be married on Saturday to a soldier, Marjorie, who looks lovely and dances like a dream at night and has two chins and slouches by day, and a little cashier whom I do not know and do not want to. The boys and manager were very nice indeed and wasted a hell of a lot of time talking to me about things in general. Tidied up the warehouse and left amid good wishes. Did lot of writing at home [including a new Will where he left a third of his money plus his beloved little black pistol and ammunition to Babe Cooper, his bicycle to Donald and the rest to his parents].

Diary

Wednesday 13ᵗʰ March Had another special shave and went and met Babe and had a glorious time. We started off awkward and then started digging an allotment (literally I mean). Then we had tea and then the pictures and then – love, lots and lots and then some more. Of this I shall say no more except that it is all too rare an occasion in my young life.

Thursday 14ᵗʰ March Went down to the shop to see Mrs Picton and stayed there most of the morning talking to various people, mainly the females. In the afternoon went over to see Granny Scott and Uncle Arthur and stayed there quite late arguing about one thing and another, mainly about Arthur getting young Gale off as a conscientious objector. Not that I have anything against a conchie, personally I think that they are a very brave lot when they put up with what some of them do but I have very grave doubts as to whether young Gale would have thought of it had it not been for Arthur and I certainly do not believe that he would have had the wit to defend his own case without Arthur's moral (and oral) support. Still he has got off so that is all there is to it.

Saturday 16ᵗʰ March Miss Olive Catchpole married some soldier at the Weston Green Church. I was back in Barracks or I should have seen it so I wrote a most beautiful letter, quite a masterpiece in which not a word was wasted, quite the best that I have ever read or written.

Sunday 17ᵗʰ March We were all paraded at Ormand Lodge and told that we were to be split into the platoons that we should be in if we ever go to France, supposed to be in less than a fortnight. Then one of the officers, a Captain Thomson, of whom more shall be written later, asked if any of us would like to be his batman. There was no reply although I thought of volunteering. I was put in a platoon commanded by Orible Orace whose real name is Sergeant Piet, a queer little bloke with glasses so I immediately went up to Sergeant

Diary

Cassels and asked if I could change into his lot. He said 'Yes' but the CSM Weston wouldn't have any of it, so I had to stop. Just as we were going out a stentorian voice bellowed 'Janes – Private Janes' and Weston leads me up to Captain Thomson and he asks me 'Would you like to be my servant? Sometimes you will have more to do than the boys and sometimes not so much but it is not a bad job on the whole'. So I, knowing that Cassels had got a word in for me, accepted. So begins a new chapter in my young life. (He sent two other batmen to help carry my stuff)

Thursday 21st March Had a day at the Officers Mess, they had a Regimental dinner, quite a slap up affair with the Mayor of Richmond and speeches and all. I did not get away before eleven and was very tired. One of the noticeable things about the dinner was the huge amounts of Hock that was drunk, over thirty bottles of it to fifty men. Drinking the Hun's damnation in his own damned booze I suppose.

Saturday 23rd March Had the big Parade that we have been waiting for for some time on Richmond Green. It was quite a posh affair, band and flags and bayonets and a huge crowd and press photographer and Mayor and Alderman, quite a do.

Thursday 28th March Was at home for some reason that I have forgotten but managed to see Kitten and waste about half an hour of her time. Her Jack has had to join up too. Pity that one of us is not left to go out with her. Mrs Gillingham knitted me a very nice Balaclava helmet, went over and thanked her for it. Have managed to pinch a lovely woollen blanket from a bloke named Major Palmer, trouble is how to move it.

Friday 29th March Surprised my officer by darning his socks for him, also labelled all of his kit ready to move. In the evening went on a night manoeuvre. I was the Captain's runner but didn't do any but we did cover some miles in the dark. I was lost completely at times but my officer managed to contact seven different patrols with only one of them seeing us, and that was led by the inimitable Cassels. Got back very tired.

Babe claims that she has really come back to me and wears her ring and is very loving to prove it. Don't know yet whether I am glad or sorry, which has been my trouble all along. Last Thursday we had a long route march, from Richmond nearly into Cobham and back, or very nearly twenty-three miles all told. I managed it all right and we passed Babe's shop and the International. I didn't see Babe but they did turn out most of the staff from the Inter. to wave. Cassels wanted me to come back and introduce him to Pet. Turned round and we had our dinner by the Orleans Arms, bread and margarine, tea and chicken and ham roll, rough fare but welcome. Was off on Saturday afternoon till Monday morning and had Babe over, also Roland and his girl Doris as he has lost his ship and is going to have special training for a landing party. He is not much struck on the idea. Managed to get Major Palmer's blanket home, also my woollen vests and a forage cap for Mum. Have a bad foot, the right one, aches badly and have blisters between the toes. Went to the MO on Monday, told me that I have Athletes Foot. Hope it soon gets well anyway.

Tuesday 2nd April Went again to the MO and got caught for a job in the kitchen, which happened to be washing up the plates and mugs for the whole Bloody Battalion, got fed up with them. Stayed at Wick House for Dinner.

*You who read this book have no right to, it was never written for
publication; in it are things that may shock you but which
nevertheless are an integral part of the story. Myself I have never
shyed at the truth, that is why I do not hesitate to write it.*

Peter Scott Janes

Gibraltar November 1941

Honi soit qui mal y pense

This first part of my diary can only be a remembered resume of what
I wrote out from day to day in my other books which, owing to
circumstances beyond my control, had to be left in Marseilles. I do
not intend to write much about the war, beyond only this: I came to
Le Havre on the 28th of April 1940 and passed four more or less
eventful weeks at Roalles just outside of town. There I learnt a
meagre smattering of French as well as a good deal about the Army.
Had my teeth seen to, five filled in the town, bought cartridges for
my automatic and got drunk more times than I should have done.
Babe wrote me many loving letters, all of which I kept and which
are now in France. From there we heard the news of the invasion of
the Low Countries and were afterwards mixed up in the bombing of
Abbeville when we lost a dispatch rider.

Afterwards we moved to Dieppe and stayed at Arques la Bataille in
a large chateau. There I saw the bombing of the two hospital ships
that formed such a big item of the news and fired my first shots at
the attacking planes. From there I also raided the bombed warehouse
of the docks with Lofty and little Redfern in order to get the rations
which we could neither draw nor buy. Then up to St Valery near
Aumale[1] when our battalion was shot to pieces by a Panzer Division.
I helped Captain Thomson rescue the wounded men, Sergeant Stone,

---

[1] St Valery-sur-Bresle is a tiny hamlet next to the village of Rothois mentioned in
Capt Thomson's report

Nethercat and another of the Royal Artillery, Fry and Heywood of our own battalion and one other man whose name I do not remember. Then the death of Richardson, the wounding or death of Captain Thomson and the awful retreat. My rescue by the Royal Engineers and subsequent reunion to the Surreys took only half an hour before our flight to St Valery en Caux.

During this journey through the fleeing French and Belgian armies Riley was accidentally shot by a burst from a Bren gun, one man went crazy and nearly shot both myself and the police sergeant. All of the cigarettes were then issued, each man getting about four hundred each and also a muster made of all available ammunition and weapons. Then we came to St Valery en Caux, even then being shelled to pieces by German long-range guns. This was on the morning of the 11th of June. We passed the day, I myself sleeping most of the morning, in fields about two miles from the town. Here I bought another automatic pistol and found some more of my regiment. Then we moved into a field where we found two French wireless vans with the sets in one swimming in the blood of its operators. One of the MPs here told me that he had helped to make the film "The Four Feathers". At midnight we moved into the town, a nightmare march that I shall never forget. The road for two miles was blocked with motor and horse-drawn vehicles as well as dozens of dead bodies of men and horses. The town was blazing in several places while shells of heavy calibre were still crashing into it. I have been told that these shells were fired from British ships out at sea but do not know how much truth there is in this. The harbour was a fantastic sight, littered with wrecked boats of every size, the whole scene lit by blazing warehouses with every few minutes a whistling scream as another enormous shell crashed into the stricken town. Then also several machine-guns started firing tracer bullets at short intervals and star shells went up to complete the fantastic scene. Into this we went: no-one had washed or shaved for several days, every one of us wearing steel helmets, several already wounded, with rifles and machine-guns at the ready. I had a Bren gun which I had already cocked, intending to fire from the hip if the chance came. We saw a long line of stretcher-bearers and first-aid men also a good few dead men of all nationalities. Then our little force, we were only twenty-eight in all, entered an already hit house and passed the night in utter misery being soaked through with drizzling rain.

In the morning of the 12th a sergeant came and took our names and numbers and when I asked him if we were going to have a real go in the morning to my surprise saw tears running down his face. Just before six o'clock we crept out of the house loaded with as much stuff as we could carry and went through a town the like of which I have never imagined in any dream. The place had been blown to hell, not one single house or building was complete. The roads were littered with debris feet deep in which were dead men and horses, guns and other equipment and the whole place stank with the horrible smell of powder smoke, blood and burnt wood. There were hundreds of small bombs of a peculiar type scattered everywhere. In the shadow of the house was a Hotchkiss machine-gun with hundreds of rounds and dozens of steel strips scattered around it while the bodies of eight men showed that this town at least was not sold out.

Another thing I saw was a dead man with a 12 bore shotgun in his hand. I was so weak from starvation and loaded with ammunition that another fellow who was carrying absolutely nothing helped carry my Bren gun. At last we got to an orchard and several of us started digging little holes as usual but the sergeant major told us 'never mind' which was the first intimation of what was coming. Then came the order 'unload your guns' and we all stared in amazement. Then the truth dawned on us, that we, like most of the Allied Armies, were surrendering.

Gibraltar 1941

THE BATTLE OF AUMALE - or -

'A' COMPANY 2/6 SURREYS v ROMMEL

On the doubling up of the Territorial Army in 1938 and 1939 the Chertsey detachment of the 6th Surreys was expanded to produce 'A' Company of the second line battalion the 2/6th.

The declaration of war on 3rd September 1939 found the Company already in position defending the Navy's fuel tanks, ammunition magazines and communications around Chatham. It spent the first six months of the war there. During this time it had no field or weapon training. In March 1940 the Battalion had been concentrated in Richmond and on 21st April it set sail for Le Havre with the other Battalions of the second line 12th Division. It was to unload cargoes in the Channel ports and carry out other line-of-communication duties. The mobilisation of the French Army had so reduced the dock labour force that they were unable to service the needs of the British Expeditionary Force, whilst the French Army was concentrated on the French-Germany frontier. Captain Alex Thomson, formerly of the Kingston detachment and Lt John Redfern, from the Richmond detachment had joined the Company in March 1940. 2nd Lt John Naylor, CSM Weston and the majority of NCO's and men were from the Chertsey detachment. All told there were three Officers, the CSM and 96 NCO's and men.

On arrival in France, the Battalion's CO Lt Col Burgess, had made strenuous efforts to get some of the Battalion freed from duties for military training. 'A' Company was the beneficiary of his efforts and spent a strenuous two weeks in the Foret de Montgeon, two miles to the north of Le Havre.

Alec Thomson's Diary

The Property of

PETER SCOTT JANES 6145479

If found, will the finder be good enough to return to

50 VALE ROAD CLAYGATE SURREY (ENG)

Stamps to cover postage in the back

Thanks Pal

RICHMOND

Saturday 20th April 1940 With the change from foolscap to a pocket book comes also a change in my so far uneventful life. Tomorrow morning we should sail for France but whether we do or not remains to be seen. We knew that we were going on Thursday but took very little notice as we have been going on and off for over a month. This time however half the lads have really gone and the cooks and stores and weapons have gone on before us. Also most of the lads have been issued with fifty rounds of rifle ammunition and are now feeling very proud of themselves. I wonder who will have the first accident?

I managed to get off for a few hours on Friday and went home, I had sent a telegram to Doreen in the morning and she came over, very hot and bothered about twenty past six. She has been very different lately to what she has been at other times and is altogether a very charming person. We went for a short walk after tea and met Kitten on the way up the road. Of course we had to stop and have a talk about nothing in particular, also swap a few subtle wisecracks. Wynne is letting herself go a trifle lately and I was not slow to tell her about it, it is one of the very few things that I could not forgive her for. She wanted a shampoo and a spot of powder on her face and she would have looked very different altogether. We went on up to Winny Hill and had a look round from the top. The view from there is lovely even on a somewhat dull evening and somehow Claygate looked very attractive. Babe at least was very sensible about it all, she did not have any silliness or tears. I have only once known her cry and then it was very dark and I did not let her know that I knew she was crying.

Came home and had supper and then said goodbye to everyone including Mr Potts and went over to Esher with Babe. I stayed so late that I missed the train and did not know when the next bus would come along. Had a bit of luck though for an ARP Warden stopped his Austin and gave me a lift, incidentally the first lift that anyone has ever given me without asking. Caught the 65 bus easily enough and got back to Richmond by about 12.00. Did not know what the first parade was in the morning so spent quite a long time putting my equipment together properly. Got in bed about 1.20.

Saturday 20th April Very busy and tiring day, also very tough on the nerves. Everyone seems to feel the tension of this bloody waiting, we do not know if we are really going or not. The food has got very bad indeed lately and is hardly eatable. On Friday I took Captain Thomson's car over to St Marks Hill, Surbiton and had quite a thrilling drive over. Actually I am not much of a driver and the car not much more of a car but we got along quite well this time. Came back by bus.

Sunday 21st April Got up at ten to five, which is somewhat of a record for me, had a very busy two hours getting the Captain's valise packed (I packed all of my own last night). There was so much of his kit and mine and the Company's that it was quite impossible to pack it all, but luckily we had a kit bag and I put most of the books and a typewriter into that. Had to be at Ormand Lodge at 7.00 and just did it. Made more history by telling the CSM that I had no 'slugs' meaning cartridges. I got them all right, fifty rounds in a bandoleer that I am wearing round my neck at the moment (I am writing this page in the train). Had a very hot and tiring march in full equipment and then had breakfast, bread and sausage and tea, sitting on my steel helmet. Then the Padre told two short prayers which I thought was superfluous and insincere and then amid cheers and smiles and 'Good-lucks' we went down to the station. We had a special train to ourselves and as we were only six to a compartment we were quite comfortable. We were allowed to take off all of our kit except the ammo belt, which incidentally is of very little practical use as it is only made of thin cloth on a tape.

The lads tried to sing *Auld Lang Syne* as we were steaming out of the station but somehow it did not come very well. The lads hung out of the windows as we went by the stations as many of them came from the places. One of the lads cheered us all up by saying that Old Moores Almanack foretold that a troopship would be sunk today. I do think he might have kept it to himself as most of them are only keeping cheerful by a real effort. What has made it worse is that last night we had only one blanket and most of us packed that in our packs to save time in the morning. I slept in Thomson's valise which was quite warm but did not sleep very well because of nerves which I did not think that I possessed. Also this morning I found that I had a pimple on my forehead which is the first since before Xmas. I wonder if I shall write about my next Christmas and also what will be the position between Babe and Myself. I hope that we shall be married.

2.30 We are now on the boat which I believe is named the Ulster Belle but am not sure as we have not been allowed on deck yet. When we first came on board we were as hot as hell in our equipment and going down below into a stifling cabin nearly killed me at least. The sweat was pouring off in streams. We were three in a small third class cabin and it was very difficult to walk or even to turn round. I proceeded to strip down, take off my thick vest and felt a lot cooler. We will have to wear our lifebelts and respirators as soon as we are out of harbour. We are now at Southampton which is a bit of a surprise as we did not expect to go across so much water as that. We have been told that we shall be over six hours on the boat. We have a basin and hot and cold water in our little cabin and I have just had a shave, a wash, done my nails and hair and taken off my boots. The other boys are following suit. Can hear the engines turning over steadily from here as we are below the water-line. The boat is a Dublin one and quite a big job. Going to try and have a sleep now. I have my little black automatic with me and for some reason that I cannot explain have kept it in my outside coat pocket all of the time.

9.00 We have been on the boat now for seven and a half hours but she has only gone about three miles and is now just off of the Isle of Wight. The water is like a mill pond and there are about six other troopships quite near to us; we are waiting for the destroyers to come and escort us over. It is a very queer feeling knowing that we are far below the surface of the water, a feeling of being closed in and not very nice, I believe the correct term is claustrophobia. When I came down from on deck I was wearing a life float and a cartridge bandoleer and they got tangled up. For one moment I lost control and tore at the strap of the bandoleer and had to fight down an impulse to run back on deck. It was only for a single moment but I suddenly realised what a feeling must have come over the men on boats when they are below for perhaps weeks. Have just been to a canteen and had a cup of very hot tea and a huge corned beef sandwich which is the first bully that I have had in the Army. We have only two bunks here and three chaps and no blankets so it is not going to be so good.

10.00 Have just been up on the top deck and had a look around. The night is very light and we can see about ten boats, big indistinct shapes in the dark like big friendly ghosts, no lights, and then miles away the two flashing lights of a ship's semaphore. Some of the lads were singing about an hour ago and it was very nice, particularly they sang 'Abide with Me' and 'God Save the King' as if they meant it. I can't sing at all today don't know why. We were all chased off the deck at 10.00. The moon is very lovely and throws a great silver path across the water, a path that has been much written about and talked of and which like so many other paths, leads to nowhere at all, just out to the wastes of water of the Channel and the Atlantic Ocean. Still it is nice to think that one could really step over the side and walk away, over a rainbow as it were to a land where wars and strife and poverty are not heard of. Such is the imagination of youth. And now Goodnight, turning in for my first night at sea.

8.00pm Monday Well at 12.00 last night we sailed, the motor's note rose higher and higher and I heard the swish of water along the side of the boat, water and it seems bubbles. The sound was un-nerving in the space that we were in, a feeling of helplessness swept over me for the ship's side seemed to be very thin. If anything did hit her, a mine or torpedo or a shell we should not have a chance, the passages are so narrow that we could not pass one another and we should never get on deck in time. At least, that is what I thought. We had no breakfast and I slept with another chap and had an uncomfortable night all round. Up at 4.30 and on deck in time to see the sun rise. It came up red and lovely and we could see the other five troopships zig-zagging about and the swift grey phantoms that were our torpedo escort. Also two autogiros circling round.[2] Just woke up Thomson and cleaned his buttons and up on deck again for breakfast at 6.00. It was a tin of Maconochies ration and was a queer breakfast but at least it was satisfying.

---

[2] Presumably these were Cierva C.30 aircraft being used for calibrating land based radar systems

We docked at Le Havre at ten to eight amid other grey ships and so we were in France for the first time in most of our lives. The putting on of equipment over our overcoats was a nightmare in that space. We marched about two miles and nearly died from the heat. The place was quite unimpressive, only the sloppily dressed French policemen with their revolvers were strange. Had another ration from a tin in a huge luggage room and then a six mile nightmare run in a lorry, twenty of us together. The traffic was chaotic, trains run down the centre of the street and carts and barrows wander about without rhythm or reason. At last we came to the open country and then our new camp. It is at a Chateau and the boys live in tents. We batmen are lucky in a way because we have a room to ourselves, just the three of us and we are all friends, Howard, Morris and me. Then we began the hardest day's work that I have ever had in the Army. Everything of Thomson's had to be carried up five flights of stairs and my own up six. Then we had to unpack it all and our own, which took us until gone seven. I hope to God that we stay here now. We had another tin of Maconochie for tea and had to wait for nearly an hour for it. The boys are getting very discontented and the quartermaster and one sergeant at least do not help things. The sergeant in question is named Kingsbury and I doubt if he will ever see England again. The bullet that kills him may be a .303 or it may even be a .32 but I bet a dollar that it is not a 7mm Mauser slug. The boys sleep ten to a tent which must be very bad as there is not room to move round at all and I really do not know what they will do with their kit. Had a YMCA tea car come round tonight and everyone seemed to have a cup of it. I hope that the food improves. We have to up at 6.00 tomorrow and I am dead beat now. I am writing this whilst waiting for Captain Thomson to come up to his room. We were all given 50 francs today, the residue of our last weeks pay.

Thursday 25ᵗʰ April Are just about settled down now. On Wednesday it rained like hell and the whole camp has been a quagmire ever since. There have been no parades for two days. On Tuesday we went for a route march and although we had no equipment and only carried our rifles we were sweating very badly, mainly heat but partly the steep hills and very rough roads that we had to go over. The French children ran alongside of us begging for *'Souvenir Tommy, cigarette Tommy'* and the lads got rid of most of their loose change that way. It gets a bit monotonous though after the hundredth time. Also the boys kept on *'Bon jour Monsieur, bon jour Madame'* to everyone they passed. One lad who knows a smattering of French called out to a baker something like *'Good morning baker, greetings to one of my own trade'* and the man answered *'Good day to you soldier, I also have been in your trade'*.

The number of cafes and wineshops is amazing, as is also the price of wine, five francs – about sixpence ha'penny – buys a pint and a half of quite good red or white wine and half of it makes one very drunk indeed. We are forbidden to buy spirits or whole bottles of wine to take away with us but we manage, or at least I do. I have managed quite a few things for my own and my mates' comfort lately, we have a five gallon drum of drinking water in our room and a mat and a beer crate to sleep on, also two big drawers to put stuff in and a lot of nails which I had to drive in with a rifle butt to hang stuff on. Also I have an extra blanket to sleep on and have a big cup of tea every morning and share it with the boys. The water position here is terrible, there are no taps in the house at all, no bath, no wash basins and the water from the pump is so filthy that it is useless to contemplate doing anything with it. The smell alone is discernible a yard away. Fortunately the MO has condemned it and no-one may use it now, but he was a bit late as several of the lads have had very bad skin troubles that it may have caused. I say may because the food has been appalling right up to today.

We had an air raid the first night that we were here but just said 'Damn it' (or worse) and turned round and went back to sleep. We are at the top of a big hill which Sergeant Major Weston calls Heartbreak Hill and he is not far wrong. The village is about a mile and a half away and the town of Le Havre is about five miles. We are not allowed in Le Havre and about right too. We have been told that thirty-eight British soldiers have been murdered there since the war started, knifed or sandbagged and robbed. The worst place is the Red Light district which is down by the docks and of course the bloody fools must go down there. At home they would not dream of going out to find a prostitute but here that is the paramount thought in their minds. I shall make sure that my little black sweetheart goes with me if I get down there and there will be a cartridge in the breach too. I must get some more cartridges for it too which should not be too hard here.

Today I have been in the officers mess and have been working pretty hard but at the moment I am laying on top of the flat roof in the warm sun on a blanket. The weather today is lovely but yesterday it rained continuously all day. In the afternoon I put on my tin hat and took a chopper and made Captain Thomson a lovely fire. It was quite a feat with only green wet wood and a cigarette carton for paper but I did it all right and he was very pleased and sat in front of it and drunk himself silly on *vin rouge*. Went to bed about nine and slept like a log. I have just started to grow a moustache to see what I look like with it, after all, it does not take five minutes to shave it off. I have eaten so much today that I want to lay down and sleep it off but I'm afraid that it is out of the question as I have to go back to the mess at 6.00. We are forbidden to tell anyone who we are but if we take off our overcoats we have 'ESURREY' on our shoulders in bright brass but then I suppose that Nazi agents can't read English. So sure are they of that that below me they are putting up a big pole with the Regimental Flag on it. I have had the stopping come out of one of my front teeth and went down to Le Havre to have a Service dentist fix it for me. He is very busy however and I have to go back in a week's time. We are told that we are the only fighting unit anywhere near here so that we have to be prepared for parachute troops at any moment. We all have fifty rounds of ammo but not ten men in the company have ever fired one before.

Friday 26th April More rain but a busy day for us anyway, were all paraded and had to clean the Chateau up from top to bottom and some job it was too. Got paid 70 francs in the afternoon and felt rich again. Went out in the evening down to Le Havre to try and buy some cartridges for my automatic but could not find a shop that looked anything like possible so came back and nearly got canned at a café on red wine. Bought a bottle of brandy quite illegally for 15 francs and came home happy. Tried to light the Captain's fire but could not because of wet wood. Wrote to Flo, Kitten and Babe and got a letter from Little Lady, all in one day. Went to bed a bit dizzy in the head.

Saturday 27th April Had another day in the officers mess and another very busy day. It was not really my turn but I jumped at the chance because it means that for one day one is not responsible for anything at all. It has stopped raining today and was very hot in the afternoon. I am writing this sitting in the sun on the flat roof of the Chateau d'Epremesnil which seems to indicate that being a soldier on active service is rather fun. So it is but I hear that we are to start work seriously on Monday although at what I was not told. Opened my bottle of brandy and found it excellent but it really needs a drop of soda water in it. From where we are I can see about 30 balloons which form the balloon barrage that guards Le Havre's harbour. They are of exactly the same pattern as our own ones at home. One thing that is new to me in camp is the number of bugle calls that I have never heard before. I know 'Cookhouse' 'Reveille' 'Last Post'

'Lights Out' and 'Jankers'. Now they sound 'Orderly Officer' 'Orderly Sergeant' 'Orderly Corporal'. The last is in 'No Parade' and 'Officers Mess' as well as one or two peculiar ones.

I have been wondering all day just how many bottles of brandy I can take home with me and it has just occurred to me that the bloody stuff won't be of any use as none of us ever drink it. Perhaps it would be more to the point to get about a thousand cigarettes over but even then I do not smoke and why the hell should I risk getting put in the glasshouse for somebody else. I have had about three goes at reading Betty's letter but it is nearly impossible to read it owing to her very peculiar style of writing. She tells me that she is in love but that is not news, she always is anyway, she was with me once, or so she believed. I have started to grow a moustache and have made a very good show in five days. I have already heard funny remarks about it from half of the company. I bet I saw it off before I go home (I am still sticking to the pathetic belief that I shall go home one day even with a war on).

Sunday 28th April Only one Parade, that was Church Parade which we held in front of the Chateau. We had the Battalion Padre and he was really very good and spoke nothing but the truth. It made some of the officers wriggle I can tell you. The singing was very good except for one hymn which most of us had never heard of. Don't like the Army version of the 23rd Psalm, it's a bit cockeyed. It has stopped raining but the ground is still covered with mud and it is very hard to get round the camp. Tried hard to get a haircut but couldn't. My Captain and Mr Redfern can't go out as they are confined to barracks for being drunk and disorderly or something like that. The boys say that Piss-Hole Naylor the One Pip Man put them on a charge, it wouldn't surprise me at all, he's capable of worse than that. Didn't feel very good so went to bed for a couple of hours in the afternoon and so missed tea. Had a supper of biscuits and butter and brandy. Went to bed.

Monday 29th April Up early and packed up the captain's bed and a lot of stuff which he need not have carried. Went out on manoeuvres and had a pretty hard day. The food has improved a lot lately and we even had tea after dinner which is something new to me. Was very glad to have a ride round on the company truck with the captain. Finished about 6.00 and was darned glad of that too. Went out in the evening for a drink and smuggled Captain Thomson back six bottles of wine for which he was truly thankful. Must remember to ask him for some money, he owes me 130 francs which is quite a lot of money. Went to bed rather happy, partly due to the fact that I got a four page letter from Babe and partly to the *'vin rouge'*. These manoeuvres are all right but bloody tiring.

Tuesday 30th April A long march followed by more manoeuvres of which only the Company HQ with myself had any fun at all, we just had a kip. The dinner was a tin of corned beef and a slice of bread and it was quite enjoyable in the open. We had a little white dog follow us all the way and I believe that he is still in the camp at the moment. The country is ideal round here for such games as we play and we were all very tired when we got in at night. These shows would be better in direct proportion to the quality of the food we get. Made the captain a fire and wrote two letters. Had a parcel from Babe and got a haircut from LC Marriot.

Wednesday 1st May Did not go out but had an easy morning and wrote two more letters. Went to the dentist in an ambulance driven by a crazy driver, he did fifty everywhere and seventy in most places and I don't mean kilometres either. Had four teeth filled, a painful job but the dentist was very good indeed. Came out and went to a gunsmiths and bought fifty .32 automatic pistol cartridges far easier than buying a pound of nails in England. Could have bought a thousand just as easy. They cost me 50 francs. Over in England I would cheerfully have paid a pound for one box of cartridges but here it seems as easy as kiss your hand to buy both guns and the shells for them. Was as pleased as Punch and loaded the gun up in the NAAFI. Met a bloke named Alman whom I knew at Esher there, he is going on leave on Saturday. Found out the manager of the canteen's name and sent it on to Mum hoping that Donald [who was then working for the NAAFI at Ruxley Towers, Claygate] will be able to trace it and tell her where I am. Had a drop of brandy and so to bed.

Thursday 2nd May Back to work and quite a good day. Started rather late and did not move off until nearly 10.00. The Company HQ, which includes me, rode on the CHQ truck which was rather nice. Had the job of making a HQ in a wood and made rather a good job of it. The trouble was that we had to fill it all in before we came away. Got ganged up with a couple of twats who kept talking but did SFA in the way of work. I got stripped out and was working in just my trousers. Got talking and found that they had read much the same books as I have and got into a lovely argument about them. Had an easy afternoon and rode back on the truck. The driver took her along at a terrific speed and we got a real thrill riding on the back. It was very easy to realise how the Germans conquered Polish and Czech and Austrian towns by speedy motor transport and machine-guns on them. I honestly believe that with two MGs, one heavy, say a Vickers .5 and a Colt-Browning .303 and each man armed with an automatic and half a dozen bombs we could have decimated a town as big as Esher easily.

Lit a huge fire for the captain and drunk a bottle of red wine and got merry on it. Had a parcel from Dad with which I was more than pleased, had a shave and went to bed. We are going on a two day scheme tomorrow so have to be up early. Don't know quite what it is going to be like but it should be fun. Managed to pinch three .303 cartridges which may come in handy. Some of the boys keep saying that they wish they had just one live one for some person or another so perhaps they would be worth ten francs each. Went to bed early and had a good night.

Friday 3rd May Started early and had a hell of a lot of rush but when it was all over we hung about for hours in one place. Packed myself four blankets instead of two and four groundsheets to say nixes of a huge piece of sacking for a bivvy. Should be comfortable, although its not what they want. But a batman gets a hell of a lot of extra work here and should take things as they come. I can rough it with the rest if necessary but why should I if I can get out of it. Had a queer dream last night, I dreamt that I was spying and saw a group of Nazis insulting and assaulting a young woman who was very like Miss Catchpole. As I was alone I went back and fetched up the section and later armed with a submachine-gun and my automatic was told to get what information I could from them as they in turn were now prisoners. The officer in charge I shoved into a chair and said to him 'I don't want you to tell yet you bastard I'm going to see how you like your own medicine'. With that I swiped him across the bridge of the nose with the barrel of the pistol and as the blood ran out of his nose, smashed his teeth in with the butt. I do not know if I should really do it but I do know that the stories of the Nazi atrocities make me feel that I shall not take many prisoners. The unfortunate part is that the men that I shall meet will not be the people who were responsible for them, but perhaps as CHQ I shall meet a few SS men of importance. And they won't get much small change from me.

As I said we did not do much in the morning but I had to go and get some brandy for Captain Thomson and had about four of them myself. After a huge mug of very good French coffee I felt a different man. Was so very happy that a number of people remarked about it. My moustache is growing at an alarming rate and the Captain remarks about it four times a day. At the moment I am sitting on a dirty clay bank by an old water mill about a mile from the Chateau. We have been here for nearly two hours and do not know quite how long this joke is going to last. Shall be glad when dinner time comes and we get something to eat. My mate Morris is wandering about with a huge Verey Light Pistol hung from his respirator and looking like an ancient highwayman with a blunderbuss. The officers think that I am making notes on the scheme otherwise they would bloody soon find me some pissbowling job or another.

Saturday 4th May What a bloody day we did have yesterday after all. We did not get any dinner until after 4.00 and I at least was working bleeding hard all afternoon. I made bivouacs for all the Company HQ including a real beauty for the CSM and one of the ground sheets for the Captain. I also made a lovely one for four of us out of a huge piece of sacking and stakes and string. They told me right at the last moment that I was cook of the officers mess and had to produce some sort of a meal. Didn't do so bad with it either. Then when we were all dog tired and just going to turn in for the night a message came through that we were on night manoeuvres. Talk about swear, no-one was happy about it. We were told that there would be twenty-five francs paid for every prisoner taken so we went out to take them. The CSM carried a huge knobbly club of oak and the Captain had a machete weighing about six pounds. I have a rifle and bayonet and with no scabbard on the bayonet either. Also my automatic, which put the breeze up my mate who was with me. We challenged three lots of people in whispers but they were not the right ones. One bloke whom I put a bayonet into his throat and said 'Halt and give the password' answered 'Oh fuck off - I'm bleeding tired of this bleeding game of soldiers'. No one was contacted at all and as I had no food since four I sat down at the officer's mess table and started to tuck in. About 12.00 a bloke named Lieutenant Russell slunk in and gasped 'For Christ's sake, have you any food or drink, I'm bloody near all in' so we tucked in together and had bread and cheese and salmon and red wine and corned beef and cointreau (this is a strong oily liqueur which tastes like almonds and costs thirty bob for half a pint, which is enough for four drinks: can't drink much of it though as it very choking and strong). Then to bed with overcoat on and trousers and automatic slung on my lanyard and the only difference being that I took my boots off.

Did not sleep very well though but at least it kept dry and fine. Woke Captain Thomson up at 4.30 and found that none of the guards had been mounted at all but had slept through. Bloody good job too, nothing happened anyway. Got up at 6.30 myself and lit a fire to cook the officers' breakfast on. Upset the water into it and cooked on the Company Cooks fire. Still the fire gave me plenty of boiling water for washing shaving and washing up. Then a glorious breakfast for myself, bacon, tomatoes, fried bread, tea, as much as I could eat, beer, wine, and more cointreau. Then we sat about for a hell of a time and got cold again. I'm still sitting now on the illustrious Mr Russell's valise. He is the Signal Officer and this is the first time that I have seen signals in action. They lay wires everywhere and wag flags and use unintelligible jargon. One calls to another *'Hello, hello, this is Nuts Orange who are you: Beer Ack, no, I don't want you but Zip Emma has been trying to contact you: Goodbye – hello hello – ah is that Beer Nuts good, take this down. Let us have your monthly return of men wishing to change their religion by twenty oh oh hours'*. And they keep this up all night, talk about fun.[3] Still most of the signals are rather nice fellows which is

---

[3] Lt R H L Russell was to win a Military Cross for his part in the fighting of 11 June - Regimental History

more than can be said of the Intelligence men who are mainly bastards of the first water and who get very peeved when they find that the Commanders won't let them run the scheme their own way. These jobs are all right for the experience but the lads do an awful lot of damage to trees and things of necessity. I have spent most of my time slashing with a machete.

Sunday 5th May Well we got back after doing very little on Saturday, but had a lot to do when I got back cleaning up. Captain Thomson carries bloody nearly all he owns when he goes camping. Went to bed early and feel a lot better for it. Had a good church parade this morning and spent most of the rest of the day on the roof in the sun. I'm there now, have been writing letters and am just going down for some wine.

Monday 6th May Well I had my wine, two bottles of it and was very happy, so happy that I had to make some toast over a primus stove to get sober enough to sleep. And did I sleep, I'll say I did. Well, got left behind today and the lorry had to come back with me and pick up the rest of our kit. Made a really good dinner for the officers today, a huge lobster salad and Lord knows what else beside. Anyway its going to cost somebody 63 francs for it, including the wine. Had a glorious day myself and came back on the lorry. Went down to Le Havre to get my watch mended but could not find a shop open. Got merry again with two sergeant majors and blasted off four rounds of .32 ammo into the air. Had a bit of a clean up of my kit. Babe sent me another parcel, I wish she wouldn't, I'm darned sure that they cost more than she can afford.

Tuesday 7th May Turned them out another super dinner, soup, omelettes, new potatoes, asparagus, camembert, tea, french bread and wine also bananas and oranges among other details, also took them tea in the afternoon. This is war. Got five extra eggs and boiled two for myself and made two omelettes for my room mates on a primus stove that I have obtained (good word that). Went to bed happy after lighting them a huge fire in their room. Seem to be doing well lately with both NCOs and officers. Had a terrific ride back in our truck behind a driver who is quite mad, tearing round corners at about forty in the middle of the road and scraping obstacles then up winding lanes while the driver wound up his watch and filled his pipe and searched his haversack for oddments. Quite mad, I'm sure of it. But we enjoyed it. Boiled some water and had a good wash all over as we are getting a bit milo [sic]. One of the men has scabies and another impetigo, both no doubt from the food and lack of water. The men are not having an easy time, especially in the bad weather and most of them drink too much.

Wednesday 8th May Another easy day. Wrote three letters while waiting for my truck this morning. Had pork chops, new potatoes, fruit salad, soup, cream, camembert, brandy, red wine and french bread for the officers dinner. We had a most glorious stew of potatoes and onions and steak and kidney, it was really delicious. Bought myself a bottle of brandy, cost me 19.50 or about two and four pence in English money, would have cost 13/8 at home. Pity can't get any Schweppes ginger ale to drink it with. Hear that we shall be in a cottage in Bolbec when we get there, don't know quite what the batmen will do but I hope we have some more cooking to do, I rather like it. Also hope that I get my money, they owe me about two hundred francs all told. Damn this game, I'm not learning a thing but its great fun here. Wrote this and four letters this afternoon. Have got a beautiful moustache now, its only taken me a fortnight.

Thursday 9th May Stayed at the Chateau all of the morning which was just as well as I did not wake up until nearly eight. Cleaned up the rooms and then had a good read, don't often get a read now and went to have a bath and haircut in the afternoon. The bath was really a shower which was very hot indeed. We were all packed into a lorry like sardines in a tin but it was great fun. The officers came in very bad tempered but cheered up a bit after tea. Drunk a large amount of brandy and lime-soda which is pretty good stuff and cheered up myself. Just going to bed when the captain called down to say that he had company coming and could I let him have some red wine. I hadn't any but soon went and bought some. On the way met two very thirsty fellows Cole and Adler who asked if I could get them a drink. Told them that I could and got four bottles, two of ordinary red wine and two of Bordeaux. They had one of each in their tent and the captain had one of each. I went to bed after writing a long letter to Babe. Collected four hundred francs.

> On the 10th May, whilst 'A' Company was happily training in the Foret de Montgeon, the German Army invaded Belgium and Holland. In a few days the B.E.F. and French Armies were retreating.

Friday 10th May Day started at 4.20 when the air raid sirens went and the Regimental Police scrambled out of bed swearing and cursing. Went up on the roof, the guns were roaring over at Fecamp and Le Havre and great balls of white wool were spotted all over the blue sky, could not see any planes but heard them, also saw a long streak of white smoke that was probably a plane taking its pilot and crew down to hell. The sirens keep on and so do the guns, seems to be no end to the stuff they keep firing. Haven't heard any bombs yet. Should have started off on another jaunt today at 8.30 but we are still here at 9.30 waiting for orders to move. The bloody fools have still given out the orders that Bren guns will not be loaded with live ammo. I am carrying my pistol and have fifty rounds of .303 round my neck and ten spare in my pocket, also fifty rounds for the pistol. That, together with bayonet and jackknife should make me a pretty awkward customer. Heard that Germany had invaded both Holland and Belgium at four this morning. Still do not know if it is true. Am writing this from the top of a lorry and waiting to go places, everyone is dolled up in tin hat and gas mask and cape as well as rifle and bandoleer. Well, the guns did not stop but neither did we. We were all loaded on to a huge RASC lorry and taken about twenty kilometres away to a place by the sea called *'blank'* near Yvètot. The place is infested with vipers which are not Jews handkerchiefs but pretty snakes about two feet long with a perfect diamond on their ugly flat heads and a bite that either kills in about two hours or makes the bitten one wish he had died. We killed one about two yards from our camp, quite a big brute as vipers go (a viper is an adder).

Have done practically nothing all day except lay in the sun and make tea for practically everyone within sight. About five the CC sent a message to bring his towel down to the beach as he was bathing. Meant to have one myself but did not get as far as the sea although like Moses and the Promised Land I saw it in the distance. Then more writing. Its this ragtime army all over to use the Signals to send for a towel, by semaphore, by Morse on the wires and then by heliograph the last lap. Anyway I got there too late. The Sergeant Major has had my pistol all of the afternoon in case we meet a real enemy. The Germans have invaded Holland and Belgium today and over three hundred people have been killed in Brussels. Our moves are all cancelled and we do not know what we are supposed to do now.

8.00 Had a lot of unexpected requests for food from a number of people and was able to comply with most of them. Packed up all the filthy crocks and things and came away. Tried to shoot rabbits with my pistol from a moving truck and believe that I got one of them at least. The trouble is that the gun fires in bursts of about three or four rounds and it is very hard to fire on shot. The first shots were fired over the two drivers heads and they both ducked down and so did the rear passengers as the empty cases rattled into the truck. The drivers were all for it and would have run me round the country for hours shooting if necessary but the corporal got the wind up and made us pack it up.

Got a glorious ride home on top of the truck, a lovely evening with a nice cool breeze. The sky was an ethereal blue, a colour that I have rarely seen before and the whole country looked really lovely. Each of the farms seemed to have a clump of trees round them and when the sun goes down behind them they look so beautiful that they do not seem earthly at all, rather like the Morning of the World when all was fresh and young, no sin or rottenness of any kind but everything clean and pure. The queer thought came to me that it was on just such a farm that the scene of Ruth and Boaz was enacted, Ruth who was so much in love that she forgot everything else, and Boaz who is perhaps the only man in the Old Testament, if not the whole Bible, whom one can call a gentleman. There are bigger men and greater and more holy men but he alone shared a breeding and refinement that are the hallmark of a gentleman.

Still enough of that, I am here to get twelve notches on my pistol butt, not to write a beautiful story. Maybe I'll come back one day and do both. I've already decided what my book will be called, it is to be 'Conscript Heroes' and will be just an account of what happens without any moral to it. Some of the stuff will come from my diary but of course the main story will be imaginary, started from that memorable day when Chamberlain stepped from his plane, just back from Munich and in his rather self-centred voice proclaim 'I bring you peace in our time'. Chamberlain, that third rate politician, who banking on the reputations that Austin Chamberlain and Joseph Chamberlain made, imagines himself to be the voice of the people and who promises us what Christ alone could give (and never does give) 'Peace in our Time'.

Reminds me of the cartoon of Hitler showing the recording angel Czechoslovakia with its rows of graves: 'I promised them Peace for Xmas and I hope I have kept my word; they are resting in Peace.' Of course later he gave us another slogan 'Time is on our side'. And of course this is still another Holy War, they always are now, just as our men wore on the brass of their belts *Dieu Et Mon Droit* (God and my right) and the Germans who shot them and were bayoneted in turn had on theirs *Gott Mitt Uns* (God with us). And I bet God laughed like blazes at all the silly blasphemy, or was he angry at the cynical genius who started taking advantage of mans beliefs? And then on to the weeks of feverish hoarding of food, the rocketing of prices, no candles, joining groups to make sure of getting petrol and then the sunny morning when the announcers calm cold voice told England 'His Majesties Government is at war with the State Third Reich of Germany'. People turned to one another with changed faces, the young with - 'well thank the Lord we know where we are' - but the people who remember the last war were silent and looked at a world suddenly turned grey and cold. And while they all stood and thought their thoughts the wailing of the Air Raid Warning sent all England into action with the thought in their minds surely they are not here already. Then the months of comparative inaction, the sinking of the Athenia, then the Courageous, the mines and the stories of the British submarines, the futile leaflet raids over Germany, the not so futile raid on Keil when relays of Blenheims manned by boys of my age bombed the ships to hell and came back without many of their comrades, the boasting of 'The Lion has Wings' and then the calling of all ages of lads, the BEF in the Maginot Line and the fall of Denmark and Norway, the immense mine field laid down in the North Sea. Well hundreds of books will be written about it, some true, some false, and some pure propaganda, some showing what fun we had, all wine and pretty Mademoiselles with red lips and no morals, some making out that life was just plain hell with the boys grown old suddenly and praying for the end. Well Chamberlain resigned today and Winston Churchill took his job. That was one more mistake he made, he was six years too late.

Saturday 11th May The sirens are still going, have been all day. We are not going to Bolbec after all because of it. Had an easy day and was sunbathing on the roof when the news came that parachute troops were dropped about five miles away. Rushed to get dressed and grab rifle, ammo, tin hat, respirator, pistol and more ammo and then missed the truck. Am waiting to go now.

Were all put on Parade at 8.00. The officers had no revolvers or ammo and either had to borrow rifles or carry sticks. The Captain did not go out and as I asked to be allowed to go, even if it meant going in the ranks, I was made bodyguard to little Mr Redfern. The real reason for going out was that nearly every other aerodrome in France has been bombed and four parachutists were supposed to have landed here today with the intention of guiding the bombers by flares or lights. Knowing the inaccuracy of German air bombing I should call such men either a suicide squad or just plain bloody heroes. We went plunging through scrub and forest, corn and brambles, over farms, round cows and down quarries and had a glorious evening. In the middle of it Mr Redfern halted the whole battalion and went forward 'to have a shit' as he put it. This is a game I'll tell you. We all had live ammo in the magazine and most of us had the gun cocked. I was carrying my rifle in my left hand so as to get my pistol into action long before the catches were off the rifles. At close range the twelve shots in that would be as good as a Bren gun. We found a lone Scout camping on a hill in a white tent and about four sections interrogated him in turn. The poor little bugger was not much more than twenty and looked scared stiff at all the loaded rifles. He had an old German bayonet cut down to make a sheath knife which made us suspicious. Anyway we searched until dark and found no one but came on home. Then the CO sent out the Liaison Officer to check up on the Scout again but he proved to be all right after all. We went to bed but were dug out again to look for more troops. Still no luck, but it would have been rough on any that we found. Have just read a message from Brigade HQ. TROOPS LANDED IN BELGIUM HAVE COME DOWN WITH HANDS RAISED TO GIVE IMPRESSION OF SURRENDERING STOP HANDS HOLD GRENADES STOP WEARING KHAKI STOP MORE THAN SIX MEN LANDING FROM PLANES TO BE DEFINITELY ENEMY STOP FIRE WITHOUT WARNING STOP FIRE TO BE EFFECTIVE STOP MESSAGE ENDS. They needn't worry, our fire will be effective after all the trouble we have had.

There was a voluntary church parade and only five men turned up, including the three from our room. Later on sixteen men from the RASC came in and made a better congregation. The Padre was unperturbed and carried on as if we were a Battalion. Spent the rest of the morning cleaning up and after dinner got into my bathing trunks and went up on the roof to sunbathe. The sirens went incessantly and guns roared in the distance. Kept hearing bursts of machine-gun fire but did not see any planes. Then at four-thirty came the order 'Pack everything you own, we're moving.' Talk about scramble round, packing both the Captain's and my own but it got done by tea time. Stood by all the evening and had a sleep but got woken up to unpack all the stuff off of the lorry. Had a bottle of wine with Captain Thomson and went to bed tired.

Monday 13th May 1940 Whit Monday. Had a day in the officers mess and as we had one too many had a very easy day. After dinner told them that I wanted to go to town and do some shopping for the Captain. Had a lot of trouble finding out what I had to carry. First of all it was rifle, bayonet, respirator, gas cape, ammo and haversack. Then it was R A Re and finished up with tin hat and respirator. The

Captain had my pistol as he was down at Le Havre at the docks. The boys were doing navvy's work there, that is unloading stuff from the boats. Today they picked on a clothing boat and the boys came sweating with three shirts on, four pairs of socks, new gaiters and what ever else they could lay their thieving hands on. Don't blame them. I have plenty of kit myself but most of the boys are very short of stuff to change into. Had a parcel from Babe and a good sleep on the roof in the sun. Wrote to both her and Roland and went to bed. Then came calamity. The Captain called for me and said that the Colonel wanted to see my gun. I took it down to the Mess and he took one look at it and said 'That's my pistol that I had in the last war, it was pinched from Richmond Drill Hall, where did you get it?' I told him how long I had had it but also told him that I got it from a Mr Portel of the Royal Mills [at Lower Green, Esher]. Really of course I got it from Sergeant Dawkins of the Hersham Territorials and it is quite possible that it really was his gun. If it is it is the most amazing coincidence that I have ever heard of, Dawky was in this regiment and he bought it for about nothing from a bloke in the canteen. Anyway I got my gun back which is all that matters.

Tuesday 14th May Up at 6.00 and breakfast at 6.30. Perfect hell of a rush round but I made it. The boys went away at 7.30 but I had an easy day. Had a tiny brown spot in my eye so went to the MO, really because Morris has had eye trouble.[4] He said that it was nothing but put three drops of some brown stuff into each eye. Christ I thought I would go mad, the eyes burnt like liquid fire and I was blind for two hours. Then it went off a bit and I went down to town in a RASC ambulance to go shopping. Bought towels and dusters, safety pins and a litre of brandy. Had a terrible job to buy the pins, also the dusters but no trouble at all with the cognac. Then went sunbathing

---

[4] Pte J W Morris' eye trouble was later to become something of a blessing in disguise - see historic notes

on the roof again. Have just had the order 'Pack everything but say nothing to anyone'. Wonder what it means. The war has really started now and we should be in action very soon. Hope so anyway, the only thing I have used my rifle for is to knock in nails and toast bread on the bayonet. The Captain has my gun again.

Wednesday 15th May More trouble in the night, Naylor rushed up to borrow my rifle and ammo and I asked him what the hell I was to fight with if I was called out. Up at 6.00 and a glorious rush round that got us nowhere. Had an orange and about half a tumbler of brandy for breakfast as couldn't get down in time for it at 6.15. Another air raid and the rumour that Holland is surrendering to the Germans at 12.00 today.

8.00 Haven't done anything at all today but have had a lovely sunbathe on the roof. The flat roof of the Chateaux seems to be the rendezvous for all the batmen and many of the officers and it is really lovely up there. Had a bad thunderstorm in the evening and went for a walk with a groundsheet as a cape and tin hat to keep the rain off to get two bottles of wine. On the way back my lip touched the steel buckle of the helmet and I got a slight but definite electric shock from it. Had two letters, one from Babe and one from Mrs Picton [wife of the manager of the International Stores] and wrote to both of them this afternoon. Mr Redfern has bought an absurd little .25, a dirty little toy and is very proud of it. He let off one shot in the grounds and came running up to me like an excited school boy with the gun under his hat to see what I thought of it. I couldn't take it to pieces in spite of my knowledge of such toys. May have a chance to do that later on. Went to bed at 9.10 hoping to get some sleep at least tonight.

Thursday 16th May Had my night's rest. Have made a sleeping bag from my blankets and it not only saves a lot of trouble in the morning but is very much warmer at night. Another easy day, chopped a lot of wood and got chatty with Sergeant Kingsbury who so far has been the only man whom I dislike in this mob. Had a lot of new trucks come in and B Company are wandering round in a flying column. The Germans are reported to have killed 100,000 Dutch people. We are expecting to go into action at any moment now and although no one is actually nervous there is a sort of tension in the air, waiting for something to crack, much the same sort of thing as when we were ordered over the water only deeper. People who have hitherto been very snooty seem to muck in more and we are all closer together than we have ever been before. Far less talk of putting blokes on a 'blue one', haven't heard it at all today. I should like to see some action myself but am not too sure of either officers or men, they do not give the impression of strength that they will need to. They will fight like hell, I do know that though. I've got a pistol with a virgin butt, not one notch in it yet and am just longing to take it home with 21 on it, one to every quarter inch, it will be easier to hold then.

10.30 No, didn't do a stroke all day, cadged a new pair of socks from Mr Redfern and had a letter from Granny. Had quite a meal of peaches and cream and went to bed very happy after cleaning my pistol. Have just been up on the roof to look at the stars but although it is a lovely night it is rather cold. Have had a number of new 8 cwt trucks come today, one of them should belong to A Company, in which case I shall ride in it, hope so case not. They are twenty-six horsepower Humber Snipes.

Saturday 18th May Didn't have a chance to write anything yesterday as was busy right up to gone midnight. At first we were given the order to pack and be ready to move at 12.00. We did this and at 4.00 were given the order to unpack the lot. I didn't do either so was where the others were with no waste of energy but I did pack my own stuff up a bit more tidy than usual. Then at gone 9.00pm came the order 'Pack everything, we shall move by 8.00 Saturday morning.' Had to pack the bloody lot of the officer's kitchen and then Captain Thomson's stuff and then my own. Had a good half pint of neat brandy and tried to get some sleep. Was woken up at just before 4.00 by a policeman and told that the time had been changed to 6.00. Hell of a rush round and managed to get done by 7.00. The stuff we took with us had to be seen to be believed, dart-boards, bottles of God knows what, letters and calendars and spare kit of every description. Roughly speaking we only left dirty paper and eight nut jugs, which nearly broke my heart. Was going to leave half a pint of brandy but drank it instead and for the first time went on a parade stone bloody drunk. Not that anyone cared much, there was too much confusion to worry about a drunken batman. Got on CHQ truck and had a very cold ride for the first couple of hours, until the sun came out at about 9.00. Am writing this as the convoy is halted by the side of the road, don't know why but there seems to be an air raid on near here. One poor bloody dispatch rider has had trouble with his motor bike all of the time, he patches her up and then belts past at about eighty only to be passed later on up the road as he is tinkering with his motor. Darned uncomfortable in this barrow, all guns and ammo and other blokes feet.

1.00 Well after losing our way and having to come back over the Seine we have arrived at a big hutment camp [Le Manoir] about four miles from Rouen or some such place. There do not seem to be many soldiers about, only a few prisoners. The boys have made a bee line for the canteen. Do not know how long we are to stay here but do not expect it to be long. The road this morning has been full of Belgian refugees with cars full of household goods and packed with people, there are hundreds of them, don't know where they are all going or even coming from. The country seems to be very flat and level except for a few chalk hills and occasional unexpected walls of chalk. The people are cheering as we go by, the favourite greeting seems to be 'thumbs up' and they all seem to know it. One woman threw a beautifully scented rose into our truck. Further on was a road block of farm carts and behind a stone was a *poilu* [French soldier] with a heavy calibre Hotchkiss machine-gun. 'They shall not pass'. Should not like to be the person who tried to pass.

Sunday 19th May Up at 7.30 and then a cushy time up until about four in the afternoon, but I am going a bit fast. Yesterday we stopped at a hutment camp, of Nissen huts and tents. We put our officers in one large hut and then I found a whole hut for myself. We were to have the other two A Company batmen with us but they slept with their platoons in the end. Slept like a log for I was very tired indeed and woke up at 7.30 fresh as a daisy. Then after, as I said an easy morning, had a sun bathe even, all hell broke loose. First of all we had to change huts and then when all was quiet again and I thought that I could go down for a drink, the bugle gave the general alarm and we were told that we had to get going within a quarter of an hour. We were ready to go and all primed up to kill somebody but the order was never given to move and we stood about and chopped and changed about until nearly twelve and then we were told to unpack and get some sleep. We needed it I can tell you. Have got to be ready by 6.00

A whole regiment has just marched past us, going towards Germany and the stream of refugees has not stopped yet, some of the motor cars are drawing farm carts loaded with stuff and many of them have been wounded by machine-gun bullets from aeroplanes. The Germans made a terrific push today and got into France but tonight we are holding them back. Going to sleep bleeding tired.

2.30 Not much good going to bed as I've just been dug out as I was getting really comfortable. Still dark, we are to move by four. Another rush and tear in the extremely cold hours before dawn. Then an angel from heaven appeared unto the cook saying 'Fear not, rise and for Christ's sake make a cup of tea'. He did and very welcome it was, in fact I had two of them. Then off, leaving behind nearly everything that we own, blankets, shirts, cleaning stuff, all of it.

On the 24th May the Battalion came under the command of improvised Brigade "Beauforce". It was equipped with 3 ton lorries and ordered north to join the B.E.F. It was to cross the river Somme at Abbeville, and receive further orders at Montreuil, 25 miles further north. 'A' Company, together with the rest of the Battalion (less 'D' Company who were still guarding a dump of mustard gas at Fecamp, near Le Havre), motored northwards towards Abbeville at the mouth of the Somme. A few miles south of the river at Fressenville, the Battalion was halted by an officer from Beauforce. "German tanks are in Abbeville". 'B' Company under Capt Tebay had found Germans in Abbeville and returned to HQ with the information.

'A' Company was ordered back to hold a bridgehead at Gamache, on the north bank of the river Bresle, whilst the rest of the Battalion took up positions along the south bank of the river. In the dark we deployed in a semi-circle round the hamlet.

The convoy was about three miles long and consisted mainly of Dispatch Riders who had had their bikes about three hours and Humber Snipe drivers who had known their wagons a day. One wagon, a three tonner, broke down because it had no oil in it and another dropped out because of engine trouble. Then a DR lost all his petrol. But we still went on and our first halt was about twenty-five miles away in a thick wood. It was bloody cold so I took off all my stuff and put on my overcoat, but it's still cold. Expect it will be as hot as hell today, later on. Had a letter from Babe and one from Mother, both given at two-thirty this morning so read them as soon as it got light enough. Felt rather worried that I haven't any more kit with me, but hope it will, like our crimes, follow us. The officers have burned their maps of the route. They still have no revolvers. The Captain is trying to sleep in the front seat, wish him luck with it, I'd like to myself. Do not know why we are halted but we have been here for some time. Just had a talk with the Padre who wants to know why I have an automatic with me. I told him that it might be useful. He has no weapon of any sort, damn that for a game of soldiers.

1.00 We stopped for about three hours and then came a change of orders. We are to join the BEF as a fighting unit. The main body of the enemy are equipped with armoured fighting vehicles and we have only sixteen cartridges for each anti-tank rifle, which is our only weapon against them. We have no AT guns or heavy machine-guns at all and not nearly enough SAA. Also no grenades at all, in fact we shall have to rely on our rifles and bayonets. All day long the roads have been blocked by refugees from Belgium, hundreds upon hundreds of them, some on cycles, walking with prams, on farm carts and cars and even on tractors. All I haven't seen is Just Jake's Patent Sheep Dipper. They all look thoroughly despondent but a few manage to give us the old thumbs up salute. Managed to buy twelve bottles of rather dry cider for fifty francs.

4.30 We have just finished passing a rather terrible sight, for over eight miles we have been passing a pathetic stream of cars that have been jammed as the folk try to get out of the bombed villages. Their belongings are all tied to the tops of the cars and people are clinging to the running boards as cars go along. Then out of the blue came the terrific explosions of about thirty odd bombs, huge columns of smoke blew in the air and from out of sight came the stutter of machine-guns and the bang bang bang of an aeroplane's cannon. We all got out and spread out in the grass and got ready in case he came low enough. I only caught a fleeting glimpse but whether it was enemy or Allied I do not know. The village[5] was bombed for the ninth time in one day and huge gouts of black smoke rose in the air. It took about ten minutes and then was all over.

Then we found that we had lost most of the convoy and had no food or spare clothes or ammo or cooks and then began a nightmare ride round over a mile of unknown country, always with the same query, 'Have you seen the East Surrey's convoy, are you East Surreys?' and always it seemed the same answer 'No - we are the Buffs'. The Bold Bloody Bastard Buffs seem to be everywhere but no East Surreys at all. We went round until two in the morning and then called it a bad job and came back to our base. Then the boys had to be guards for vulnerable points after that. I was told to find Mr Redfern and was strolling round with my pistol in my hand looking for him. There was no password and no-one thought of challenging me. I didn't find him until I came back, he had been asleep within ten feet of me. It was as cold as the devil and I could not get warm. I managed to buy a quart of brandy and gave a sergeant, Kingsbury, about a pint to give to the guard which he did. I drank most of the rest.

Tried to get some sleep on a ground sheet as we have lost our store truck but could only doze for about twenty minutes. Woke up frozen and we were on the move again. Drove for about twenty miles and nearly froze solid. Then we pulled up at a hospital base and then another and still another. At the last one a man put his hand under the flap and in broad Scottish asked 'Why don't you cunts go and get some tea with your mates?'

Tea, my God. I promised to shoot him if he was pulling our legs. He is still alive. Not only did we get as much hot tea as we could drink

---

[5] Although the diary pages 71 & 72 are headed 'Abbeville' the village was actually Fressenneville

but sat in front of an enormous fire and had a gigantic marmalade tart about two feet in diameter. Captain Thomson was there too and the four of us finished it off. Truly I have never tasted food like it, it was ambrosia from heaven, as it was the first food for twenty-four hours apart from a corned beef sandwich. Felt altogether a new man.

Before dawn we were ordered back to the south bank of the Bresle, to occupy the high ground south of Le Treport on the coast road, in support of 'B' and 'C' Companies, on the line of the river. Cpl Fearson, our despatch rider, shepherded our ungainly lorries on the narrow road like a well trained sheep dog. Dawn was breaking as we drove up the hill to the south of Le Treport. A quarry at the top, fringed with trees, provided a magnificent view over the river valley in front and cover for the vehicles. We deployed and dug in again.

We moved further along to the sea shore and picked out a good post. Then we had time to sleep as best we could but we did not sleep, we were beyond it. Then we withdrew still further back, don't know what we are doing but we seem to be retreating as fast as we can. And the entire French and Belgian Armies seem to be doing the same. After having had to abandon two motor cycles and take the drivers with us because of lack of petrol, we had two thousand gallons come in a tanker, more than we could do with. Gallons of the precious stuff went into the gutter and every tank was filled with it, also every gallon we could store in cans. Then came the order 'Get going' and that is what we are now doing.

11.15 The refugees are still streaming past clutching a few rags and sometimes a long loaf of French bread. Then we were moving again, with the stream of fugitives this time. We took simply appalling risks and roared in and out of everything. The number of French and Belgian soldiers is amazing. There are hundreds of them, sometimes thirty on one car, lying on the bonnet, on the wings, on the top, clinging to the running boards, anything as long as they move, hundreds of them are walking or two on a bike together. Most of them have lost their rifles but all have two pairs of boots.

> Before the day was out we were on the move again, south by the coast road to Dieppe. At the southern edge of the town we were halted by a level-crossing. Head to tail in our crowded vehicles in the tree lined road, we watched, with some apprehension, as a dozen or so Stukas bombed the docks. Unscathed, we motored on.

At last we came to Dieppe and took up our positions on a small farm. The trucks made a magnificent target, about sixty packed head to tail. We had a look round the farm which was a very small house and huge fields of wheat and clover. Bought some eggs and had them boiled. Then, from the sea came a terrific explosion and a huge mass of spray went up into the air. We thought at first that it was a mine, but we were wrong. Then about an hour later came two more explosions and huge clouds of smoke went up from Dieppe. Four bombers roared overhead. Then some fool cut loose with a rifle and then everyone started. The Bren guns and the big Vickers guns roared and stuttered and rifles cracked all round. I waited until one came over extra low and pumped six rounds at it as fast as I could work the bolt. One lad fired two inches from my face and the blast scorched my eyes. Smoke burst from the plane I fired on and then another from one that was fired on by two Vickers guns. One went down into the sea and six seaplanes chased off the rest. Then one came over very deliberately and dropped four huge bombs exactly onto a hospital ship [Maid of Kent] and blew it in half. Three people were killed instantly and dozens injured. As the plane came away we poured bullets at it as fast as we could work our bolts but it did not come down. The huge clouds of black smoke hung in the air for nearly an hour. Then came three Spitfires, hours too late, who made a leisurely reconnaissance and then flew off, as they went some fool let off three shots as fast as he could. Then came the order to move and away we went within ten minutes. We passed the bombed ship and also cars and trees smashed to splinters by the explosion. I think that the bombs must have weighed about five hundred pounds, they were a lot bigger than those used at Abbeville.

We stopped at the corner of a road and when it became known that we were to be there for some time we rushed out and bought up chocolate and loaves of very hot bread. The boys were actually starving, they had had nothing for four days, they tore at the hot bread and wolfed it down as fast as they could. I was not too bad as I had had a packet of dog biscuits and some spring onions from a field the day before. Also we had been drinking all sorts and qualities of wine all of the time, also brandy and were in a glorious condition. We camped out in the open and woke up at three when the rain came down at a steady drizzle. I took my groundsheet and slept under a car, afraid that it would move and kill me at any moment.

All of the next morning it rained and rained. We had nothing to eat or drink and were wet through. We crowded together thirty and more on a lorry out of the driving rain. Rifles and equipment, gas masks and capes and ammo all lay in the mud. Then at last we moved only a mile and had a farm and Chateau handed to us.

The Battalion was to defend the line of the river Bethune which ran westwards to the sea at Dieppe, against attack from the north. 'A' Company's position was in the centre of the Battalion line at the hamlet of Martigny. Here the river Bethune flowed through a flat marshy valley almost a mile wide; an excellent defence against tanks. The river was split into several channels and Martigny itself was on a tributary, the Varenne, flowing almost parallel to the main river. The Company dug in along the south side of the river valley, 7 Platoon on the left towards Arques-la-Bataille, 8 Platoon in the centre, north of Martigny, 9

Platoon to the right towards St Aubin-le-Cauf. A small chateau provided cover for our vehicles, the cooks and Company HQ.

Four peaceful days were spent here whilst we improved our defences and prepared bridges for demolition. Doves cooed as we drove in and out of the chateau yard.

I got busy, took charge of the kitchen, requisitioned men to do this and that and got water boiling. I hadn't washed or shaved for three days and most of the boys not for six and we needed that water. I dished out tea and bread and God knows what until I could hardly stand on my feet. Then the cooks came and turned me out of it and took over.

I then went over to the chateau and set to work to establish an officer's kitchen. I did bloody well at it. The people have left everything in place ready to use, plates, glasses, cutlery, a radio, furniture and everything, sheer extravagant luxury of the first water. Made a good job of cooking but darned well ought to with everything to hand as it was. We solved the meat problem quite simply, took a pig, shot him between the eyes with my pistol and cut his throat. In half an hour he was all in joints. I took a leg for my kitchen, about ten pounds. Found a way into the other Chateau and the Surreys had what must be the grandest looting of all their history. The fact that we have to carry everything made quite a bit of difference. I got a pair of chamois gloves and some 12 bore cartridges that I intend selling to Captain Tebay. And wine, one house had about four thousand bottles and the other six or seven thousand and some barrels.

Have not cleaned my rifle since I fired at the planes and it is in a wicked state, all red rust but I can't do much about it yet. The food that I dish them up with here is far better than they ever dreamed of at Richmond and they eat until they can't move. And drink, I myself have been living on rare vintage wines and sherries and brandies for a week now, have had no sleep but it seems not to matter. I have sent out over two hundred bottles to the boys.

Am rather worried because I have not been able to send a letter to Babe yet and only a field card to Mother, am bloody sure that they are both worrying their guts out. Have not had any pay but have had more to eat than I ever dreamed of before. I can cook just what I want when I want to, that is of course, if I have what I want. Good Old Ireland, or should I say Eire? Had a glorious loot one night all over a huge place and the stuff left had to be seen to be believed. Among other things was a case of three hundred silver spoons and nearly as many forks and innumerable silver mounted steel knives, all I swiped was as I say 80 12 bore cartridges and gloves and a huge white blanket. The place was locked up about an hour after I got clear. Was told that Company HQ was going to be moved to BHQ and had to pack all up. Also pinched two knives, one real beauty. Then the whole bloody lot was altered and I had to unpack again *Ca na la rien* [sic] I like this place.

Saturday 25th May Glorious day, slept in the best bed in the place and like a log. Cooked some wonderful food and had another ride round on the lorry. Found a most beautiful twin barrelled twelve bore hammer shot gun and wrapped it up ready to pinch. It is as nice a weapon as I have ever seen and not a mark on it, all engraved on bright steel and a Damascened barrel. I should say that it cost about a hundred and twenty pounds when new as it is definitely handmade. I only hope that I shall be able to get it back to England. Sent a lorry to Rouen and they pinched eight thousand rounds of .303 ammo and twenty cases of pineapples (Mills hand grenades). The bombs nearly sent half a dozen of us crazy, we danced for joy. They are no bigger than an orange, lovely little things. I got hold of a case of twelve and primed them and hid them in my dining room cupboard.

Gave them a marvellous meal, five courses of it and it took them nearly an hour and a half to finish it off. Naturally I also have been eating as much as humanly possible and exactly what I want, in fact I need at least eight eggs a day to boil for myself and get them too. I have a staff of three now and about all I have to do is to plan out a meal and tell them how to do it. Actually I am using all of my imagination on their meals and am producing food beyond my wildest dreams.

Monday 27th May Went on another looting raid and looted a house that had been occupied by a nursing corp. The mess there was simply sickening, I have never seen anything like it, dresses and wool, underwear and kind were scattered in confusion a foot thick on the floor. The fact that some girl had paid for it all made it just horrible, there were hundreds of pounds worth of stuff in the place. Someone had cut open suit cases and bags and thrown the contents all over the room. I took a leather case and a dress and cardigan that I hope I can get back to Babe, also some oatmeal, tea, custard powder and curry and currants. Then we went to an RE dump and the same appalling waste was evident. We took two hundredweight of nails and as much corrugated iron as we could put on the truck. Also got six tin drums of curry powder and some American magazines.

Then on to the docks and the most horrible sight that I have seen, a hospital ship and train side by side, both burnt out, the ship at the bottom of the quay and the train burnt down to the iron. Among the wreckage of just one coach I picked up eleven steel helmets, eleven respirator canisters and eighteen barrels and stocks of Lee Enfield rifles. In the next one was about two gross of Brands essence of chicken and no end of essences of such stuff as vanilla, peppermint, raspberry and so forth, also hundreds of tins of corned beef, burnt to hell by the enormous incendiary bombs that I myself saw dropped on them. All I can hope is that my own bullets went home to the Heinkel that sent us all behind cover and that terrible day when we, starved and desperate were trying to dig a pit to cover us. So hungry that I went looking for food with my pistol in one hand and a handful of money in the other and finished up by eating Army biscuits and spring onions from a field. It will be a long time before I forget the feeling of exhilaration that surged through me as I pumped bullets at the roaring sky monster that dived and poured machine-gun bullets at us as we sought cover. I laughed like a fool and smashed home the bolt as fast as I could pull the trigger.

Well the Red Cross ship lay, a black and smoking derelict in the harbour and the iridescent oil lay everywhere. The only other things to be seen were tall cranes and blackened buildings with shattered windows and huge bomb craters about thirty feet across. And still someone had scrawled across a board the indomitable message that originated at Verdun - *No Passaral* - they shall not pass. And believe me, They shall not pass!

Then we came back and bought some fruit, oranges cost me nearly fourpence each and onions about a shilling a pound. Got into a terrific temper about the seemingly endless jobs that have to be done in my kitchen. Got really drunk before I served dinner and do not know how I managed to get through it. Drank a whole bottle of wine and half of one of port. Went to bed very happy and slept like a log.

Tuesday 28th May Had a general exodus of men from my kitchen all the morning but they nearly all crept back. Had a general clear out and wash down. Had a row with the quarter-master and served up a corned beef dinner with lettuce and new potatoes, the first scratch meal that we have had since we came here. In the afternoon commandeered a truck and after a bit of bother with the driver went down to the DID which has been bombed and destroyed. Had a lot of bother with some of the men with the truck who were obviously on the same stunt as we were, that is looting.

Although I had an officer on hand, Mr Redfern, he would not take any part in the operations but stayed in the truck. I made out that I had all the authority in the world and ordered corporals and men and drivers to do this that and the other thing. I also had complete charge of the truck and told the driver just what I wanted - and got it too. We pinched sugar, tea, about four hundred and fifty Nestles milk and four cases of Hollands gin and four cases of port wine as well as shirts, cap comforters and knives, forks and spoons galore. I also got a number of treasure bags and playing cards. Then we took a hundredweight of coffee and forty pounds of Orange Pekoe tea. Then we came home. I was so happy that I sang all the way back and only refrained from shooting my pistol from the truck because of lack of cartridges. In the evening we all had a glorious binge and several of them were very badly drunk, one lad at least got into a fearful state and couldn't stand at all. I drank with them and finished up cold sober. Then went to bed.

Wednesday 29th May Had a fairly easy day. One of the lads who was at the binge took us all morning to sober him up but we did it and kept him off of booze all day. One of the drivers brought in a Belgian made Browning automatic and I spent nearly two hours putting it back together again, it is a terribly tricky little weapon and as it is only a .25, not in my opinion worth bothering about. Still I did it and took it outside to make sure that it worked. The sergeant major had pinched mine until I could mend this one so we had to go down and collect mine. Then we had a shooting match to see which was the best gun. I knew. Had the CO and the Adjutant to dinner and they said it was the best dinner that they had had in France. The CO said, give my compliments to the cook, tell him that the meal was excellently cooked. Quite imperturbably I said 'Thank you Sir, I am the cook'. Wrote a long letter to Babe and went off to bed happy.

Thursday 30th May Was told that we had to move tomorrow, which is a bastard. I have got an enormous stock of food and am just getting used to this joint. Had an enormous breakfast. Packed up a lot of stuff ready for tomorrow, including quite a number of things that I had pinched while here, my double-barrelled gun and some knives, a girl's night dress, two pairs of forceps, twenty-four cartridges 12 bore, a scalpel and a pair of hair clippers. I hope I get some, at least, of them home. Had seven officers to dinner and was darned glad when they went away, the buggers had seven sets of wine glasses for one thing.

On 31st May we were relieved by a Foresters Battalion and ordered back to Rouen on the river Seine.

Friday 31st May The usual rush and tear on the morning of departure. Got everything packed and then had to unpack it all again for something that was in the wrong packet. Then the putting of it all on the trucks 'That can't go on here' 'Fuck old Thomson, make the bastard carry it' and 'You're a bleeding nuisance, bugger off and drown yourself'. But I got it all on. Had the Sherwood Foresters move in on us and made a very good deal with one of their officers, we sold him a case of gin that I pinched for two hundred francs. He wanted to make it 100 but I told him that I would put my rifle butt into each bottle and put it into the river rather than leave it behind. We got the money and were thankful.

Moved off with an enormous load of booze on board, a bottle of port, whisky, sherry, white port, four of gin, two ciders and two white wines, also a small one of rum in my haversack. I have got a case of port on one of the motors but do not know if I shall ever see it again, I hope so for it is by far the best wine that I have ever tasted and we got it for nothing. What almost breaks my heart is that I left thirty cases of it in the warehouse when I could have had the lot, also about twenty more cases of gin and twenty-six radio sets. Still, we can't carry them anyhow so we have to leave them behind.

Well the first stage of the journey brought us to Neuve Chappelle, about six miles from Arques la Battaille which is where we were. The name of the lady who owned the place was Baroness de Sainte Claire and she was something important in the Swiss Red Cross Society. We were told to get settled down for the night at Neuve Chappelle at about 2.30 and I went and found a lovely barn full of straw and put the whole company into it. Went down to the nearest café about a mile away and had a drink, also got Captain Thomson some of the inferior wine that he likes so much. When we got back everyone was packing again ready to move. So I had all the bleeding job of packing again. Then off and we did not stop until we got to the race-course at Rouen at about 8.00.

The boys were put into a brickfield and bloody draughty I bet it was. It took us about two hours to find our billet and it was not much of a place when we did find it. The Captain invited myself and the driver in and we had some sort of supper, coffee, bread, butter, wine and tinned meat. The quarter-master tells me that he has not got any blankets for me so it is just as well that I have a big one that I pinched. Slept on the Captain's Li Lo in the hall of the place but did not sleep very well. Got up at 7.00 and managed to get the good lady to fix me up with a mug of coffee and some bread. Am writing this while waiting to know what to do.

Well, I got my orders and they were simple enough 'Janes, we can't do anything, we eat and sleep and eat and then go to bed'. Suits me. The cafés round here used not to serve troops until after 12.00 noon and as I was not going to walk three miles for breakfast, I bought a loaf and tomatoes and with cider and sardines made quite a good meal. Then a leisurely walk with the Captain up to the boys, cadged a tin of beans and a cup of tea and came back and lay in the sun. There has just been another air raid, bombs bursting and shells screaming up and some bloody fool blasting away with a heavy machine-gun. I say fool because the big Dornier did not come lower than a mile up and even I did not bother to get my rifle. Talking about that, I seem to be the only man who carries both rifle and ammunition with me, most of them only carry the ammo. The Captain has got one of the two Sniper's rifles in the Company and a gorgeous tool it is too. I'll have a go with that, somehow or another. Am writing in this stuff because my pen has run out of ink [pages 105 & 106 are written in a different colour] I found this one in the nurses place at Arques la Battaille. Have just been counting my money, in cash I have 208.35 francs. And the officers owe me 407.10 so I am worth a good deal, also have 6/8½ in English money.

3.30 Have had a good sleep in the sun, a wash, shave and a clean up and have first had dinner, an orange, a long loaf of french bread and a tin of beans. As soon as I sat down one of the girls brought me a bottle of quite drinkable cider from the cellar. These people seem to be very hospitable. I got brought coffee and butter this morning and the woman did not want to take any thing for it. There is a lad here who has the most marvellous head of hair that I have ever seen and he knows rather more English than I know French, which is not much. The number of crucifixes and pictures of Christ in this place is amazing, there must be twenty-five and more. Everyone seems very polite and only too anxious to do anything to make us feel at home. Shouldn't mind staying here for a bit, in spite of the air raids as I believe that it could be made quite homely. I have a silk night gown for Babe which I hope to get back to England and the girls all chattered like monkeys when I packed it and four of them rushed to get paper to wrap it up in. Of such is the kingdom of heaven. Am going to see if I have any thing at all to do today now, also to try and get some tea out of the quarter bloke. Am worried about my case of port, I'm afraid I'm going to lose it. Can still hear the drone of motors and the roar of bombs but am past worrying about them.

Sunday 2nd June Quite a nice day as regards the weather. The Captain got drunk last night and woke up feeling funny so one of the first things that he wants is his service dress cleaned up so I had to unpack the uniform and cleaning kit. Had a Church Parade in a huge natural drying kiln of the brickworks. It was rather silly really because air raids were on the whole time and one two-thousand pound bomb would have wiped out the whole battalion. Fortunately it did not fall so we are still here. Only the drivers were exempt and they were taking the governors off their motors. Got thoroughly browned off with the whole affair because he kept wanting silly things all day and in the end he took a bottle of inferior white wine with him and went on a tour of Rouen on a back-pedalling cycle. He has stripped two corporals since we have been out here and I feel sure that someone will shoot him as soon as it is safe. I promise that it will not be me, he is too useful to me for that but sometimes I feel like chucking it all up. Had a good sleep in the afternoon and ate a tin of peaches for dinner. Slept again and went down to the camp, which is about a mile and a half away and had a talk with the boys. Most of them are cheerful enough but we do feel that we have no real leaders and not nearly enough weapons or ammo. The lack of good men to follow is the worst and we can't help remembering the awful blunders that have been made. When the convoy reached Abbeville they were already six miles BEHIND the Germans and if the road had not been blocked by refugees we should have been cut off, in which case we should either have been killed or would have all got bleeding medals. The truck that I was in then, was at one time ten miles behind the Germans, who were less than four hundred yards to our left. Neither they nor we knew it though so we went on to Dieppe. There we were on the wrong side of the river and our convoy was packed nose to tail. If the bombers had not bombed what they came for, that is the Red Cross ships, we should have been wiped out. Now we don't know what we are going to do or be. Major Palmer, whose blanket I have pinched, is now a prisoner of war in Germany. So much for that.

The NAAFI have opened a small stall in the brickfields and are well patronised. Had a glorious evening in a café with some HQ lads and two girls and a woman who speaks both English and French. One of the girls was very like Wynne, which made her untouchable anyway. I have never attempted to touch Kitten, Lord knows why. I like her enough to want to sleep with her but somehow she is just, well, adored. Don't love her as I love Babe, but Babe is with me in my heart and Wynne is with the angels. Anyway it was a glorious party and we all parted good friends. Came home and went to bed and wrote this tripe. And I'm sober too (10.10pm)

Early in the morning of the 3rd June, Company Commanders were told that we were to join the 1st Armoured Division as their motorised infantry battalion, and to be ready to move later that morning. Britain's only armoured division had been re-equipping at Le Mans when the Germans attacked on the 10th of May. Their own infantry battalion had been diverted to garrison Calais, and the 4th Borders had taken their place: we were to take on their job. The 51st Highland Division had also been a long way from the B.E.F. on the 10th May: occupying a sector of the Franco-German frontier in the Saar. Those two divisions were now on their way north from the Seine to fight their way across the Somme and join the B.E.F. At 10.00, Lt Redfern with an officer from each Company set off with Major Spearing (who had taken over from Major Adams as Second in Command), as advance party. At Grattenoix, a hamlet a few miles east of Neufchatel, set amongst orchards, woods and a maze of minor roads, Major Spearing explained the situation.

German forces with tanks were believed to be on the Somme, preparing to attack from Amiens, south-east towards Poix. The 1st Armoured Division support group had established a line of 44 2-pounder anti-tank guns, facing east, between Aumale in the north and Forges-les-Eaux in the south. This was a distance of fifteen miles as the crow flies. The line, however, followed the contours and was more than twenty miles on the ground: about one gun every half-mile.

The 51st Division were at Abbeville on the south bank of the Somme, the 4th Borders, when we had relieved them, would be on our left, north of Aumale. Two French regiments were thought to be east of Aumale. 'A' Company was to provide infantry protection to the 11 guns in the sector between Aumale and Abancourt, a distance of about five miles. Battalion HQ was to be at Gratenoix and rations to be drawn from there at night. 'A' Company HQ would be at the hamlet of Rothois at the source of the river Bresle, half-way between Aumale and Abancourt. That evening guides from the 4th Borders met us at Rothois. In the dark they led us to their positions and we doubled up for the few hours of the short summer night. Before dawn, on the 4th June, they stole away. The occupation had gone remarkably smoothly. We stood-to at dawn and surveyed our battlefield.

At the village of Aumale the main road from Poix, running westwards, crossed the river Bresle. A road from the north crossed this road at the village and continued southwards on the high ground for the five miles to Abancourt. To the east of this latter road mainly open country stretched eastwards to a railway which curved south-eastwards to a railway junction south-east of Abancourt.

This open country was the field of fire for our anti-tank guns. To the west of this road a shallow valley, the head waters of the Bresle (although without any water), rose gently to the high ground at Abancourt. The eastern side of this valley was heavily wooded: the bottom was open meadowland: whilst on the east it sloped upwards, with orchards, fields and woods. It was on this western slope, half-way between Aumale and Abancourt, that Company HQ was sited in the hamlet of Rothois. A minor road ran to each of these villages whilst a lane ran east and west across the valley. The gunners had dug in and camouflaged their guns well. On either flank of each gun, two-men weapon pits had been dug by the Borders. These were 50 yards or so away to avoid disclosing the gun positions, and we decided not to occupy them by day for the same reason. East post had three or four gunners and an infantry section. Some of the posts also had two men of a L/A/A Regiment with a Lewis gun mounted on a 'music stand'. Both 7 Platoon and 9 Platoon had four guns to protect; so their Platoon Headquarters took this duty.

Monday 3rd June Had what one lad termed the height of imbecility, we had an RSMs parade and had arms drill and piling arms and all the rest of the balls that we thought that we had left behind at Richmond. The whole Battalion was again in one spot, again a dream of a target for aeroplanes. It was soon broken up by the news that we were to move straight away which was later changed to Wednesday morning. Am resting again now, which is about all that we can do here. Can't bear the idea of going up to the Somme with dirty brass and no blanco, to say nothing of no crease in my trousers. Have an awful load of food and booze to move with me, don't know if I shall be able to move it with me. We have had a lot of trouble with corporals today, three full corporals and two lance jacks have thrown their stripes in and the Captain has answered by making five new unpaid temporary lance corporals, three of them from the Army class, one of whom is Winter, who should make good even if the others don't. We had a standing joke about stripes, claimed that we could get one for 1 franc 50 and two for 5 francs and make a sergeant for 10 francs, that is about 1/3^d. I feel sure that the Captain will never see England again, too many blokes have threatened to shoot him and the trouble is that they have the ammo to do it with too. Bishop, who has been stripped of two stripes, has a buckshee grenade which he says is for Thomson and the bloody thing is primed and all ready. Billy Bean [Sergeant Major Broad] has been made a CSM which is quite a jump from PSM of the TA.

> We spent Tuesday, 4th June, improving our defences: and noticed German reconnaissance planes overhead.
> Rations arrived from Battalion Headquarters that night. It was a long job distributing them to our widely separated posts in the darkness. Unbeknown to us this was the day when, twenty miles to our north, the 51st Highland Division, with which the Battalion's fate was to be linked and the 1st Armoured Division failed in their attacks on the German bridgehead south of the Somme at St. Valery-sur-Somme and at Abbeville, suffered heavy casualties, and themselves came under attack.

Tuesday 4th June Slept out in the open with only me white blanket that I pinched and it was bloody cold, only kept alive by drinking neat rum. Got up at 4.00 and had a walk round the camp before anyone was awake. All were sleeping peacefully under everything that they could pile on themselves, groundsheets, overcoats, sandbags even tarpaulins. When I got back the cooks had got the petrol cookers going and had made a very welcome cup of tea ready for us. Again I had two and then we got ready to move off. The CSM has been bollocking me all the last twenty-four hours over one thing or another. Had a nice smooth journey and got very hungry so I shucked out a packet of chocolate biscuits and the SM said that he took back all the harsh things he had said to me and he would see that I got the Military Medal. IF, of course he is able to see anything by then.

We are now on top of a hill in the middle of a huge wood about eighteen miles from Forge [Forges-les-Eaux]. From there we moved down to a small cottage in the valley that has belonged to rather poor people. It was occupied by the Borders, that is a Scottish regiment and quite a decent lot of men they were really. They had a rather nice French liaison officer who was kindness itself and showed me where to get most of the stuff that could be got at all about here, which is not much. Bought four small chicken for dinner and was surprised at the horrible way they kill them here. The first two the farmer put a knife down their throats and then swung them until they bled to death. I took the other two by the feet, one swipe with my pistol barrel and wrung their necks, altogether a more humane method to my way of thinking. The dinner was simple, just potatoes and chicken and bread and butter but I think that they enjoyed it. There was a fowl left over so I gave it to the Borders batmen. Went to bed in the kitchen.

Wednesday 5th June. At first light, German planes bombed Aumale station and the railway line along our front. They returned again and again during the day. A final dive-bombing attack in the evening completely destroyed Aumale station. None of our posts were hit. On 7 Platoon's front, French troops began withdrawing westwards through Aumale. We heard artillery firing from the east. Cpl Moore and his assistant, who had worked incessantly laying cable to Battalion HQ - eight miles away - finally got through. In the late evening the Company Commander was called to Battalion HQ. The roads were jammed with refugees, it took two hours to get there. There was hope of a French counter-attack. We must hold our positions. On the return journey he noticed a Royal Engineers sign by the side of the road. He was warmly welcomed by two Sappers as much in the dark as he was.

Wednesday 5th June (St Valerie's day) Starting from 1.30 this morning we have been subjected to almost continuous air raids, not warnings but bombs and machine-gun bullets. The worst danger though is from AA fire. Whilst we were at dinner the worst raid of all came. The very ground shook with the roar of HE and when I looked round for my mates they were all crouching behind food containers, I laughed at them and stayed where I was. Two pieces of shrap crashed through the tree that we were under and another whistled through the hedge. The scream of shells did not stop and I alone saw the planes. There were eight of them and they came down in vertical dives from the sun, laying their eggs at the bottom and going up like bats from hell, only to be followed by another. They dropped about four or five bombs each in this way and then roared over with machine-guns pouring out nickel as fast as possible. They bombed a French station [Aumale] and a convoy and we believe that they shot up one of our posts. The Signals were shit scared and as soon as it was over rushed up for shovels to dig a shelter. Not me, not in this heat.

Well, they dug a beauty in record time and sandbagged it over. Had a lot of bother with our meals as the Captain goes poodling about all over the country. Had to stand to at 3.30 but forgot.

Thursday 6th June started with heavy dive-bombing along the line of our posts and our Company HQ. We had seen Stukas in action at Dieppe: but this time we were their target. The bombs were bad enough but the machine-gunning was terrifying: bullets everywhere: but no one was hit. Our deep weapon-pits had been worth the labour! None of the Stukas was brought down by our Lewis guns. It was disappointing that, after all our efforts at concealment, so many of our positions had been located. Disturbing too: if enemy planes knew where we were so would their tanks and guns. Cpl Moore reported that he could no longer get through to Battalion HQ. A despatch rider arrived with a written order signed by Major Adams. It repeated the hope of a French counter-attack, and ended 'You will hold your positions to the last round and the last man.'

Thursday 6th June Started the day with a terrific air raid. Six three motored bombers came down and dropped bombs on anything they wanted to. The scream of HE and AA shells was deafening and the whole house shook. Huge lumps of red hot steel rained down and two pieces went within a foot of myself. I picked them both up and dropped them quick. One bomb hit the stream and blew up a willow tree on the bank. The Captain and Mr Redfern were flat on their faces in the muck and I just sat on the step. Then the last plane machine-gunned the lane and went home. Soon afterwards I was called out to see what I could do with a lad with shell shock. Did what I could with him and made [?] and got him to sleep quite comfortably. They did not shell us again today.

Friday 7th June. The sun rose in a cloudless sky. All was quiet. At 7.00 Stukas appeared overhead; they bombed and machine-gunned our positions along the Aumale-Abancourt road. Our Company HQ was also bombed. At 10.00 2/Lt John Naylor arrived. He had visited his three sections and reported that there were no casualties from the air attack. He also told me that during the night Lt Wilkinson had withdrawn the L.A.A. Lewis guns from the posts in 8 Platoon area and had evacuated his troop headquarters. At 11.00 we heard very heavy gunfire and machine-gun fire from No 8 Platoon's front and, more to the right, from 9 Platoon's area.

Saturday 8th June. Dawn, no French counter-attack. An occasional shot from the '75' and burst of machine-gun fire kept the Germans at bay until mid-morning. Then they started shelling us whilst their infantry pressed forward along the hedgerows and through the wood in front. We had only one Bren and our rifles, but the French were well armed with machine-guns and their heavy fire prevented any attack across the open meadows. Gradually, however, the German gunners located our positions and we began to have men wounded.

Saturday 8th June Absolute hell of a day, shells and bombs and machine-gun fire all day. We have had no sleep for four days and not a lot of food. Then the war started, huge tanks of over 70 tons crossed the valley on the other side of the hill. We had four big two-pounder anti-tank guns, beautiful weapons that fire a shell that really weighs about eight pounds. These opened up on the tanks and put some at least out of action. The other tanks replied with pom-pom fire, awful stuff that pours out of them at the rate of about four hundred a minute and each shell weighs roughly two pounds. They wrecked the guns and killed the crews.

In the afternoon [of Friday 7th June] when things were a bit quiet, the Captain, myself and Monk went out on a patrol, we had rifles and grenades and my pistol. We wandered all over the country until we got sick and tired of wandering round. We saw a house that had been bombed and trees all over the show, also two huge bomb craters in the road that were about twenty-five feet across. Then we found an antitank gun and hundreds of rounds of ammo (2"). Then we found a pit with three wounded men in it, they were part of the crew of the gun. One had only a broken leg but the other two were badly shot up. The stench of blood was awful. We found an abandoned truck full of kit and ammo and chucked the bloody lot overboard. Then came the fearful job of putting them on the truck. I reckon that we lost a pint of sweat each, but we did it. Down in the valley was a sixty ton tank, a monster with three turrets and we did not know if it was occupied or not. Got the motor going and I had the heartbreaking job of smashing up the gun, a brand new job and beautifully made. The sights were valued at thirty pounds alone and I put a hammer through them and then got to work on the controls. I had to be careful because there was a live shell in the breech and I could not get it out. That gun will never fire again. On the way back we found two of our men, Fry and Heywood who were absolutely panic stricken. Fry had a bad cut from shrap on his chin but Heywood was unhurt. Neither had as much as a rifle or tin hat even. They had lost the lot. We took them on board but had to smash down several fences because of the roads being mined. This bloody mining is a joke, although it had all been carried out, we got the lorry back over the places, and they expected to stop a tank. Then we had to stop because we came down a road that was covered by an AT gun. We sent Monk back to stop them from firing.

While we were doing all this a motorcyclist roared by and fired a revolver at us. We heard a tank in the distance and were afraid that the cyclist would bring them back. So I stood in front of the wagon and waved a rag like blazes expecting to be blown to hell at any moment. Actually it stopped about a foot from a bunch of anti-tank mines. While laying these mines two days ago a bunch of RE laid them and then backed over them. The whole lot, those already laid and those on the truck as well as four thousand rounds of SAA went up in smoke. Anyway we found a French Red Cross man and he did not take long to patch the men up and take them away. Then we heard that the Jerries were about three miles away and had to stand to all day and night.[6]

Sunday 9th June We all slept in the orchard in hastily dug trenches, which was done in the night. At four in the morning a French officer rushed round to us and shouted *'Les Allemands, Les Boches'*. Then all hell broke loose. We were bombed by planes, shelled by artillery and bombed by trench mortars. And the machine-gun fire was incessant. Two Allied posts were firing over our heads into the valley and the Germans absolutely plastered us with bullets. Then three of us, Mr Naylor, another of the Heywoods and myself took the front post. We had only our rifles and grenades. The bombs fell all of the time, some of them ten yards away. Naylor was scared but was sticking it well. Heywood was panicky but he also did his best to keep cool. I was actually happy and got out of the trench and got a couple of blankets to make it more comfortable. I did not see a German at all and did not fire a single shot. The French machine-guns were firing continuously in bursts of about twenty rounds. They have a beautiful crack crack crack sound to them and it is very easy to distinguish from the Brens roaring chatter or the big Vickers bellow. Then things got too hot and we got the order to retreat. Naylor and Heywood went like scared rabbits at the double, I stayed and collected all ammo and Mills bombs in the various trenches, also all of my kit and overcoat. At this time I was the last man left in the line and was last from the field.

> 2/Lt John Naylor: After Capt Thomson had been away a little time we came under heavy mortar-bombing or shelling. Pte Monk crawled up to me and told me Capt Thomson had been hit, he believed killed, during their return from the French HQ. When there was a lull in the bombing I looked for and found the French Commandant.

---

[6] Captain Alec Thomson also wrote about this patrol in great detail in his diary

He told me that Capt Thomson had been wounded and was being evacuated: and that he proposed to withdraw. I told him I would withdraw with him.

I arranged a RV for the remnants of the Company, at the sunken track running westwards up the hill. At the RV we mustered CSM Weston and about 20 NCOs and men. We had rifles but very little ammunition. The withdrawal went smoothly and we and the French halted half a mile or so to the west of our original position. I then had another conference with the Commandant and told him it was my intention to try and find my Battalion HQ. I do not know where he was making for but we shook hands and wished each other luck.

Outside of the orchard was a fearful sight, the 12ᵗʰ Division of the French Army and our lads were in full retreat. Let me say here and now that the French showed an order and discipline that was terrific. They took all of their kit and machine-guns with them, ours left with nothing, sometimes throwing rifle and ammo away in a mad scramble. I believe that again I alone had equipment. Just inside of the field was Richardson, the best looking lad of the Army class, his whole face below his forehead was blown away ..

This was the last page of this diary but it is continued on some loose pages that were tucked into the back cover. These are foolscap pages, folded into four, written on both sides and numbered separately.

... and his scalp was hanging over a log like a ghastly lid. His whole head was one awful pool of brain specked blood. I looked at his rifle. Called up for Service he had never fired a shot, never in practice and never in war. He was in the front line with clean gun. Next to him was a French policeman, one clean bullet hole on the bridge of his nose, laying peacefully on his face. There were others but I was not interested enough to stop. The only officer I saw was

The Battle of Aumale - St Valery en Caux - Prisoner of War

Naylor, he was grey and would only say 'Follow the crowd, go with them'. I was sweating with the weight of overcoat and equipment, my gasmask canister was shot away from my chest by shrapnel so I threw it away. I helped two Frenchmen with a Hotchkiss gun, but we never fired it. The shells never stopped falling. I [carried] a box of Hotchkiss ammo strips for miles and dropped it down. We got a lorry across the fields full of wounded, we cut down hedges and fences and got it on to the road. A Frenchman gave me a slice of stale bread and some white wine and he spoke a little English. There were no English troops anywhere near. We talked a little but it was hard, against troops we would have fought like fury, with bayonet and grenade if necessary but all we saw was huge tanks and planes. The planes flew over and fired white flares and then we were shelled to hell by the pom-poms on the tanks. The shells were very small and only did a little damage but they came at the rate of two hundred every minute and raked the ground. I did not even see a tank. As the Frenchman, whose name was Andre said 'What can we do, we have no cannon, we have no artillery'. No British or French plane or gun was seen or used. We walked for many miles across the fields, scattering in all directions but always coming back together. A French Captain gave me a weak black coffee and loaded it with white brandy. It made a different man of me. We stopped and I took an inventory of what I had with me, rifle and one hundred and seven rounds, pistol with forty rounds, eight grenades, bayonet, steel helmet, haversack with corned beef and salmon and rum, my diary and 140 francs and 6/6 in English money, jack-knife and my overcoat. I could have fought a section myself and was quite happy about things. The Frenchmen gave me cider and wine and offered me food but I did not take it, they did not have enough themselves. And always we were shelled and bombed. We were joined by two Hotchkiss tanks, grimly efficient machines who went back to fight. We wandered until four o'clock and then I found a Signal corporal whom I knew. He had nothing at all, not even a hat. He wanted to make for Contreville but I would not go with him as I felt sure the BHQ had moved, as indeed they had. I wanted to stop with the French Army as at least we would get food. I filled my stomach and my water bottle at a stream. Then we fell in with two RA men and later on a second lieutenant named Unsworth whom I knew from his having been to dinner with Captain Thomson. He was quite demoralised and imagined that he was on a parade ground. I cocked my pistol and determined to shoot him down if necessary, necessity meaning if he was taking the unarmed men back to the front. I was prepared to go myself willingly. We found a French *Capitaine* and he promised to give us a lift on his lorries and after about an hour of walking we found the lorries. They were cook's lorries and we all got into them. Mine went twenty yards and ran into the ditch and overturned. We crawled out and got onto a private car and went for a very long way but I do not know where. We were left by the road side for three hours and then found a dispatch rider who belonged to the REs and he went and fetched two Bedford lorries and took us back to an enormous depot in the woods. The lads and officers were kindness itself, especially when they learned that I was one of the men who saved Nethercot and Stone from the gun-pit. The handshaking and welcome were terrific and Stone's pal was nearly in tears when he heard that his pal was alive and comparatively well. They asked me what I would like done and gave me stew and bread and tea and did it go down well? Amazed the officers by my armament, rifle, pistol and grenades, they wondered who the hell I was. Then they got ready to move. I pretended to go to sleep on top of one of the trucks and they put me on the MO's truck and made me a bed. I went to sleep and slept until the morning when a chap brought me a cup of tea. Felt better and learned how to mount and fire the 2pd anti-tank gun. Then we did some digging in the trenches. When we had them all dug nicely we moved, as is usual in this man's Army.

I seem to have missed the most important point, where we were in the morning we found thirty abandoned packs and looted them of all we needed. I needed everything and got it except for shaving and washing kit. Some of the lads got themselves hundreds of cigarettes and one of the prizes that I got was four brand new pairs of socks. Also a groundsheet, blanket, new pack, towels, braces, corned beef, blacking and Dubbin. Truly I am under God's protection. I do not know where my mates are but I am comfortable, well fed and happy, all I need is a shave and perhaps more rest, and I may even get that. Above all I have my pistol and diary and even my letters …

Page 134 has been torn off and is missing

After a short sleep we were taken to another Regiment and after another ride were taken to the Surreys. The first man whom I saw was the Padre and he was absolutely overjoyed and took me at once to the CO. They were both eager for news and told me in turn they we were to go home to England if only we could get to Le Havre. We may have to fight our way through. And most of us have no rifles or anything. The nine Kensingtons [Princess Louise's Kensington Regiment were a wartime battalion of The Middlesex Regiment] have three rifles and two .38 revolvers. We were told to stay in the woods until we were told to get into the lorries. It got dark and it was not possible to see even ones own rifle two feet away. We slept in everything we had which in my case was a hell of a lot. I was of a mind to sling the valise as I was the only man with one. It was awful in the wood, we expected to be left because we could not be found, there were only five of us. A bloody owl kept on hooting mournfully above my head and we were still very close to the roar of HE. I kept seeing Richardson's ghastly face, with a smile on his lips and his eyes and forehead blown away and kept hearing his cultured voice saying 'I never fired a shot, not one round'. We were called by the Police Sergeant at half past one and started our way through the wood. We had to hold on to each other to avoid being lost. After an hour of mud we were on the trucks and away. It was dawn at about four and we saw the most horrible sight imaginable. The French Army was in full retreat, as of course were we, most of them were walking and they were done in absolutely. The splendid French cavalry with their magnificent horses were staggering as they rode and walked. These are the men who galloped into the tanks with grenades and put them …

Page 138 was on the back of page 134

After a lot of bother we were put on our lorries and were ready to set off. Then we heard firing and a dozen men came rushing through the woods shouting that the Germans were here. We all took up positions, I was on the right flank. The men were absolutely demoralised and the officers the same. Men grabbed Brens and had no magazines, grabbed AT rifles and no ammo. Sergeant King and myself were fired on by a Bren loaded with tracers. We shouted and I trained my gun on to the Bren gunner. One more burst and I would have shot him dead. Then there was a mad stampede for the trucks and we rushed away leaving several men. As we went past I saw Riley, Captain Thomson's DR shot between … leaning over his bike with his brains and blood running into his lamp. He was not dead. We travelled at a terrific speed for an hour, until it was dark. Suddenly a machine-gun started firing tracer bullets at us and we had to get out. There were no orders and the men left rifles and guns while I went ten yards and took up a good position behind a bank. The tracers hissed overhead. I went back to the cars, there were two men standing. I covered them with my rifle and challenged them. They were a sergeant of the Intelligence and one of his men. He said 'Good Janes you are the one man I need. Can you use a machine-gun?' I said yes and took a Bren.[7] We stayed at our posts for three hours and then got the lorries turned and moved. A house a mile from us was blazing furiously, set on fire by the incendiary bullets of the machine-gun. One of our men was in great pain. The lorries were crowded and were driven at a terrific rate by the terrified drivers. The man groaned and moaned but we simply dare not go any slower. We made for Dieppe, only to be told that it was in German hands. So we went on to Le Havre. When we were near we lost half of our lorries. Then we passed a dead horse who had been shot by a machine-gun and was lying stiff and terrible in the road. Almost at once we were joined by four terrified French soldiers who screamed out that the Germans were just round the corner. They piled onto the already crowded lorries and I stood on the running board.

Wednesday 12th June Well, the bottom has dropped out of everything, we were marched for two miles and told that we were being put on a boat for England. I was staggering along under a Bren gun and seven hundred rounds of ammo. Then we were told to unload our guns and machine-guns, also to throw away knives and bayonets. The whole French Army and our Division had surrendered to Germany. We were dumb with the misery of it all, several burst into tears. We took our guns apart and threw them away. The rounds of ammo laying about were terrible. There must have been half a million rounds there. I had to throw away two automatic pistols and a Bren. It nearly broke my heart to lose my pistol. Then we were marched away and taken over by Germans with pistols. The damage to Cannes by our guns was too awful to describe, the whole place was one terrible ruin. The HE that was poured on it had to be counted by the thousand tons. Every road was full of shattered cars

---

[7] This was probably Donald Edgar who wrote a book of his experiences up until St Valery entitled *The Day of Reckoning* (John Clare Books) in which a similar meeting is described

and tanks by the hundred. Fortunately the dead and wounded had been taken away beforehand. We were marched to a place about three miles away and all put into a huge meadow, about eight thousand of us as far as we could see. I went to sleep, there was not much else to do. They kept bringing in more and more men. They took away our knives and odds rounds of ammo and the officers field glasses but made no attempt to search us. Then we marched for about five miles and passed more burnt out lorries. I was so hungry that I picked up some Army issue biscuits from the road and ate them. There did not seem to be more than a dozen Germans all told but a number of armoured cars kept cruising up and down. We came to a sort of farm with a very high wall and were joined by a lot more men. It does not seem worth having a shot at escape as several have tried but can't get a boat. The Germans seem to be doing all that they can for us but they have an impossible job on. They gave us some very stale bread but it was very welcome, also we have some straw. I have got three hundred cigarettes which is crazy as I don't smoke. I will not part with my water bottle if I can help it.

A major of our lot was crying as he burnt his papers and one fellow put his rifle muzzle onto his forehead and shot himself. The bugler came up to the major and one of the corporals asked "Shall we have the bugler blow retreat?" and the major only nodded. I don't think I shall ever forget my own feelings when that bugle call rang out. Prisoner of war, something that none of us had ever dreamt of; it is something stunning, which strikes at one's very soul to find oneself a prisoner.[8] I lay down with my face on the wet ground, my brain would not work at all for a few minutes. Around me I could hear some of the others as they smashed up the machine-guns and other arms. For a moment the

---

[8] Brigadier James Hargest used very similar words to describe his feelings when he was captured at Sidi Aziz in November 1941 - see *"Farewell Campo 12"* (1945) Michael Joseph (p21)

thought of shooting myself passed through my brain but it was dismissed instantly. At last I roused myself sufficiently to get up and smash my Bren gun and try to smash my rifle also. All of the Bren magazines I smashed in as well and the Mills bombs were un-primed and the pins pulled out. We had hardly time to think before a German Staff car drew up and the occupants formally took us prisoner. We could see that we were covered by heavy machine-guns already although that would not have stopped us had there been any chance of doing anything. We were herded along onto another road that had not been so badly bombed and already we could see the hungry German soldiers looting the wrecked shops while others were already at work repairing our Bedford lorries. We were marched along for about three miles while men flung away all the kit that they had no use for. The road was littered with steel helmets, bayonets, gas-masks, ammunition, razors, papers, even overcoats and spare boots.

At last we came to huge field which was already full of men of all nationalities. It was impossible to lie down and we had to sit or stand as best we could. When I say that this field was about six acres in extent some idea can be gained of the number of men taken at St Valery en Caux on Wednesday the 12th of June 1940. We spent the whole day there and several men were shot because they attempted to get out from the apparently inadequately guarded field. As we had not yet been searched some of these attempts were armed ones and I believe that two guards were wounded by revolver shots from one party who tried to break away. Later in the morning more guards and armoured cars arrived making such attempts still more futile. Towards the evening we were all marched off about four miles to a large farm with very high stone walls and told to get down for the night. There were men everywhere, the vast majority sleeping in the open with no cover whatsoever. Just before dark some of us were given small pieces of bread but it was so sour and mouldy that a couple of bites was more than enough. It rained a little in the night and it was a bedraggled crew who woke up in the morning. (Gibraltar 1941)

Thursday 13th June Well, I had quite a comfortable time last night and woke up feeling cheerful. Had a wash at a pump and felt better still. Lay down for as much rest as possible and was glad of it later on. Some hardy souls did their best to wash and shave at the pump but the vast majority of us preferred to keep our already luxuriant whiskers on. When we moved off we started singing but we soon gave it up for a bad job. There were not many guards but several armoured cars and dozens of motorcycles with machine-guns mounted on them, also nearly all of the soldiers had sub-machine guns. That day's march was fearful. We were marching for nine hours without more than five minutes rest all told. The majority of the Germans were decent and when there was a chance to get food or water gave us every opportunity to get it. Water was the worst job. I carried a water bottle and drank my fill every time I could refill it. I reckon that I got rid of a gallon of it during the day. We had no food given us but were given lettuce and onions and chocolate by the French people. I also got a tin of peas and some concoction of peas and veal which went down very well indeed. I shared all of them with the lads around me who had none, also some of my cigarettes.

On the way down we passed by the sea and as we passed it one bloke made a dive into the bushes and as far as we know he got away. One of the cars came rushing past with klaxon going full pelt, knocked down a Frenchman and crashed over the cliff. There were six Germans on board and most of them must have been killed. It made me laugh. Then we turned back and made for Rouen. This is the third time that I have been to this beautiful cathedral city, but now it is no longer beautiful, it is just another sample of civilisation in the act of civilising. It has been bombed to hell.

We were all marched into an orchard and had only been there for ten minutes when we had to move again. It was not far fortunately, we have walked roughly twenty-eight miles today. Ended up in a huge field behind a big church. It was bloody cold and most of us had no blankets but slept in batches so as to keep as warm as possible. Actually I had quite a decent night. If only we had been ordinary prisoners of war there would be a chance of getting away but as the only place to go is Spain, four hundred miles away, and even that very doubtful, we are better off as we are. One day perhaps we shall again have Allied troops here and then we will at least have a chance. Till then - Heil Hitler.

The only food we have had so far is a lump of black bread, an ounce or so of lard and a smoked herring, all of which went down well. We made fires and I made a sort of thick sweet glorious hot cocoa from a few scraps of chocolate. They have taken some of the lads away in lorries, pity we don't know where they are going.

Friday 14th June 1940 We have had an easy day, done nothing but lay in the very hot sun. They had a bread issue but I did not go because it takes about two hours to get our bit which is pretty awful stuff anyway. They have been taking us away in lorries, about forty in each and we have been taken about thirty miles, towards the South West as far as I can make out. The Germans seem to be very sure of themselves, there are only about forty of them guarding roughly four thousand of us here. They have lovely little Tommy guns, gorgeous little tools that fire a .32 bullet as far as I can make out. Shall have to try and buy one as a souvenir when, if ever we get back. Do not think that we shall be prisoners for long although I can't say why. I have found a new hoodoo and that is orchards, every time I get into trouble lately it is in an orchard. Incidentally I am in one now. I have a badge that I got at St Valery, I shall wear it on my belt to remind me of the place where we neither fucked nor fought.

Can't help feeling bitter about the whole turn out, the whole Battalion came out here with no training and our officers with no revolvers, no artillery support, no tanks and no air support. We have our rifles and an inadequate number of Bren guns. This is the result. The ordinary German privates have automatics and rifle stick bombs and most of them the murderous submachine guns. Their air and artillery action was perfect in every detail, nothing was missed out at all. Then they have Parabellum guns in every car and side-car and tanks by galore. And to cap it all every man seems to be well trained and well fed. The food that they gave us last night was the two things that they were supposed to be short of, lard and herrings. Makes one believe very little of what our papers and radio have said. And yet I still think that we shall get the best of this war in the end. We have heard that USA, Italy and Russia are all in it now but we are not all sure of it. It doesn't seem to matter. But I am happy anyway. I manage to keep cheerful under almost any conditions.

The next ten days were just plain hell, the marches varied in length from sixteen to nearly thirty miles and as each day went by the proportion of men unable to finish the march grew larger. Not all of the cases were genuine however and the result was that the Germans soon began to treat them all with same remedy - a rain of kicks and blows from rifle and revolver butts. The French people were extremely kind in some towns and utterly indifferent in others, in any case the amount of food or water received by any individual was never sufficient. The main worry was always water and very few of the men had had the foresight to bring their water bottles with them and every chance of water was the signal for a stampede. These mad scrambles of course upset the Germans who always thought, and often with reason, that we were attempting to escape and many a pail of water, worth its weight in silver at least to us, was kicked into the dusty road by exasperated German soldiers. Another way in which we attempted to fill our empty stomachs was by raiding the silos of betterave (clamps of mangel-wurzel) but the sweetness of them combined with the scarcity of water made them very unappetising fare.(Gibraltar 1941)

Saturday 15th June We had a really good meal last night, a lump of black bread and about ten or eleven pieces of smoked herring in olive oil. I managed to get about a cupful of the oil and it was very good indeed. Also got hold of some straw and had a lovely kip, best for weeks and weeks, we do not have to worry about whether or not we shall wake up in time now. In fact we have no worries at all now, not even aircraft, it does not matter a damn what nationality a plane is he will not do us any harm. And also we can be sure that as long as we behave ourselves we shall see the end of this war alive, which is far more than we dare say a week ago. We are hoping that England will try and do something for us in the way of exchanging prisoners, after all, to surrender a whole Army Division is unprecedented in history and at least we have some prisoners. Both prisoners are a bloody nuisance to their captors whereas if they were exchanged they would have useful men instead even if they could not fight again.

Well we had a long march today and got here very tired indeed and were glad to sit down. They gave us bread and about half a pint of quite good soup and we are happy again. Unfortunately we are very short of water although I personally have plenty. The have the whole of the field covered with very efficient looking machine-guns, with Parabellum drum and a water jacket and a butt like a rifle.

Sunday 16th June We woke up at about four and the more enterprising of us tried to light fires and very soon had about eight good ones going a treat. Then after breakfast we had a long march in front of us of about twenty miles. It was cold and the walking was not too bad but our feet are not in very good shape and a good many of them dropped out. We passed through Forge les Eaux and Gallefontaine and later on a town of which a quarter had been razed to the ground by bombs and was a truly terrifying sight. Whole blocks of houses lay in ruins and even the cathedral did not escape damage. One thing alone was unmarked, a statue of Marchel Joffre in the square stood up proudly among the ruins. Some of the cars had as many as eighty machine-gun bullet holes in them. We passed about eleven 6.2 inch howitzer guns all smashed by their crews before they left them. And carts and cars all over the show. One thing I did notice was a number of graves of soldiers of all nationalities buried with their helmets on sticks above them. We got to our new place at about 2.15 and a bloody dreary hole it is too, just a wide field with a sanitary trench at one end and two machine-guns at opposite corners. I went to have a piss at the wrong hedge and a guard fired at me with a Luger. The slug cut branches about four inches from my head, which, at eighty yards is bloody good shooting. We had some thick green soup given us but no bread and could get no water before 9.00. It was perishing cold, although I have my overcoat I could not sleep. I don't know what will happen to the men who have nothing. Got up at 2.00 and walked about until dawn when we lit a fire with what scraps we could find. It was very welcome. I have a glorious beard about an inch and a half long all over my face and look a rare sight. I wish I could let them know at home that I am alive and well. Shan't be well much longer with this grub. Have got rid of all my fags, realised 110 francs for them and gave away the rest. They were more precious than gold to the boys, one gave 50 frs for 20 Woodbines.

Monday 17th June Had a long march today and covered about 18 miles, the last two of which I literally staggered for want of food and drink. The men who were in charge of us were very decent today and gave us three good halts and one of them said 'Keep your chin up Tommy, only two more kilos to go'. When we got to the camp the whole Allied Armies seem to be congregated together and a most depressing sight it was too, English, Scots, Welsh, Irish, French, Belgians, Poles, Senegalese, a couple of Moors, hundreds of French sailors, an awful sight to me anyway. I fell down and slept for three hours, more coma than real sleep. The sun was still very hot. Then I woke with a start, someone was shouting 'The war is over, the war is over!' and as far as I know at the moment it is. I have been praying that I shall get home to say 'Jeep Jeep' to Mr Potts ever since I have been a prisoner. I hope that God will answer my prayers and let me go, no matter under what circumstances. I of course I should very much like to see an Allied victory but if not, well several things are possible. I am still praying very hard that it will still be answered. I am going light-headed and thinking chaotic thoughts, of Time and Death and God as the Eternal Trinity and of Love and Infinite Pathos and many other things, of steak and kidney pies and of Richardson and his white brains on the bank and the queer coincidence that made a Frenchman give me his AB64 [Army Book 64 - Soldiers Service & Pay Book] He will not be here to see our humiliation, to see us thankful for a scrap of mouldy bread and of refusing a mate a sip of water. But perhaps he will be with us in sympathy. The French are going mad, rushing about and packing and kissing each other. We are not happy, only apprehensive. At least, as I have said before, we can hope to see the end now whereas before we only had two alternatives, death or mutilation, this third possibility never crossed my mind. I never would have surrendered myself but would rather have gone down fighting. We were betrayed, we were sold and we bitterly regret it. Those of us who do not do so now will do so soon, when we think it all over and sort out the Dead Sea Fruit that is left to us. Perhaps God will give us some consolation from this awful affair. I would give everything I possess to see Mr Potts ugly black face again. Mine is just as black and ugly now.

Tuesday 18th June At least I believe that it is, I do not know. We rested until 2.00 and then had a terrible march in front of us. We none of us had any water in our bottles and men fell by the roadside by the dozen. Most of them were Frenchmen, also most of them were foxing. We are beginning to get a new conception of 'our gallant Allies the French' the bastards behave like pigs now that we are prisoners. And the farmhouses that were so anxious to sell us eggs and cider and anything else now refuse us a drink of water. The water position is acute, we drank from a stagnant duck pond and were glad to. Every time we saw a pump or well we rushed to it irrespective of whether or not the Germans would fulfil their promise and shoot us. They let off shots about every ten minutes at someone or other. I have had three shots fired at me but do not care a damn, I have faced bullets before. I managed to get a huge dollop of water from a pump and drank nearly a quart of the awful stuff. We got to the camp No. 4 at about 9.40 and were given some horrible soup and boiled black beans. Also some of us got a small bit of salt meat. Had quite a decent night's sleep and woke up feeling quite cheerful. Wish that we could get some news though, we hear rumours and still more rumours but know nothing. We hear that the war is suspended while Britain and Germany come to terms. I hope that it is true, above all things I pray to be home for Babe's birthday [July 1st] Even so it would be a bit of a rush. At least we have plenty of water here, a stream runs through the place. We have passed Aumale and Poix and Airmontres. Believe that we are near Abbeville. I have been to most of these places before.

Wednesday 19th June We have had a lovely rest day today, in fact we have done exactly nothing. The men have been split into groups which makes eating very easy. We have had two issues of boiled beans and one of delicious new French bread of which we have been promised more. Also I have washed my feet and one pair of socks in the river and lay in the sun for the rest of the time. I am with a lot of Scottish lads and they are wonderful in knowing just what is their own, in fact I feel far safer in leaving my stuff here than with my own crowd. I seem to be about the only one who has not shaved, shall really have to think about it. Managed to write a letter to Mother for which I am very thankful. Hope to God that I shall see them all soon. Also managed to write to Babe, I hope that they both get through, at least it will stop them from worrying a bit.

Thursday 20th June Have not moved all day. The sun has been awful and we have no protection from it. Some of us have been sunbathing and some are burnt. Also had a good wash down and felt miles better for it. Have washed my towel and found another. Have not stopped praying that God will end this awful war. I have seen some of the towns in France and should hate to think of the same thing in England. And I am afraid that it will happen if some sort of agreement is not reached. That we shall do as much if not more damage in Germany is certain but what good will that do? There is talk of a conference here all day but of course we know nothing. Have had two more issues of boiled beans and another of bread, one loaf between ten. We were given both lard and salt with the bread and it was lovely. I was almost delirious this morning, what with the sun and the lack of food. They have just brought a poor devil in who has been loose for eight days and he is nearly starved. Still no news.

Friday 21st June Had quite a decent night and got up at 6.30. We had to clean up the field and had some breakfast of the inevitable boiled beans and a piece of meat and luxury of luxuries another piece of French bread. We got going at 8.30 and marched until 4.30 with only two stops. We did not have too bad a time as the pace was easy and we were given all sorts of things by people on the route, water, wine, milk, coffee, even knobs of sugar and pieces of cake. I drank so much milk that I felt quite queer but got to the end of the march feeling quite cheerful. Managed to cadge two small scraps of bread at the end of the route and ate them straight away. This camp seems to be a lousy one, just a wide field with about eight thousand men in it. Don't quite know how they are going to dish the food out as we are in no sort of order.

During the whole of this first eight days things were not so bad as they became later on, many of us had big quantities of cigarettes (I do not smoke myself) and we generally managed to get food of some sort from the French. But then things got worse, the long marches began to tell on us, the lack of food and drinking bad water gave every second man a bad stomach. Then, on the tenth day I had a premonition, more than that, a conviction in fact, that in three days time everything would be all right.

I do not know why but this feeling was extremely strong and I had not the hope but the real assurance that on Wednesday something important would happen. As a consequence the three days that I had to wait did not seem of any importance. However the next day when we had only marched about three miles along the road my stomach and head gave so much pain that I staggered along, unable to see a thing. As a result I found myself in the rear of the column being urged to keep up by a German soldier. He was very decent, and when he saw that I was really ill and not shamming he stopped the first car, explained something to the occupant officers and I was put inside, and promptly collapsed. The next thing I remember was finding myself in the courtyard of a large house which appeared to be full of officers. From there I was taken to a hut and waited for about an hour with a great number of men, most of whom were wounded and required their dressings changed. There was an old

Commandant who struck me as being particularly courageous, he had a huge gash right across the top of his head and one man was shaving off his hair with a blunt razor. At long length it was my turn but as my command of the French language was equal to the doctor's English and time was very valuable I'm afraid that he did not understand a lot. However he gave me a draught of some liquid that did eventually put an end to the pain in my stomach. I then lay in the courtyard of the house for the rest of the day. A Scottish private brought me a good ration of soup about six o'clock. Then I was sent back to my friends in the bottom of a large gravel pit.

That night I slept under canvas (for the first time since the day the war started) in the sick tent in fact. The place was stuffy and during the night I nearly suffocated but could not get out because doing so would have meant wakening the whole tent, some of whose occupants were really ill and some wounded. The next day we did not move at all (this was at Doullens) and in the evening it started to rain very hard. Now, up to now the sleeping question had been bad but at least endurable, we slept in short rows of a dozen or so, anyone who had an overcoat or gas cape using it so that two others also shared it. I had an overcoat and a small piece of canvas from a lorry so that I was in a much better plight than many of the others, many of whom had only battle dress. But to sleep in the open, in a pit with about three inches of water in it and rising rapidly while cold piercing rain poured down was by no means a pleasant prospect to contemplate. Some of us were already in the sick tent but the water was even deeper there than outside and lying down was out of the question. Just as we had given up all hope of doing anything except stand up until morning the welcome news arrived that we were to be moved somewhere else. At first this turned out to be a short tunnel already half full of cement in bags but a few minutes afterwards we were moved into a room in a small house. There were forty-four of us in a room about ten by fifteen and yet everyone had a good night. The next morning we had a shorter march than usual and reached St Pol, Pas de Calais. One man remarked, as we got to the camp, which was in a racecourse 'I don't like the look of this place, it's the first bastard with a swastika on it'. It was in fact the first time I saw the now familiar flag, blood red with a black swastika in a white circle. As soon as we were there however we received a good big ration of soup, dished out by a laughing brown skinned French cook. The ration was so big that I was unable to eat all of mine and gave the rest to Cook, one of the Army Class who had been with me since St Valery. I was in a contented frame of mind as the next day was the day I knew something would happen. That day we heard that the French had signed an armistice with Germany and that the war was over. The French soldiers went mad, kissing and hugging each other and singing. As we had no news of the British doing the same we did not join in with them.

That day, on the march a German soldier had told me and several others that he had kept a café in Abbeville for five years, being all the time an agent of the Nazi Intelligence. The guards on the whole were not too bad, although there were some cases of individual brutality, mainly when there was a chance to get water or food some of the men were badly knocked about by rifle butts and kicked. The next morning we were given coffee at four o'clock in the morning and marched off of the racecourse. Followed a wait of an hour in the town of St Pol when we got a lot of food given to us and several fellows escaped. I was determined that if nothing happened that day that the following day I should attempt to escape. On the road I attempted to get someone to go with me but no-one would go, the answer was always the same 'Fuck it, the war is done for me, anyway it won't last long'.

The Battle of Aumale - St Valery en Caux - Prisoner of War

After a long march of about twenty kilometres we were put into a large field and given food by the French Red Cross. I had already collected about two pounds of bread in the town of St Pol. One incident occurred which I remember vividly, there was a young girl of about twenty outside one house and she had a bag of biscuits with her that she was giving away two at a time. Such was the dignity, the air of that girl that the soldiers formed a short queue and got their biscuits without grabbing or pushing. I never saw this happen before or since. She was a small well built girl, rather like Kitten and she was dressed in a pale dove grey. Little Lady in Grey, I saw you only once but you will remain in my memory as part of the France that was. (Gibraltar 1941)

Outside the village of Divion my premonition was justified. A huge crowd of people lined the route for miles, some to give us food, cigarettes and drink, some even soap, towels and razors, some merely to watch us. Then an absolutely mad thing happened. I had just been given a pint of beer by a man which is mad enough anyway when a girl grabbed me and hissed *"Toots Sweet, Ally Ally, Toots Sweet"* and seizing my arm, gave me a shirt and a pair of miner's trousers. She took me behind a low wall and tried by signs to make me put them on. I took off my overcoat and started taking off my jacket but she got angry and made me put the clothes on top of them. My mind was in a confused whirl until it came to me that this was Wednesday and the 'something' that I knew would come on that day. I followed the girl, who was joined by another.[9] They hid my pack, steel helmet, water bottle and overcoat and made me go to a house about two hundred yards away. My first impression of the house was that it was full of people, mainly children, in all about thirty of them, all of whom were drinking coffee. Not one of them knew a word of English and my knowledge of French consisted of

---

[9] The two girls were Mathilde Bodlet and her cousin Solange Devise

about thirty words. I was also given a cup of coffee which was more than half rum and then another until my empty stomach could take no more. Then a young fellow proceeded to shave me, a painful business as it was the first time in at least three weeks but at last most of it was off, but I retained a moustache. I learned then that my new home was not to be here but some way away. Then we each took a bundle and walked for about four miles where they completed the transformation and I got rid of the rest of my clothes.

Colonne Ricouart June 1940

Now here it is necessary to make something clear otherwise the following will not make sense. At this time, although it was the 26th of June I had no inkling of the defeat of the Allied Armies, no idea that the battle of Dunkirk had taken place, no realisation that the surrender at St Valery en Caux was more than a small local affair. Furthermore, in common with the vast majority of other prisoners I believed that a large British force was still operating in Calais and that it was only necessary to reach that point to be able to take part in future operations. So that I had the idea that this was all part of a scheme and that before night at least I should find myself well on the way back to my regiment. (Gibraltar 1941)

They gave me plenty of food, as much as I could eat although they are obviously poor, and also a very comfortable bed which I appreciate after sleeping in open fields for so long. It does not seem that I shall be able to leave yet for some time but no doubt something will turn up. We are only about thirty odd miles from Calais which, dressed as I am and with the roads full of returning refugees and soldiers should not be too hard to cover but the problem of that twenty odd miles of water is not to be solved as easily as that.

Only God can really help me and I know that he will but how I do not know. I hope that it will be by some sort of peace between Germany and England, can't understand why they did not get one with France, it would be awful to have both lands bombed to blazes like this part of France has been and the problem still not at an end. If Chamberlain was in power I believe that he would scrape together some sort of Pact but Winny is made of sterner stuff, unfortunately for us. We can give Germany more than she can send but it will lead nowhere.

I am very comfortable indeed here, it fact it does not seem to be real at all but I do hope that these people do not get into trouble over it. I do not know just what the Germans are doing here, whether they are staying or going away but they have made things very bad. The people can't get the lovely French bread that they used to and have the hard dry German stuff that we have been having as prisoners. All around are terrific heaps of earth from the coal mines. When I looked out of the window the first thing I saw were the words Alsace Lorraine and as my impression was that this interesting place was some hundreds of miles away, it took me some time to find out that it was only the name of the road, Rue de Alsace-Lorraine. The family consists of a miner Alfred Bodlet, his wife Emma and two daughters, Mathilde aged seventeen and Solange aged fifteen and a boy Alfred of about six. The house is an ordinary miner's cottage but larger than the average council house. They keep a number of rabbits in the back yard.[10]

Friday 28th June Yesterday had the most enjoyable day for months, started by having coffee in bed and then spent the morning writing and playing a dice game with the young son. Had an excellent dinner and slept in the afternoon. In the evening they dressed me up in a black suit and wide sweeping sombrero hat and we walked about three miles and went to the house of a man who has been in France since the last war. He is a motor mechanic and has a French wife. We talked for about an hour and he filled me up with both tea and hope. He says that he believes that in a fortnights time we shall hear how the war is going on and that it may be possible to get home or at least get to some English troops by then. I hope to God that he is right. He reckons that either the French officers sold out to the

---

[10] Rue d'Alsace Lorraine is on the outskirts of Auchel and number 200 is the last house on the left. It may also be approached across open fields from the main village of Colonne Ricouart which is about half a mile away.

Germans or else what we thought were French soldiers were really
Fifth Column merchants which is more than possible. I simply do
not believe that the French Army is as yellow as we have seen them.
I think that they would have fought had they been given the chance
to do so. England seems to be Hitler's next objective and I think that
that is where he is going to fall down. He will have to land troops
somehow and the Navy will prevent him from doing that in any
numbers while there are enough soldiers there to deal with any
relatively small lots who do get through. And if he bombs us, as no
doubt he will as a last resource, we can swop him bomb for bomb
and see if our reconnaissance flights were for nothing. I am not
altogether happy about the result, it must mean thousands of people
and their homes destroyed in any case unless we act first and bomb
his air bases and factories first in one terrific drive. There is good
reason to suppose that we are doing something like that already, the
RAF have bombed the Channel Ports and bombs have been dropped
not far from here, that is Colonne Ricouart or so I do believe,
anyway it was near Divion not far from St Pol and Bethune in the
Pas de Calais. Also the BBC said that they have broadcast a message
to the German people telling them to take cover when the British
bombers come for the Germans will not give any air raid warnings
and in plain speech we mean business, no more leaflets. About time
too, the German people do not want a continuation of this war any
more than we do and the only way to stop it is to paralyse the Nazi
war machinery, bomb factories and munitions, airfields and
submarine and surface vessel bases. This we can do and I hope that
we will.

*The food of these people seemed to consist of bread, coffee and
soup. The coffee is made in all sorts of strengths to make several
different drinks of it. In the morning it is strong and bitter with no
milk, it gets weaker as the day goes on until the evening meal
when it consists of about two thirds of a pint of hot milk and just*

a dash of coffee, with plenty of good French bread to go with it. The girl Mathilde was rather a pretty girl, big and solidly built and she and her sister slept in the same room as I did. I had a big double bed and there was only a curtain between that and the next in which the two girls slept. In spite of this we never as much as held hands the whole time I was there. Beats me, an arrangement like that but no one seemed to find anything out of the ordinary in it. (Gibraltar 1941)

Hear a lot of stories about the Germans, in fact the way we manage to make each other understand is nothing short of a miracle. It appears from the radio that both France and Belgium mean to enter the war again with England. One thing is certain, unless we lose the war in a very short time we shall win for verily time is on our side. Time will give us the Colonial help, will allow the conscripts to be trained and perhaps even bring America in. And always at the back is the huge shadow menace of Russia, a vague indistinct shape that no one knows the power of, that does not know its own power and possibly does not know which side to take and what territory to grab. She is not a menace in the lightning sense, she cannot strike quickly and cleanly but she can crush and cannot be hurt herself. No power on earth could ever smash Russia, the very size on the map is frightening. True most of it is arid waste and most of the people could not understand each another but her potential power is stupendous. Which way will she turn or will she go back to sleep?

Time and God alone can tell and both smile at the futile attempts of man as the Sphinx smiles across the desert. 'We know and we could tell, but you have not learned our language, and you are so few moments here that it is not worth our learning yours'. Just as I saw the far famed roses of Picardy blooming on a trellis oblivious to the fact that the air was putrid with the stench of dead horse and man and the howitzer shells lay on the lush grass, instruments of death, the third member of the Great Trinity, death that man thinks he can control but which laughs in his face. Remember Kipling 'Oh faithless faith that puts its trust in reeking tube and iron shard, faithless as dust that builds on dust, and guarding calls not Thee to guard'. The roses will die and the shells remain but in a thousand years the roses will still be there and the brass will return to the earth from which it came. Such is war.

Thursday 4th July 1940 Have been here just over a week and seem to have settled down as if I had been a year. Nearly every day they take me out to visit some of their innumerable relations all round. I have met about a hundred different people who seem to know all about me and take it all as a matter of course. Queer people, the majority of them do not seem to have any money but all own a good radio set and every house is spotlessly clean. Although this is one of the poorer mining districts such a thing as a slum street just does not exist. And their hospitality is wonderful, at no matter what hour of the day we drop in on them they make coffee and usually produce red wine and fruit. And nearly always food. The food mainly consists of bread, I have not seen any cake or anything of that sort at all.

Went to see a man named Teddy whose other name appears to be *Ceasure*. He is English and married to a French woman who makes dresses in Auchel. Had an enormous meal of roast pork, broad beans and potatoes, tapioca pudding and coffee and fruit to follow. Felt quite uncomfortable after that. He came in just a trifle drunk, don't know why and was too polite to ask. This lady has about six girls who work for her and they seemed very interested in me. I shall really have to come back to the Pas de Calais when this lousy war is over. Had a long jaw as they both speak English and know what is going on around. He also keeps rabbits, *lappuns* [sic] they call them here, another local habit, they have them for food as they cost very little to keep and breed like flies. It was dark before we left and it was a lovely walk home as the wind was cool and balmy.

As we were crossing a field of green grass something caught at my heart, on just such a night three years ago I was with Babe in just such a meadow. And between you and me I shall again be in such a field about a hundred miles from here with her but I shall be a different man then. None of us could see what we have seen and done what we have done and remain the same as before. Can't be done. And Babe too, can she take the strain that she is no doubt under, she cannot as I used to, feel my pistol and say 'Well if they won't let me live as I want to at least I will choose the time when I die'. I can't say that now for my pistol probably lies in grass with the dew rusting the delicate machining that I oiled and cleaned so often.

Saturday 6th July Was rather ill yesterday, mainly through eating as much as normally and doing nothing to use it all up. Cured that by eating nothing at all all day, not even a cup of coffee. This coffee is a racket, we drink on an average nine different cups of various sizes and strengths, some with sugar and plenty of milk and some with neither and some again with one or the other Sometimes it is made with coffee, sometimes from coffee and chicory, chicory and malt, malt and coffee, malt alone and chicory alone, also there are three grades of malt. Altogether the best plan is to forget it all and drink it down. Then again, nearly every house has an unlimited supply of what they call *byrrh*, or beer, a bitter acrid brown liquid that is only fit for drowning bugs on a horses neck.[11] They drink quarts of it with gusto and then come back for more. It is of course a different place from the *Seinne Infereiur*, that is round about Le Havre. That is a wine drinking place and there it is hard to escape the bitter *Vin Rouge Ordinaire*. This district is a mining area as I have written

---

[11] Some confusion here - Byrrh is a popular aperitif whilst the French for beer is simply biere

before and one can see all around mine mountains of dirt and debris from them. They range up to about four hundred feet high and the muck is ran to the top by a narrow gauge railway of two tracks. The heaps are roughly conical, the older ones having one arc of the cones base elongated, as the tipping point moves up and out. The country seems to be nearly flat and devoid of natural hills and the villages are of nearly straight streets each of 200 houses or so. The villages are really about the size of Esher and are Divion, Auchel, Colonne Ricouart and two others. They look like models in the sun with the huge pithead wheels overtopping all except the muck heaps. These pithead works look huge and inspiring somehow against the sky as one approaches them as there is no background for them, just clear sky. It rained rather heavily today and I had to borrow an overcoat to get back with. Hope that I will not have to stay here for the winter, it must be a dreary place apart from the danger. We passed two German soldiers this afternoon on the road.

Wednesday 10th July I have been here a fortnight today and am just beginning to feel part of the place. A lot has happened since then but in the censor riddled place it is hard to get a true perspective of it. The British Navy presented the French Navy with four alternatives which boiled down roughly to 'Come in with us or we sink you.' And they were sunk.[12] The good old Nelson-Churchill touch. The Nazis and Italians are of course furious but is that anything new? The Germans had given a guarantee that the boats would not be used for war purposes. This of course made it essential that they be sunk at the earliest moment. They were I believe sunk by a new method, for the first time in history a live torpedo was launched from an aircraft in the air and the attack was very successful. The Germans are bombing Britain pretty badly as far as I can make out and losing

---

[12] On 3rd July 1940 the Royal Navy sank the French fleet at Mers el Kabir in Operation Catapult

a high proportion of machines in the process. The bombers however seem, as always, to get through. The fact that they do not return is but little consolation for us. It's a pity that the Germans do not hear our broadcasts, it would have a deterrent effect on the pilots of the Luftwaffe if they knew that they had only one chance in two of seeing the Fatherland again once they set out. Unfortunately many are picked up and put into infinitely better prison camps than our men will see. This is a mistake, Britain should make it clear that the reward of failure is Death, the German who invades Britain comes to kill and should be treated as a murderer. Likewise if they land from ship the order should be 'No prisoners'. We can't afford to keep them and we appear to be too soft-hearted to make good use of them. At any moment now the attack may be launched, I don't think that Germany can face another winter without a decision. Hope not anyway. Our own bombers make daily raids on Germany and muck up factories and railways and docks. Good work, hope they keep it up.

Yesterday I went and saw three Scottish lads[13] who are in the same position as myself but are in a very poor house together. Lord above knows how they manage to live there. Also met an English professor who said that his name was Paul Dickerson. He has the crazy idea of trying to walk to Portugal or Switzerland in the hope of getting home to England and asked me if I would care to join him. The distance to Portugal is roughly fourteen hundred kilometres, Heaven only knows how he will keep himself in food and above all boots all that way, it will take five weeks at least. And Spain is Fascist and may quite possibly be in the war on the wrong side by then. And he will be in danger of being caught every minute of the day. True he is

---

[13] Believe these men were 2879108 Pte A F D Harper, his cousin 2879107 Pte R Dunbar and 2879102 Pte Stanley Westland - all Gordon Highlanders - and that they were sheltered by a Mme Bouillez

a civilian and has a passport but I don't think that that will help him a lot. Not me, if I travel at all I want to go north or else west to America. Neither is possible yet or likely to be for a bit.

Friday 12th July The war appears to be waking up again. The Germans have begun sending very large fleets of planes to Britain and we have started shooting them into the sea at a rate that, if it is true, will very soon end this war, roughly thirty or more are claimed each day and many more are damaged and as the announcer says in his emotionless voice 'unlikely to reach their base'.

On Wednesday, which is *Mercredi* to me now, forty eight (ie. *Quarante Huite*) bombers set out in lovely formation from the nearby aerodrome. An hour and a half later twenty-three came back, two of them obviously in trouble. As far I can see this bombing on both sides still leads nowhere, it will not have a decisive effect but no country can lose planes at the rate that Germany has and still keep going. The very cost of machines and the training of the men must present immense difficulties. The money does not seem to worry them because of the countries that they have invaded, there is no doubt that not only is France being systematically looted but her currency is being undermined also. The German mark has to be valued at twenty francs which seems to be a very high value apart from the fact that it is all paper money and probably not backed by anything at all. Europe is going to be in a nasty mess when all this is finished. The entry of Italy has further complicated things, she obviously never meant to fight but counted on getting a huge slice of good land just for the asking. The fact that we are now at war with her brings up the old question of Abysinnia for there is now fighting there.

The Canadians have promised us a very large force of men within a few days but do not state where they are coming to or what they are going to do. The sympathies of the USA are obviously with us but still they do not enter the war actively. It will, of course take a long time for the whole of the Empire to throw in its weight but that weight will be enormous when it does come. Then again, Germany has been at war for nearly three years in one sense or another and no doubt the people of Germany anyway are sick of it. The countries of Czecho-Slovakia, Austria and Poland present a problem to me, I do not know if they are still active enemies on a real scale or whether they show the indifference that France does. France has surprised and pained me beyond measure, that a nation, so famed for its patriotism and valour, should knuckle under so easily and be so indifferent to its fate is incomprehensible to me.

The Germans are here in very small numbers but seem to be treated more as friends than enemies. Teddy says that in Paris they are welcome everywhere and that the people shrug their shoulders *'La Guerre est fini - bon'*. Whether they really do not care or if they are expecting England to deliver them in some unexplained way I do not know but they have allowed themselves to be deprived of every weapon that they possessed. Even the Navy had to be sunk by the Royal Navy, they had neither the courage to join us or to copy the Jerry tradition and scuttle it. I hope that something turns up that allows me to get out of here before the winter comes, things are going to be pretty bad if the war lasts for another year. It has been told to me that the airmen of the aerodrome near here have refused to fly to England because they do not return. Also many of them complain that they have had no leave for years in some cases. One officer blew his brains out in front of his men. I hope that these stories are true, internal trouble is the one factor that we need now, if they seek an Armistice as they did last time the terms will be no more tender than Versailles. And I hope that I am one of the Army of Occupation, I should like to learn German. Besides I was once their prisoner.

Monday 15th July Went out visiting again on Friday to Teddy. When I got there he was out but his wife was there with two very large young ladies. Incidentally it was the first time that I have been out by myself, about four miles I should say, it was quite an experience to know that if a Jerry stopped me I should be in clink again. Anyway it didn't happen. Teddy came in very full of liquor again for which I can't blame him, he also will be in prison if he is caught in spite of the fact that he has been in France for twenty years. He and his wife seemed very confident that the war would not last long and she produced a copy of a leaflet supposed to have been dropped from a British plane. I doubt it, as also did her husband, it told in flamboyant language of a British victory at Dunkirk. Where it came from I do not know but it was not a genuine leaflet. I sat and drank large cups of tea and ate three boiled eggs until it was very late. Came home feeling quite happy.

On Sunday Mr Churchill broadcast to the world and I had the privilege of hearing him for the first time. He did not sound very optimistic about an early end of war but stated quite simply that we should win and why. The very fact that he spoke so confidently showed that as far as he knew he was speaking the truth. One phrase stuck in my mind, when speaking of Hitler and his crew he said "We will have no parley with them, we will show them no mercy, and we shall ask none". If that policy is carried out we must win. We have all along been working on the assumption that it will be a very long war while the Nazis haven't. If we win we must carry out the latter part of his words, there must be no mercy, they have terrorised a Continent and they must be made an example of so that would-be imitators will know what to expect. Germany must be dissolved in bits again as she was before, each bit of which must work so hard to keep their backbone from their navel that never again will they even contemplate going to war. The Germans are a great nation, let them prove it by work and more work, they said that they could not pay their war debts but found money for another war. How much better it would have been to have exacted the last *pffenig* from them. And if Winny Churchill is still in command I believe that we shall, this time.

Today, Monday I heard a commentary on the air battle that took part over the Straights of Dover yesterday, it was very real and one could hear the Ack Ack guns as well as the *Emma Gees* rattling away. He described how one Messerschmitt dived clean from over twenty-five thousand feet into the sea and how a Junkers 87 [Stuka] went into the sea while its pilot was floating down on his parachute. Of course he was rescued, he would be, its just as if a murderer tried to kill me and my family and when I had taken away his weapon I got him a cup of tea because he was cold. So I should.

Tuesday 16th July Like most mornings now I did not get up until gone 11.00. Lord only knows what I am going to do when I get back into the Army and reveille is at 6.00. I still cling somewhat pathetically to the belief that one day this will happen. The German troops are moving about a lot now and everyone who comes in seems to have fresh news of troop movements. The RAF keep bombing hell out of the aerodrome at Reuley, every day one or more bombers leisurely fly over and in eight minutes time we hear the 'woof woof woof woo woo woof Whoof' of the Jerry ack ack gun then the 'Whoom, Whoooom' of bombs then away flies the plane quite content. The other day a small detachment of Jerries were marching along a road when the plane came over. An officer was fool enough to open up with his tommy gun on it. The plane went slowly up in a climb and then came down in a shallow dive. Tata ta ta ta ta tack, tatatatatatata tack and away home after saluting with his gloved hand. The Jerries climbed out of the hedge and found fourteen had gone to hell and thirty were injured by British nickel. That gunner was good, although I wasn't there they say that he only used two bursts of five seconds each, say a hundred and fifty rounds. A lot better use for them than leaving them out in the open like the millions of rounds near Formerie. I can't forget that somehow, long belts of lovely new armour piercing cartridges in steel belts just pulled out of their cases and laying in the grass.

Thursday 18th July Went to supper with Teddy again yesterday, he was not very cheerful, said that he expected to be interned any day. Told me to come over when I liked and asked me to come over on Friday and help him with a car. Came home by myself, the place was full of Jerries, they have been on the move for the last week or so. One of them told a civilian in Auchel that they would be in London by the 22nd of this month. I hope they are, I shall not be there but quite a number of other people will. They are a scruffy lot here, not a bit like the men who captured us. The RAF blew up a double viaduct on the Dortmund canal yesterday and claim to have done a lot of good by it, the reason being that since they started blowing up railways and bridges Jerry has been using canals a lot and they have built very big barges for the purpose. It will cost them so much more petrol to move the stuff from the barges now as they say on the radio that part of the canal has run dry as a result. Nice work, keep it up. The wireless has had no news at all lately, just reports about nothing at all and then filling in the odd four minutes with a gramophone record. I feel that something is going to happen before the weather breaks up and hope it does.

Saturday 20th July Yesterday I went over to Teddy and helped him to dismantle a van. When I got there he was hopelessly drunk and insisted upon my going out with him to have another one. The one meant four and by the time we got back he did not know what he was doing and did not care, he had already knocked a Frenchman down in an *estaminet* [café] who was going to report him to the Mairie. Worse than that, all foreigners, of which of course he is one, had to report to the Mairie anyway. Well, we took quite a lot off the car and made ourselves lovely and black, also had an enormous amount to eat. Left then about 9.00 and came on home.

This morning I went over again although I did not feel that it was safe and we finished stripping the car down. About two o'clock one of the girls (who works for his wife) came out and said that the Germans had come and that I was to hide. So I went quietly down the garden and hopped over to next door and started weeding the garden in the nonchalant 'don't care if I do' sort of way that the French do. About a quarter of hour later he came down the garden and said "Goodbye Pierre, I've got to go". All I could answer was "Goodbye sir" and the Germans took him away.

His wife took it very well but she was obviously very much upset. I stayed for another three hours and then the lady and daughter whom I am with came for me. I called on the three Scotsmen on the way back and warned them and they said that they had not been out for two days. That evening Mathilde took me for a walk to the Mairie of Colonne Ricouart, I shall not forget that evening easily. The sunset was a blaze of glory, lighting up the toy houses and the gigantic pit-heads and dumps into a fantastically beautiful scene, the soft evening breeze blew in our faces and there was a good looking young woman with me. *I squeezed her hand and she looked at me, my belief is that in that moment was planted a seed that did not show itself above ground until a year later.*

Passed several German soldiers on the way home, the ones here are all very badly dressed and not in the least smart. Yesterday, when we were sweeping up coal in front of Teddy's house one of them asked us the way to Cushy [Cauchy-a-la-Tour] a town not very far away. Teddy said when he had gone "I wonder what the bastard would say if he knew that we were both Englishmen". The pocket and side of his very dirty tunic were torn and done up with a pin. I haven't heard the news for some time now. Its rotten about Teddy. And the man who owns the car will not be very happy about it either, the whole thing is in at least six hundred pieces. His wife tells the future by ones coffee cups and a large number of people come to her to have it told because mainly it turns out correct. She told me that for three weeks I shall be in danger but that after that I shall go for a very long walk and shall return to England before the War is finished. I hope that it turns out as she said, I want to fight again.

Tuesday 23rd July The day before yesterday the small Baltic States of Latvia, Estonia and Lithuania asked to be incorporated in the USSR, or so they say. Anyway they are now part of it. I, together with many others, do not know quite what the Russians game is but she has gained a terrific acreage of ground in the last twelve months, Poland, Finland, part of Roumania and now these three countries. I am not sure but I do feel that Hitler does not like the Hammer and Sickle Boys right on his doorstep as they are now, and I don't think that they will do us any harm. I look at it like this, Germany would have had all of Poland and no doubt would have had both Bessarabia and the Baltic countries as soon as an opportunity showed itself. And I don't think that he will tangle with Russia if he can avoid it. So what? So we've got to wait.

I heard the speech of both Lord Halifax and Aneurin Bevan yesterday. Bevan's was the best because he talked like a man to man but Halifax put too much emphasis on the Holy Crusade line. We like to think that we are fighting for the right thing but we have no evidence that God is on our side at all, after all, the Germans are being doped up with the same line of talk. It is an old cynicism that God is with the Big Battalions, and I'm not sure quite which side that puts Him on. So I'm drawing consolation from the fact that we always lose all except the last battle. So far we have lost them all but I really fail to see how we can lose Britain unless she is riddled with

Fifth Column merchants like France was. I don't believe that she is but it is possible. Another point that bothers me is the passage in the Lords Prayer 'And forgive us our trespasses as we forgive them that trespass against us'. That does not give me much hope for I do not forgive the Nazis one atom of what they have done and I shall exact a very terrible price from any who fall into my hands. And at the same time I hope that there are many of them.

To come back to earth again, The Germans are very numerous here now, so much so that I can't go out at all, they appear to be moving towards the coast for the invasion of England although only they know how they will get there. An American newshound who has reported on several wars already wrote that for the Germans to get into Britain was risky but possible, but that it would make Gallipoli look like a Sunday school treat. And he's right.

Wednesday 24th July Have moved again, the girl Mathilde came home with the story that someone had reported to the Mairie that they had a stranger in the house. So Madame Beven (Teddy's wife) came over in a hurry to get me moved out of it. She had been to see her husband at Bethune and was very upset about it, he was of course very miserable. He is in a civil prison and I should say that he is far better off than our lads were. Still, it is being hard at his age, he is 59 and has not seen England for twenty-five years. Still, we have done the same in England. The house that I am in now, Madame Decobert's [at 69 rue Emile Vandervelde, Auchel] is a much larger one and the people, that is Mde Bodlet's mother and father are quite well off as these people go. Their daughter-in-law, Yvonne François is the real owner of the house, a young woman of twenty-five with dark hair and a good skin but although she is kindness itself we keep an absolutely proper distance between us, although we are often alone for long periods. She has a young daughter, Anne Marie, quite a nice little child of two years old and

Peter Janes for his Carte d'Identitie in the name of Pierre Bertinchon.

12 August 1941

It was sent to him after the war with the message "Souvenir d'une Francaise que pense a vous" written on the back and signed "Mathilde".

Mde Emma Françoise Bodlet, Mathilde Bodlet, Peter Janes and Anne Marie Françoise.

28 June 1940 outside the Bodlet home at 200 Alsace Lorraine, Colonne Ricouart

Gilberte Guilberte, Peter Janes, Barbara and Hélène MacLeod
and Arthur Fraser.

January 1941 behind the MacLeod family home at rue Wagner,
St Pierre-des-Auchel.

Peter Janes with the "little lady", Gilberte
Guilbert and Yvonne
Françoise.

Sains-les-Pernes 1941

Yvonne Françoise, Berthe Gournay, Gilberte Guilbert, Fred Wilkinson,
Jean Eviad and Peter Janes.

May 1941 at Corné Malo near Locon

Gilberte Guilbert

Date unknown but this picture, or more
likely the negative, was brought back to
England by Peter Janes in 1942

Yvonne Françoise, Fred Wilkinson, Bernadette, Peter Janes
and Gilberte Guilbert.
April 1941 in Louisa's garden at Sains-les-Pernes

Peter Scott Janes with Yvonne
and Albert Françoise
September 1946 at Auchel

had lost another one, Therese. The only disadvantage is that the
Germans have about three hundred troops in the same road and they
keep on passing all day, making it a bit risky to go out. The point is
that the first one who speaks to me, even if he only asks the way or
for a light has every chance of catching me as my French is not a lot
of good even now.

The wireless was a bit more cheerful, the Americans refuse to allow
Germany to touch the colonies of France and Belgium in America at
any price and we shot down at least twelve planes yesterday. Some
of the French are now flying with the RAF and much has been made
of it. Jerry now claims that Britain was responsible for the war and
for its continuance, they refused the magnificent offer of the *Fuhrer*
for peace, an offer that simply means that he wants all of Europe
without fighting any more. The RAF have dropped leaflets on
France now, I don't know with what object for France will not fight
again in this war in my opinion, they would not fight when they had
the *Maginot* and all of their weapons, now they have nothing. Hitler
wants to settle the 'Balkan problem' before he starts on us and
claims terrific success for his planes, to hear the broadcasts one
would believe that little of Britain is left standing. And now the
Italians have sunk the poor old *Ark Royal* and *Hood* again, they have
been sunk eleven times by the Germans, they deserve to float now.
And by the Italians too, who have never sunk anything but a well in
their lives. Then some of the Fleet Air Arm torpedoed three units of
the German navy that poked their noses out of harbour, didn't even
bother to call a real ship to do it, just called one to pick up the
survivors. They might have saved a tinfish though they cost money,
at the sight of a destroyer they would have scuttled themselves. I
hear too that the Nazi leaders, who have always been good
employers of Nancy boys have been learning how to back scuttle
themselves, thus releasing the boys for the Army. Seriously though,
we have simply got to win this war and equally seriously the Yanks

have got to help us. They will come in at the end so why don't they help to shorten what Aneuren Bevan calls 'this wretched affair'.

Have just heard on the wireless that the Nazis have torpedoed a ship containing 1300 French officers and men who were returning to France under the terms of the Armistice. They were told all about the boat and could make no mistake about it, the bastards. I hope that it will prove to be as big a shock as the Lusitania was but I'm afraid it won't be, there wasn't a Yank on board.

Also heard a very rousing singsong from Highgate, all the old patriotic dope ladled out, Land of Hope and Glory, Blakes Jerusalem, Pack up your Troubles, and O God our Help in Ages Past, surely a cynical finale in war time - 'Sufficient is Thine Arm alone and our defence is sure' but we still need Brens and Hurricanes, torpedoes and even our bayonets. Jerry hates cold steel and my only regret is that I have not so far used it on them, I regard it as one of the finest weapons that we have. Sir John Reith once said 'Vengeance is Mine sayeth the Lord, I will repay - yes, but I should like to be the Lord's instrument'. And I feel exactly the same but perhaps could not express it as well as he did. Queer about myself, I have always loved firearms but always thought of killing in the light of something to be done with cold steel, I had a lovely collection of knives, razors and bayonets in civil life. Well, the singing was very good indeed, quite enjoyed it, also the fellow who has just told me that *Tippary* [sic] is the National Anthem of Britain.

Saturday 27th July Went and visited Madame Teddy again yesterday but she was busy most of the day, she tells fortunes from peoples coffee cups and about twenty odd came. She said that Friday was always a busy day for her in this respect as they thought that it was a lucky day. I don't like to laugh at these people, at least it cheers them up a bit and I hope that there is some truth in it for my sake. The Germans here have put up a notice and if I am caught now

I get shot anyway. Not very comforting thought that, still, I've faced their guns before and was not scared. If I do cop one my troubles will be over which is one consolation if a poor one. If I get out of this I shall apply the same law to them, should have done anyway.

Tuesday 30th July Have visited the three Scotsmen several times in the last few days, am not much impressed by them or the house, which is only swapping one prison for another. One of them is fed up while the other two do not seem to be very bright. Once they sent for me, the two houses are about four hundred yards apart, and introduced me to a Belgian who claimed to be in the Belgian Secret Service and still willing to help in the war. He had very bad breath and somehow I did not trust him although he seemed genuine enough. After all, he could give us away at any moment, there is no need to wait any longer. The Germans seem to be in a queer state round here, there are many stories of men disobeying orders to go to England, even to have shot their officers in two cases. Also hundreds of them are stated to have been sent back to Germany as prisoners because they will not fight. Although the people round here seem delighted about it and pass the stories on with relish, I do not believe much of them, The Germans have had too many successes that they can be excused for believing themselves invincible. True, they have lost thousands of men but I doubt if they know how many, any more than I know how many British got wiped out in Belgium. The pilots at Reuly [sic - assume Rely, about 10 kms north-west of Auchel] are supposed to have refused to fly again and certainly the planes don't come over from there. None of this however really means that there is only hope of revolt among them. The main grievance seems to be that they have had no leave for, in some cases, four years.

Now for something solid in the way of news. I will bet five hundred francs that USA are in the war before Xmas. All of the 21 republics of the New World have agreed upon an Anti-Axis programme.

Germany and Italy can't touch ships or colonies belonging to her by right of conquest over France and the others, there is to be a repression of Nazi propaganda in America and above all the President, who incidentally is the third time elected Franklin Delano Roosevelt, has asked Congress to grant permission to call up all Reservists and so on, in fact conscription looks like being a fact there as well. (I wonder if the reader knew the middle name of the President). Of one thing I am afraid, and that is that Germany will be able to cause such damage to Britain in a short time that our people chuck it in. If they do I shall carry out my intention at St Valery, rather than live as a slave I will die, like a coward if you like, but I prefer to say too proud to be anything but free. But I feel that it will not be necessary, we always lose all the battles but equally always win the wars. The day will come again when I can sing 'Deep Purple' without fear and when once again we can drink beer and say what we bloody well like. It is a peculiar feeling to walk along and feel that at any moment a bullet will crash through your back, peculiar and not altogether disagreeable. What Britain will be like *'après la guerre est fini'* I do not venture to guess but I don't suppose that it will be any different from the mad years after '18. And Germany? I'm afraid I don't believe in the Brotherhood of Man, in loving kindness and all the other beautiful abstractions that have been going to create a New Era since Noah landed his private zoo. He knew better than our capitalists how to create a 'corner' or a monopoly.

Friday 2nd August Visited Madame Teddy again yesterday, Teddy has been sent to Germany, much to her distress, as she cannot visit him now. Didn't have quite such a lonely day as before but we did have quite a lot of visitors. She has a most exquisite piece of loveliness who comes to sleep with her at night, I'm sorry that she doesn't sleep with me but that is being rude. She is rather like Betty Rogers in build and also habits but she is a really beautiful girl, a

Hellenic type of beauty if I may use the phrase, and I know that I can because this is my diary and I write what I bloody well like. As I told Mde Bevan, I shall have to learn French if only to 'tell her the old old story of Peter and his love'. This learning is not easy, often I read and understand a paper or book or a speech but cannot reply because of lack of knowledge as to the pronunciation. I shall learn however, I have always prided myself on speaking English correctly (when suitable opportunities arise) and French is a much easier language to learn.

There does not seem to be much news lately, the Americans have decided to conscript untold millions of men and to refuse to lend any food to countries under totalitarian domination. I liked Roosevelt's speech 'We are only interested in protecting America, but she will only need protection if Britain is conquered' is what he said in effect. The Germans dropped thousands of leaflets on Britain today, quoting Hitler's speech of July 16th - 'A last appeal to reason'. In Germany you are liable to the death penalty for reading leaflets, in England they are sold for 3d each in aid of the Red Cross. Just the difference. It seems hard to realise that a hard headed race like the Jerries should waste men's lives and petrol to drop these because the speech had already been printed in the daily papers and I heard it on the radio. The Jerry controlled paper that is sold in Auchel claims that Dover is razed to the ground but they haven't sunk the *'Hood'* for a long time now, also 'oh where oh where has the *'Deutchsland'* gone, oh where oh where can it be?' The British radio confirmed the existence of heavy calibre guns on the coast of France but said that the government did not regard them very seriously. Much in the light of Big Bertha, she must have cost an astronomical figure but the damage she did could have been done by one planeload of bombs. The radio also said that 'many thousands' of tons of bombs had been dropped on Bremen. Sounds nice to me, also I would like to stand a pint to the crew of a Blenheim who after they had used up all of their bombs on a drome came down to 50 feet and machine-gunned it. Oh boy, I'd give a year of my life to use a machine-gun on German or Italian troops now, *peut etre* I shall give all of it for the pleasure.

Saturday 10th August No real news to put down, we seem to be having some trouble with the Japanese and to be getting far more help from the Yanks, in fact short of sending squadrons over they are in the war now. The RAF had a peach of a day yesterday, they have officially shot down 60 planes, Lord knows how many were really lost. And the Italians lost 15 and so did we. Jerry of course claims it as a great victory and claims to have sunk 67,000 tons of ships, a trifle over twice the amount that he attacked even. They used to claim five times what they got but the figure now is 13; hope its lucky for us. Keep on hearing the most fantastic stories myself but don't believe any. Have been to see Madame Teddy twice and her lovely little lady. Borrowed a book, Sabatinis 'Stalking Horse' nearly know it by heart now, it has some very good phrases that I must use, if I live to. He is the best master of the English language whom I have ever read the works of. One sticks in my mind particularly 'As marvellous image of 'Love' by a superb craftsman, ebony and ivory and gold'. I could have written that of someone upon one occasion but didn't, now it would just be copying. And if she hasn't had the shampoo that she needed when last I beheld her it will no longer be appropriate, the ebony will be changed for something more romantic.

When will I cease being a fool about her in my thoughts? War will change most of what it cannot destroy but will it change my opinions or merely render it impossible for me to have any? I don't care, it has never mattered to me whether I live or not, I ask nothing and am content with what I receive above that modest amount. This alone I would ask, if I am to live I want something to live for, if not, well, the choice is mine. This sounds like cheap heroics but at the moment it is truth itself, I consider that my life ended at St Valery en Caux, the rest is borrowed time. If a civilian life awaits me when I go back it will be dull and disappointing at first, but not for long, I am too inconsistent and changeable and easily made happy to be miserable for long. Many things have given me infinite pleasure that were insignificant in themselves, a sharp knife, one particular dance, my bike when it was clean, the leg of pork that I roasted at Dieppe, the fact of being the only one to laugh at our surrender and above all my little gun.

Wednesday 14th August In the paper this morning I read that I daily commit one more crime against laws of the *Third Reich*, I listen to radio transmissions from England which render me liable to still further penalties. I wonder if they will allow the sentence to run concurrently with the death penalty for being a soldier in civilian clothing and for not reporting to the Mairie when Teddy did. I hope so, I should hate to die owing Germany five years penal servitude, in fact should hate to die owing her anything at all, owing for Richardson and my gun, for Teddy and the strain of living like this. To pray for the chance to repay would be hypocritical for my payment will be more just than holy. I think a lot here, there is not much else to do. May God help the first German who is so unfortunate as to fall to my mercy, for I shall have none, just as they have none. These sentiments may have been written in here before but they have been in my mind so long that now they are burned in as if by fire.

The aeroplanes have been flying over here continuously for the last two days and the RAF got 63 of them yesterday. Jerry is upset about the 60 he lost the other day, he makes it 10 and 49 of ours down but they must know how many did not return even if the people don't. As Raymond Gram Swing said on Saturday the British Air Ministry is responsible to Parliament as well as other offices for the truth of their statements while the Nazi propaganda merchants are responsible to no one and anyone who has read *Mein Kampf* realises the futility of expecting truth from them. The end justifies the means, as Mr Aldous Huxley has so truly written 'Vile means may be justified by a noble end but what if the end be base also?' What my friends? I'm glad that I am old fashioned enough to believe in a Hell, for most of the Nazi leaders will not pay for all of their crimes in this life, there isn't time if they started now. I am afraid that even when we win they will be allowed to go and chop wood at Doorn or some such silly idea. Hitler wants to be thought a God and his *Mein Kampf* a Bible, why not then carry the thing to its logical conclusion and crucify him with Goebells and Himmler as the two malefactors? Surely this would be poetic justice at it finest, it would do no harm because he would surely rise on the third day.

8.30: Madame Teddy has just visited here together with her lovely Little Lady whose name I do not know yet. With one single possible exception I have never seen anyone look so breath-takingly lovely. She was dressed in white, a one piece costume of material like towelling with small cut glass buttons and a short birds egg blue knitted jumper underneath. Heavy gauge silk stockings and black shoes and a tiny gold chain round her neck, truly she looked wonderful, a queenly dignity but none of the distant *hauture* of a queen, her light brown hair piled up on her head and what was exposed of her skin very slightly sun-browned, her arms, neck and the cleavage of her dress. Little Lady I thought that you reminded me of Betty but you now make me forget her, she never achieved one per cent of the sheer loveliness that you have without trying to, I do not worry about the insuperable barrier of our language because if I were French I should not get far with you, only the fact that an escaped prisoner of war, especially now that Britain is France's only hope, has a certain romantic glamour makes you think and look at me in a favourable light. Nevertheless, because a lily does not live for ever is no reason why we should not be cheered by its beauty so I will think of you for some time as the only really beautiful woman whom I have seen in France, supposed to be the land of gorgeous women and patriots and really the land of hags and prostitutes, of cowards and Judas's. And if you never gain any more honour for your beauty at least you are the only female to have over thirty lines in my diary devoted to you alone consecutively.

Tuesday 13th August Another big series of air fights yesterday and Jerry lost at least 39 planes. He is most indignant about things in today's papers, according to Berlin 89 British planes were shot down on Sunday alone as against two Germans. What beats me is the terrible damage that his bombs cause while ours either miss the target and land in fields or at most injure only civilians. Rudolf Hess made the breathtaking announcement that Germany is now certain of victory, the report does not say that anyone is surprised at this. I suppose they will be sure right up until the day that peace is declared and then declare that Germany was stabbed in the back at home. Little incident on the radio yesterday, Ex President Hoover declared that owing to the British blockade 18,000,000 people are starving in Europe and the announcer pointed out that this cannot be our fault as Hitler has often declared that the blockade does Germany no harm at all and that she has plenty of everything, therefore all he has to do is feed these people from his 'plenty'. Of course the German blockade of Britain is complete, nothing reaches us from outside without his consent, must say he is very generous with consenting as quite a lot filters through. The position though is a nasty one, these poor devils will get nothing from Germany, on the contrary Germany is taking every ounce that she can lay her hands on and nothing from Britain for that reason alone. The papers every day are full of reports of the quantities of food for France that have been stopped by the British. America is now sending us pilots but only for training purposes, subtle difference because it will release our trainers for fighting so the result is the same.

Thursday 15th August Visited Mde Teddy yesterday and met a couple who believe that they are going to come to England with me. I hope that they do. They are both only twenty and the young wife is one of the few women I have seen who look better under electric light than by daylight, mainly due to very large eyes of speckled brown and black, like Wynne's only a lot larger. They seem to have this trip to England all cut and dried but I am still not convinced, as I remarked my name is that of one of the Apostles but it should be that of another, not Peter but Thomas. Talking about Apostles I have a Protestant Bible in French here and am struck by the way that some of the speeches in it sound better in French than in English, at the beginning of Ester for instance is the phrase *'Qu'on cherche pour le roi des jeunnes filles, vierges et belles figure'* which sounds lovely in French. The again in John (*Jean*) 8 *'Que celui de vous qui est sans péché, jette la premier pierre contra elle'*. Again in *Matthieu* 3 John the Baptist says *'Races de vipères, qui vous a appris á fuir la colère a venir?'* (The English for these is at the end of this book)[14] But perhaps I am biased, I have always held that some of the biblical passages cannot be beaten for sheer drama, take Paul for instance when he said 'I am Saul of Tarsus, a citizen of no mean city' and later the officer saying to him 'With a great sum obtained I this freedom' and Paul's answer 'But I was free born'. The world of pitying contempt in that 'But'. What a play it would make, given the right actors, there are several actors who could take the title role and it would make them.

---

[14] They are in the original but you can translate them for yourself

Friday 16th August Yesterday the RAF shot down 144 *(cent quarante quatre)* Jerry planes, the best day so far.[15] Over a thousand planes came (or rather went) over and of course some got through, it is impossible that they could all be stopped. I would give a lot to know the real truth, how many planes did get home, how many airmen were lost because many planes must get back with dead men on board. One pilot who came to England had with him a suit case filled with kit and a big fur coat. He had come to stay. The lads at Stations Bremen, Hamburg and the short wave station DBG are full of the air raids. Most of Britain lies in ruins according to them.

Went and saw the Scottish lads yesterday. They have managed to get identity cards for themselves but I don't like the slap dash way that they are filled in. The Jerries are patrolling the roads tonight with rifles, an English officer had had his photo on the daily papers and on hoardings lately, he is still at large though. The night was a rather peculiar one, absolutely still and the air full of low clouds of black smoke but the view clear, not a leaf moved, I had the feeling that some awful force had taken away all life from the world and left it empty, that all was dead but not yet decayed, that soon the air would be full of the reek of decaying bodies and plants and that as time marched inexorably on only the bare earth would show. No philosophy on this, its just what I thought.

Friday 23rd August. Still here, not much to my surprise and still the war has not taken any real turn, it fact it has gone back to the old apathetic inertia of last year. Jerry planes seem to have given up raiding the country in any numbers and the RAF still make their daily and nightly raids on Germany. Mr Churchill talks quite cheerfully about 'The campaigns of 1941 and 1942' while Jerry is

---

[15] It was the events of 15 August when Germany lost 75 aircraft and the RAF lost 34 fighters, that inspired Churchill's famous 'Never in the field of human conflict ..' speech.

sure that it will all be over by November. Now I don't want to seem ungrateful but the idea of spending a couple more years here does not make me very happy. True, I should be infinitely worse off in a prison camp and I do not lose sight of it but this eternal waiting is not doing me much good. I have been hearing of a method of getting back to Britain for many weeks now but am not very hopeful about it as I do not believe that it is possible.

Go and see the Scottish lads quite often but am not in the least impressed by them, half of what they say is lost on me and they have the most (to me) peculiar ideas. Both assert that they will do all that they can to keep out of the Army if and when they get back and both take the most foolish risks. I admit that I am perhaps more cautious than necessary but the penalty for failure is not only death for me but for the people who have helped me, and once enquiries are started Lord only knows what the finish may be. But these lads not only cycle and walk about everywhere but go to dances and get drunk, insult German soldiers and do all such silly things as that. Me, I am and always will be, as polite to any German as I would be to my best friend, shall not dream of insulting one even if there was no chance of his having the last laugh. From me any Jerry from Hitler to one of his ragged privates can confidently expect politeness and death.

This afternoon I heard heavy explosions and went out to see what it was all about. A barrage balloon has broken away and came over at about seven thousand feet. A heavy AA (or as they say here DCA) battery started lobbing heavy stuff up, at least 4" I should say. The shooting was awful, out of seventeen shells only one was within a hundred yards of it. Then a Stuka bomber went up and machine-gunned it. It came down at Colonne Ricouart about a mile and a half from here. This is a another great German victory, a poor gasbag, no harm or use to anyone and they imperil the lives of all around by HE shells, really, anyone as hopelessly a bad shot as that gunner ought not to be allowed a firearm at all. Yesterday the Jerries used heavy guns on the French coast to shell British ships, more bad shooting for again they missed. To everyone's surprise British guns answered and to use the communiqué verbatim 'fired a few rounds'. Just the same as they did at St Valery en Caux I suppose, a few rounds that raze the town down to ground level. Never mind its nice to know we are doing something.

Monday 26th August. Well on Saturday I went and dug potatoes for Madame Teddy and was also told that I should be going home any day now. There were quite a lot of spuds and I was bleedin' tired by the time they were all up stairs. Saw here lovely Little Lady again who, as usual, blushed every time I looked at her.

The Jerries have been fairly quiet this last few days but yesterday we got fifty-seven of them which is not bad. Better still, our own planes bombed Berlin last night, evidently pretty heavily but not nearly heavily enough, otherwise there would not be a Berlin agency or radio left to report the news.[16] Still I'm always like this lately, it gives me exquisite pleasure to think of the heavy Blenheims and Hamiltons tipping overboard the big black bombs. I've seen them drop, first of all they wobble and turn and then straighten out and start to scream, louder and louder and then - WOOOOF, and up goes the smoke and down come the buildings. The AA guns were reported to be terrific and numerous, well all of that fell back on Berlin too.

We are not supposed to have as many planes as Germany yet, so they are to be pitied when we have. I don't say 'God help them' because I don't want Him to in the first place and in the second I don't like all this stunt of associating him with either side. Every war

---

[16] This was a reprisal for the 'unintended' bombing of central London the previous night (Liddel Hart (1970) "History of the Second World War" p102)

lately seems to have been a Holy War when in reality they are only land grabbing enterprises. The last war was, among *douze mille trois cent quatre vante* [sic] *douze* other things, a War to stop War, to save civilisation, to make us all free, to create a land fit for heroes to live in and so on, and so is this one. It will leave behind just the same misery in all countries concerned, unemployment, depreciation of the soldiers wretched back-pay, fatherless homes and women with no men left to marry them, the bitter Dead Sea Fruit that is Victory for one side and worse still the soul searing agony of mind that is Defeat for the other. This war will utterly ruin both Germany and Britain for many years and one of them for ever, which means at the most twenty years. To say that it puts the clock back is not quite correct, the clock of Time cannot be altered by men or nations, it ticks on and on relentlessly, of the great Trinity, Time alone is without pity or feeling, Death even is sometimes a welcome visitor and I am old fashioned enough to believe that God, if not exactly a God of Love, at least knows the emotion. Time is kind in some ways but not many, all too often he washes away the beautiful parts of life and leaves only those things that we want to forget but cannot, the mere effort of trying to forget them defeating its own purpose. I ought to work out a system of philosophy on my trinity, God and Death and Time but, like all writing that I have started I should lose interest in it first, or taking into consideration my circumstances here, well, get a visit from the second of the Trinity.

Tuesday 27th August Have just got back from visiting the two Scottish lads and was surprised to find with them two Englishmen of about 38 or 40, also escaped prisoners. They seem to have had rather more fun in escaping than I have and spent a month living in a ditch in a field and have moved from place to place ever since. They have come over hoping to go to England in the aeroplane that we are all waiting for. They are very decent fellows and we had quite a jaw together. If I read in a book of three English and two Scottish escaped prisoners of war swapping yarns while a dozen German cavalrymen fed horses not a hundred yards away I should not believe it but there we were, large as life and twice as happy. They have some crazy plan of getting to liberated France and from there to Marseilles and so home. Sounds alright but I'm not very enthusiastic about the results.[17] They also were copped at St Valery but did not escape until after myself, and reached Bethune before they did so. Really, I seem to be the only one who did not make a romantic get-a-way, unless of course I am the only one to tell the truth. They were agreed with me about the Germans in general, the older men are all right but the young ones, who appear to be true Nazis, are just plain brutal. One of them told me that they are both reformed Christians and do not swear or anything of that sort because they believe that they have been helped all along by some Power that has given them more than just good luck. They told me also that for ten days they lived in the same house as the German *Kommandant* for Marines and used to sit reading in the next room to Jerry shouting and yelling orders to each other and that there were 5,000 Marines in a comparatively small village.

Had to laugh at an RAF officer who said in Air Log 'I was told by a distinguished foreign gentleman that there was a distressing lack of ceremony and dignity in the departure of our bombers to Germany but I pointed out that it would hardly be British to line up on the tarmac and sing *There'll Always be an England*.' We'll leave that to the Jerries, we often hear them singing but its not because they are happy but because they are ordered to. Heard some more stories of suicide among Germans but these yarns are not swallowed up quite so readily by me as the others, its often just a case of wishful

---

[17] Believe these men were 1859826 Spr A Cook & 1863093 Spr W G James - both Royal Engineers - in which case they did make their way to Marseille and were back in England in October 1941

thinking. Its nice to think that there are some Jerries decent enough to kill themselves but not many. I only hope that I shall live long enough to help some of them.

Friday 30th August Went and saw Madame Teddy again and dug up the rest of the potatoes, also saw two young fellows who also have the craze of wanting to go to England and the wife of one of them. Had a good deal of quite innocent fun with Betty and very nearly got canned on red wine. In the middle of supper came a thunderous knocking at the door and much against my inclination they told me to hide. Of course it was a false alarm but perhaps it was good practise, from the garden it is a fairly easy job to cross the railway and get away, at least I hope so. The night was quite the darkest that I have had to wander about in and I had a real job to find my way back, it would have been no joke to be lost here. Today the husband of the house where the Scotsmen are was pinched for half-inching coal (*pour vol de charbon*).

Went and visited a café which seemed to be full of English sympathisers, an incredible number of people such as only a French kitchen seems to hold and an extremely fat bitch of indeterminate breed but full of fuss. She was the largest dog that I have seen in France at all and I played with her for hours. Also drank quite a lot of various fluids from coffee to cherry brandy. Then there came in a little blonde lady who spoke amazingly good English and equally amazingly good French, I don't know quite who she is but legally she is as much a Scotsman as I am English. Actually she spoke the best English that I have heard in France. She said that she was to have been married to a Frenchman but broke off the engagement, she didn't say why but I guessed, probably incorrectly. Another very large young woman played a number of British tunes on a huge piano accordion and a young fellow cut my hair. Altogether a most satisfactory visit. Was very struck by the little lady, there was something infinitely pathetic about her and her views, her patriotism and manner, her vehement denunciation of France and her hopes of getting back to England. This bloody plane will have to be about twice as big as the 'Maxim Gorki' if it is going to hold all who want to go. Personally I doubt if it exists, but the fact remains that it is the only way to get back.[18]

A country called Chad and French Equatorial Africa have decided to continue the war against Germany, the story of the kidnapping of the governor and the release of French officers was quite an opera in its romance. Some fool at Vichy asks in the paper today if Danzig was worth all this war, a statement that needs no amplification to show its asinine stupidity.

We got another good bag of planes yesterday, forty-four before 7.30 and 85 altogether. On Sunday they only got 25 and on Saturday 67. It should be about 1,000 for the month but haven't heard the figures yet. Jerry admits losing 160 so it must be about that number. The Jerries want to use sixty boats marked with the Red Cross to pick up his airmen from the sea and is most upset because we won't let him. The BBC point out that as he only claims to have lost an average of five or six airmen a day, sixty boats is rather a lot to pick them up. Just as when he used to mark his reconnaissance planes with a red cross and raised a most pitiful cry when the RAF quite rightly shot them into the sea.

Monday 2nd September Well the war has been on for a year now and no-one can say that it has been a good year for Britain. We have lost far more men and stuff than we can afford to but worse than that we have lost France. So have the French. And Britain is not awake fully yet, nor has the British Empire thrown any real weight into the

---

[18] When it first flew in 1934 the Tupolev ANT-20 Maxim Gorki was the largest land plane in the world. These aeroplane stories are repeated by many escapers

war, in fact Jerry is smiling. We keep sending his airmen to hell and bombing his country but not in nearly effective proportions. Of course we do not know what damage a bombing raid really leaves but I'm sure that they are not on a really large scale. My idea of a bomb raid would be upwards of two thousand bombers raiding one given town systematically, not bothering about military objectives but concentrating on the laying the town flat on the ground. This raid should be at night and should be swifty and decisive, medium sized bombs, say of 100lbs each dropped indiscriminately, followed up by incendiaries and then a wave of planes to machine-gun the area. If this was carried out regularly on a different town each night it would necessarily hold up war efforts for a bit. The towns within ten or so miles from the coast could be dealt with by the Navy. While this would necessarily be a bit heavy on bombs it would produce results, all the while women work in munitions factories they are as much fighting against us as the airforce and as the Jerries have boys of sixteen and seventeen in all three services they are military targets. All this may sound nasty but only such actions can get us a quick victory and not nearly as nasty as the Nazis would be in England. The bright-eyed little lad who we say 'Poor little chap, its not his fault that his country is at war' will in three years time be able to use a rifle, a grenade, a machine-gun, to drive a tank. And don't forget that the swine who machine-gunned refugees and bombed lightships, who sink fishing boats and cargo ships were once nice little boys at school and sung *'Deutschland über Alles'* like angels. No, the days of chivalry are over and the sooner Britain forgets about playing the gentleman soldier the better; we can do that better when we have won this war, as we must.

Well to come back to earth, yesterday I went and spent a day with a man at Auchel and later went visiting to Marles, the people there had quite the biggest and best radio that I have ever seen. Drank an awful lot of drink all day but managed to keep sober. When we came away from Marles the man, to my amazement, gave me ten francs. Why I don't know but I took it as he would have been annoyed if I hadn't. Got back very tired. There has been a spot of trouble in the Balkans, Hungary has demanded a slice of Roumania and the Axis powers have made sure that she gets it. I heard that Russia has also protested about it but not officially. Trouble there might help us to get a battlefield.

Thursday 5th September The trouble seems to have blown over in the Balkans. And now for a real snip, the USA have sold 50 destroyers to us for some (to us) quite useless air bases in isolated American islands and Newfoundland. Now we are getting somewhere at last. So far however I have not heard what Jerry thinks about it but should imagine that his feelings are pretty deep. What an anniversary present! The war situation is extremely complicated now and I have trouble following it. But again it seems to be a checkmate, just as the *Maginot* and *Seigfreid* produced one before. But - Hitler can't bribe Neptune with useless paper francs and spurious honours and puppet government posts to evacuate the Channel. That Channel is as much a safeguard now as in Napoleon's (the other supernumerary lance corporal, unpaid, unwanted) time. But where is Josephine? And little Adolf has now given up his idea of a *Blitzkrieg* and told Germany to prepare for a five years war. The point is can she? And the angels sing. Also can we? And still the Sphinx smiles. After all, what does it really matter? Which ....

end of book

These pages were tucked into the back of diary number 2

It is a silly question by a silly questioner, but I came to France to get either Death or Glory and a German pistol and have not only got neither but lost my own pistol in the meanwhile, and although I have escaped it is not many thanks to me although I should have attempted to do so very soon afterwards. We have had many touching speeches on the wireless by various speakers about the anniversary of the declaration of war and are now assured once again that we shall win. The Jerry radio describes the destroyer deal and giving colonies for scrap iron: we have not given but only lent them, they are not colonies at all and anyway the boats are modern enough for our purpose, the *Graf Spee* was the most modern boat in the world but she went down under less modern boats than these. I don't like the news of the air raid results, the Jerries are evidently bombing indiscriminately and far too many people are being killed. I was amazed by the pilot of a heavy bomber who said that for an hour and a half he searched Berlin by dropping flares and looked for a military objective. He was risking the lives of his crew and a valuable plane for a quixotic idealism; there is a vast difference between a military objective and an objective of military importance, his bombs, dropped anywhere in Berlin could not failed to have caused damage to the Nazi war effort. Then, time and time again we get a pilot who brings his bombs back with him. There is no closed season for vermin.

On Thursday I had a full day, first of all I went to have my photo taken for a false passport but there were eight Jerries in the place so I went for a walk. Coming back I helped kill a pig and carve him up and then went to see some friends, especially the little Scottish girl. She is a wonderful talker in both English and French as well as quite an attractive girl, a tiny blonde with what I believe is termed a piquant face, briefly she is very pretty. They had told me that she spoke English but after about twenty minutes she had said nothing at all except to the French people in the room. I was playing with the dog when she spoke to me at last. "Do you like dogs?" she asked. Such was my introduction to Eileen MacCloud [Helene MacLeod] It appeared that she had a Scottish lad from the Camerons staying in her place. I met him about a week later, his name was Arthur Fraser and he came from Inverness and is one of the best chaps whom I have ever met.

For tea I had bread and jam and black beer and liver. A young lady with a jaw like the prow of an icebreaker played a piano accordion for me and I danced a Boomps a Daisy. A man showed me a .38 which he got from the last war, a very nice tool, I wish I had one too. On Wednesday I went and saw two more Englishmen in the rue de Rhin, Robert and Albert and had a good old jaw with them.[19] They told me that there was still another just up the road, George Pearson, but that he was sleeping with the young lady of the house and did not want to leave now. Don't blame him except for the fact that he has a wife and child in England. Well, I have neither bedmate, wife or children to go back to but I still want to go.

Friday 6th September Had fried pork, salad, bread and jam and beer for breakfast. Met three more English chaps in the afternoon. One told me how they escaped and were cooking haricot beans in a house when a Jerry came in. One of them managed to kick him downstairs and bayonet him with his own pigsticker. One less. Yvonne, the young lady here, has had about eighteen letters from her husband, one of them saying that the Jerries have got as far as Arras. And the angels sing.

Sunday 8th September Nothing much, the news very queer and confused, an American speaker gave a very encouraging speech but said that USA could not help us on a very large scale until they had got their war machine going properly. He also gave a very illuminating account of the hair splitting involved in making the destroyer deal. For the last five nights we have heard thunderous explosions from the direction of Calais where the RAF are

---

[19] Believe these men were 812356 Dvr R M Rodgers & 777195 Sig A Rodiguez - both Royal Artillery

beginning their great work of civilisation. It shakes the place and is nearly thirty miles away. Also we see the flashes of the DCA but they use them without searchlights and so invariably miss. And still we are bombing Berlin and Jerry is bombing London. Both towns are in ruins and both have received negligible damage, according to which news bulletin one listens to. I suppose both have received pretty heavy damage, they must have. Also Munich has had visits of the Holy Ghost with his cleansing fire but they do neither repent or flee from the wrath to come. For the twenty-third time the Jerry radio has told of the intended flight of Churchill and Company to Canada. Ever since Mr Knickerbocker proved that most of the Nazi leaders have big fortunes in America for when Germany falls apart they have been telling us that. Pontius Pilate asked 'what is truth'. As Shakespeare (whom Dr Goebbels claims to be a true Aryan, that is a Nazi) truly wrote in Julius Caesar 'Oh Judgement thou art fled to brutish beasts and men have but their reason' reminds me of the story of how the Swiss prime minister told Hitler that he was going to consult his First Lord of the Admiralty. The Fuhrer, for once his patience not exhausted said 'But you have no Navy'. 'What does that matter' was the reply, 'you've got a Minister of Justice and Mussolini has a Minister of Finance, why can't I have a First Lord of the Admiralty?' Switzerland is upset because we fly planes over her to bomb Italy but perhaps its only because they want to keep neutral.

Heard on the wireless of a terrific raid on London last night, over five hundred people were killed in it and a lot of damage done. A rotten business and the trouble is that we can't stop it from happening again. And yet still I don't suppose the order will be given for real bombing. Anyway the pilot who brings his bombs back from a raid now wants shooting and I don't see any good reason for not …

The third diary written in France was lost for reasons unknown and the following pages were tucked into the front cover of this fourth book.

This sheet is to record the main events covered by the lost book of my diary. The main political events were the invasion of Greece by the Italians, following which they were thrown back and in the end lost almost all of Albania as well. Then the Germans entered and the Yugoslavians declared that they would fight for the Allies. This they did but the Germans conquered both countries by using absolutely overwhelming force. The Greek and British forces fought to the last corner of Greece and then evacuated to Crete. Over Crete a terrific air battle was fought during which many thousands of parachutists, including Max Schmeling, were used and the losses must have been phenomenal. But in the end the Allied Forces were beaten and lost another 15,000 men in the second evacuation. In Africa we took town after town in Libya and thousands of prisoners, also we fought in Abysinnia and Somaliland. The fighting in Libya was mainly by mechanical [sic] forces and by planes while the Abysinnian affair was mainly patriotic forces reinforced by British officers and Colonial troops and arms. The South African and Rhodesian Air Forces were very much in the pictures and Eritrea and Somaliland were taken. At the end of the period covered by the book Abysinia had not quite fallen but there was very little resistance and the local lads were 'mopping up'.

Here we made a great number of new friends as well as losing most of the old ones. At this time I first met Jeanne Devise, granddaughter of Mme François, a tall, well built girl with nice skin and a good looking face. As however she did not understand my version of the French language things did not get beyond the *'comment ça va?'* stage. Most days I went to see the three Scotsmen at the back of the house; after about six weeks however one of them found another house and moved out, I never saw him again. Then I was told that another Englishman was coming to stay with me and the same night [19th September] he came. He was Frederick Wilkinson of the Royal Engineers and he had spent the first three months of his freedom near Calais. He had never been taken prisoner but had been left behind with a searchlight near, I believe, Wimereux and had tried to get to Dunkirk. For about a month or so we were perfectly good friends as was of course only natural under the circumstances but after that time he started paying too much attention to Yvonne. At first it did not amount to much and we went everywhere together, visiting dozens of houses in the neighbourhood. At this time the place was full of Germans, there was never less than 100 and often 500 in the village at once. Soon Wilkinson was sleeping with Yvonne regularly, which upset me a lot, not because I was jealous but because I rather liked the girl and knew that sooner or later more people than myself would know about it. It upset the whole balance of the household, often we did not speak for days on end. Madame François began to suspect something and the whole atmosphere was sour.

I started writing a book called 'Conscript Heroes' which, with a bit of polishing should be quite readable. In January we started visiting a lot of people in Lillers and Burbure and often came back loaded with supplies of food, especially bread, which was rationed strictly at the time.

By this time Matilde had gone away to work at a hospital in Roubaix and Jeanne had become rather more than a friend, although she was always on the cold side. Her mother and grandmother did all in their power to allow us to see as much as possible, which was not much as she only had about four days every three months or so.

We were getting our bread from a baker in Rimbert [Mme Prunier] and I became very friendly with the people there, the man who was very fond of a little drink particularly, and also very well with his daughter Simone, one of the very few red-heads whom I saw in France. One day however she said that Mme Yvonne would have to be very careful or else she would have good cause to remember the English and it would not be for a medal. To try and get the pair of them to throw up the dirty game that they were playing I told Yvonne but did not tell her who had said it. Nevertheless she guessed and in spite of my making her promise not to broadcast it she told Wilkinson in her bed about five minutes afterwards. He then got up early next morning and kicked up a hell of a row in the shop, entirely forgetting that she only had to call the Germans to have not only him but myself and the whole family arrested. The baker was then changed to one at Cauchy la Tour but after about a month the young woman there, whose husband was at the time in England wounded, took a passionate liking for me, invited me to come and live with her and made many attempts at persuading me that the whole family knew about it. Fortunately we never had the opportunity of being alone together so that the whole affair was dismissed as a lot of fuss over nothing. The business between the other two however became such common knowledge that we lost nearly all our friends over it. Then one day the pair of them went to Sains lès Pernes to buy some potatoes and coming back after 9.00 (the place was consigned because too many Vs and Lorraine crosses had been written up) were both arrested by the Germans. Both of them escaped however it was pouring with rain all the time, and had to spend the whole night in the fields between Floringhem and Cauchy la Tour. The next time that they went I was with them and so, for the first time met Gilberte [Guilbert] and Louisa [Gournay].

The latter is the owner[20] of a large farm at Sains les Pernes and Gilberte, the daughter of another farmer, although a tailoress by

---

[20] The farm was actually owned by Arthur Gournay - Louisa's brother

trade, was helping her run the farm until things became a little better in her trade. Louisa was thirty and Gilberte eighteen at the time and the first moment I saw the latter we mutually decided to get better acquainted. It was not easy at first but on the second visit she came with us most of the way back to help carry our bags on her cycle. She was a real beauty in a natural robust way, solidly built with beautiful eyes and perfect teeth, with a small but full lipped mouth that betrayed the latent passion in her makeup. As the other two wanted to be alone as much as we did we managed to get nearly an hour together. She did not waste time on any silly small talk but came to me as if it was someone she had known for years. After that I took every chance of seeing her, although at this time we were full of plans for getting away.

Two of the boys from the Rue du Rhin had already gone down south and in fact we two, Arthur and George were, as we thought, about the only ones left. George was getting himself a rotten bad name while Wilkinson's was not a lot better, although I do not believe that he knew this at the time, or indeed ever. We got to know many more people at Sains and district and, had it not been for what was going on in our house I should have had the happiest time of my life. Gilberte and I spent a good deal of time together.

Soon we knew a good number of the local tradesmen with the result that we did not want for much although butter was always a problem and Monsieur François used to go for about twenty odd miles to get a couple of pounds of this. Then one night we went and met Peter [Pierre Courouble] one of the nicest men I have ever known. A young man of about twenty-eight or so, he was the owner of one of the largest shops in the district and the husband of one of the few really pretty girls whom I saw. He gave us no end of stuff and would have given us more had we not refused it, money, clothes, food, toilet stuff and one day when he asked me 'Is there anything else at all that you want?' and I answered 'Yes, a good revolver'. A week later he gave us two heavy automatic pistols and sixty odd rounds of ammunition.

Madame Teddy, whose husband was arrested in July was also arrested along with Adele, one of her girls. Naturally I learned French and can talk with most people on most subjects in it. Made several attempts to write to England and got to know the surrounding district very well. In May we decided to go to Free France and made all the arrangements to go, which included collecting nearly 4,000 francs each. It was arranged that the first two should go on a Monday and meet us in Paris on the Wednesday. We told a few people that we were going but without revealing the day, destination or how we would get there. Well George and Arthur set off on the Monday and we spent the next two days twiddling our thumbs and getting bad tempered. I took my automatic back with its cartridges because this was to be a peaceful journey, or so we thought. There was a lot of tearful farewells and at last, at 6 o'clock Tuesday evening we set off to meet our guide together with Yvonne and Jeanine, George's *amorate*. We had gone only about half a mile when Monsieur François came after us on his cycle to tell us that the other two had been caught. Jeanine collapsed, Yvonne vowed that this was the last time that we made any arrangements of this sort while I swore incoherently (and uselessly).

When we got back to the house George was already there, together with Vassal telling his story in the awful corruption of the French language that he always used, a mixture of English, French, Flemish and Pas de Calais patois, mixed up with words *'que n'existé pas'*. We did not believe his story from the first, it was too egotistical, too full of what 'I' did. About ten minutes later Eileen [Helene] arrived and although she was badly upset she kept control of herself. We heard his story about six times that evening, each time with more and more frillings put on to it. We had to decide whether or not we ought to move, I was in favour of it as we would probably go to Sains. However it was in the end decided that the best plan was to keep very quiet and say that we had moved to another district. Arthur escaped, spent a night in a field near Albert and Mme MacCleod [Fernande MacLeod, Helene's mother] fetched him back two days later.[21]

We went to Sains les Pernes[22] and afterwards to Locon[23] near Bethune for two weeks but both George and Arthur escaped. George got himself disliked by going about everywhere with the young woman with whom he was staying. Then the German battle cruiser *Bismarck* sunk the *Hood*, the ship on which my brother serves and as there were no survivors I am afraid that he went down with it. When we went away I gave back my automatic and have not yet recovered it.

Tuesday 27th May 1941 Rather to my surprise Madame asked one of us to go over to Louisa and take the cycle back to Bernadette, so I jumped at the chance. On the way met Marcel who told me to go in and see his wife and demand a glass of whisky. At the time there was a hell of a lot of heavy bombing going on but where I do not know. His wife was, or at least seemed to be very glad to see me and

---

[21] A Belgian group had organised a party to head south and offered to take two of the soldiers with them. The four men drew lots and Arthur and George Pearson were chosen. They joined the group - which also included 2076242 Spr Robert Reid, 4917419 Pte W Harper and 846425 Gnr E A Hooper - on the border of the miltarised zone in the café at Corbie railway station but their attempt to board a goods train was foiled when they were spotted by a German patrol.

[22] Sains les Pernes and Tangry are tiny country villages about 10 kms west of Colonne Ricouart

[23] with Louisa's brother on his farm "Corné-Malo" just north of Bethune

I stayed about an hour and then went on over to Louisa's. She was not there but Gilberte was and I delivered the bike and stayed till about 7.00, going away in a horse and trap. Now the horse had one idea and the driver [Jules Duhem] another and the horse finished up in a ditch. I thought that he had broken his legs but he had not a scratch on him, nor was the trap broken at all. While we were disentangling harness and stuff Louisa came along and asked me to stay two or three days with her, to which of course I said yes. She told me about the trouble at Locon, it is Fred and Yvonne that they are angry about and the upshot of it is that we can go there again but *'pas de femme pour couche avec'* which is of course *'mal heurez'* as it includes Gilberte. And various other things too about the two of them, it is really marvellous that all the world knows about them but not Madame. And I heard the news that the *Bismarck*, the big 35,000 ton German battle cruiser was sunk at 11.01 this morning, but not how.

Wednesday 28th May Had a full day, carting beet and hay and weeding out thistles in the fields as well as odd jobs about the house. And went looking for dandelions (literally) in the field with Gilberte and had quite a good time. Went to bed at 12.00 darn tired.

Friday 30th May Heard how the *Bismarck* got hers, she didn't have a chance. First of all she shot it out with the *Hood* and the *Hood* blew up, killing all of her crew, possibly including my brother Roland. From then on she was the target of nearly every boat of the Atlantic Fleet. The *Prince of Wales, King George V, Rodney, Ark Royal, Dorsetshire, Nelson* and a bunch of smaller stuff closed in on her. Planes from the *Ark Royal* went in and torpedoed her from the air. She swapped 15 inch shells with the *Prince of Wales* and damaged her. Then the *Dorsetshire* closed in to 13 miles and another artillery duel took place. The *Bismarck* did everything she could to escape but there was no escape for her, sinking the *Hood* was like shooting a policeman, you can do it but you can't get away with it. God, but it must have been worth seeing, the whole of the heavy stuff of the British Navy closing in, while the big new German boat tore south at over thirty-five miles an hour. Her enormous 381 millimetre guns hit out at every boat within range, she flung out a smoke screen, dodged, tried to outrun the big boats. But they held her and again the planes went up from the old *Ark Royal* and again a torpedo hit her. Then the fire of the *Dorsetshire* smashed her decks and turrets into twisted scrap iron and at 11.00 she put her nose to the sky and dived down stern first.

Well, we lost the *Hood* for her but it was a good swap, only about ten boats in the whole world could have swapped shells with her with any hope of success and about five of them were there. A boat of her size, 35,000 tons and carrying 15" guns and 6.25 could have terrorised the trade routes and most of the fleet as well. It was her first voyage and her last but she made a good show. President Roosevelt spoke last night and his speech did not make any bones about America's sympathies in this man's war. In fact most of the papers of USA declare that the speech was tantamount to a declaration of war right now.

Sunday 1st June Haven't gone back yet, had a nice easy day and ate a good deal more than usual, haven't had such an appetite since Doullens. Go each evening with Gilberte to collect dandelions for the rabbits, they call them [the dandelions] *'pissenlit'* which is nearly a direct literal translation of the English 'piss in beds'. It usually takes us about two and a half hours. Have started learning how to milk cows and it is some job, but I do get some milk from them, usually about a gallon. One of the mares has a foal and I tried to get the two of them in from the field today which was very nearly the end of my career as a *'Varmers Bhoy'*. Two enormous hooves with iron shoes on them missed my head by about a millimetre.

On **Monday** went to visit Bernadette, a queer bird if ever there was
one. She is very like a coloured print of Saint Bernadette which
Yvonne has and I have a good deal of fun with her about it. She is
the daughter of the Maire of Tangry and I was invited to go to her
home, and went over for half a day. Bernadette, a girl of nineteen
could be described as exquisite: small, dark haired, white skin,
dainty and light as a fairy, this was Bernadette. Big brown eyes with
flecks of grey in them, like a trout's back and big white teeth in a
tiny mouth she was a dream to anyone who did not, like myself
prefer something more substantial and heavy. But at any rate she
was a good friend and did all she could to make me happy while she
was there. When I told her that I preferred coffee to tea they gave me
coffee and did not persist that Englishmen drink only tea laced with
incredible quantities of rum, as do nearly all French people. And
they cannot make tea, even after it has been explained to them, they
put it in a coffee percolator or else boil it, or they let it simmer in a
saucepan - anything in fact except put it in a teapot and pour boiling
water on it. She took a lot of trouble to find a bottle of really old
cognac, I think that it was about sixty years old and would have cost
an incredible sum for a bottle in England, it is now quite
unobtainable in France. I thought that if I tried to make love to her
she would be upset, and so didn't.

Gilb says that she is a hot little bit, it is possible but I should not say
very probable, although she can kiss very nicely. Her father is Maire
of a village and a dirty fucker at that, in fact he is rarely at home.
Monsieur Francois brought me over a clean shirt yesterday, Jeanne
has not yet come.

Wednesday 6th June Heard that some of the miners of Auchel are
out on strike because they can't get enough to eat.[24] I'm afraid that it

---

[24] After the student protests in Paris the previous November, this was only the
second organised action of what could be called 'resistance' (see "Occupied

will mean trouble with the Germans however. Also that someone has threatened to denounce George because he has spent some of the money he collected to go away with on Jeanine, whom they say is his *'poule'* which is not a nice word for a girl here.

Saturday 7ᵗʰ June Well have had to part at last, after the best twelve days that I have passed in France. Monsieur Francois has been here every two days and I have gone nearly every evening for a couple of hours with Gilberte. She is a nice girl. And *'nous parley la bêtis tous la jour'*. I have learned to milk cows very nicely as well as several other queer things. Altogether I had a full day and always sleep like a pig at night. Well, the miners of the Pas de Calais have started a strike and things look like being far from nice very soon. I got ready to go tonight but what with one thing and another did not get away before nine.

I packed up my kit, which was not very heavy, and set off back to Auchel. I went off down the road with Marcel Prevue but as we got near to Sachin it rained so heavily that he asked me to stay the night with him, which I did. He had at the time five children, the eldest about eight and the youngest about two and as it was their bath-night I took on the job of cutting their fingernails and toenails which amused me a lot. We sat up very late; late that is for me, I was in the habit of going to bed soon after ten o'clock; talking alternately in English and French and drinking really good wine. I am not a great lover of wine but both he and Louisa have really good wine always which I really enjoy drinking. In the morning had the first real bath since we were at Arques la Bataille, he had the finest house as regards comfort that I saw during the whole of my stay in France. Then he and his whole family went off to church as it was Sunday and I went off home.

France - Collaboration & Resistance" page 46 by H R Kedward published 1985 by Blackwood for the Historical Association Studies)

The actual book diary starts here

12th June 1941 A year ago today I was taken prisoner at St Valery, a year ago I heard the Regimental bugler sound the retreat and laid down the pistol that had been my best friend for five years, since I saw a British major cry as he tore up his maps and papers.

A great deal of water has flowed by since then and it has carried a good deal of detritus with it. Well I lost my last diary for the moment and have wasted a long time looking for it. I slept the night at Marcel Prevue's place and had a bath in the morning. It was not a great success as I could only get about a gallon of indifferently warm water from the tap. Had rather a scare in the morning when I thought that I found a threadworm in my stools. Hope that I was mistaken.

When I got back I found that Fred had put up new wallpaper and painted two of the rooms, it was very nice and must have been a long job. He has paid for it himself which does not seem right to me. Jeanne came in during the morning and stayed most of the day. She is a good deal prettier in my opinion than before although she always was a handsome girl, big and tall she has a peculiar stateliness that none of the rest of the family have. To my great surprise she let me get in bed with her on Monday morning for an hour and also all the other mornings too. Not that she is particularly amorous but it is a great satisfaction, I think that she is the loveliest girl whom I have ever made love to yet.

The well named Aimee has been in every day and I am in trouble because a young married woman, who has been mentioned before, badly wants what they call here *'un morceau de viande, vende sans ticket'* from me and does not hesitate to ask for it. She has already sent me a letter that should never have been written in any language never mind the highly coloured French 'Why dost thou not love me, thee whom I adore with all my soul' is lovely in French *'Pourquoi toi ne m'aime pas, toi que j'adore avec tout mon âme'*. But worse than this is that Yvonne wants to have a row with Louisa because the latter is intelligent enough to know more about her little adultery than she ought to. If she does I'm afraid that she will stir up more shit than she can stand the smell of as well as ruining my chances with Gilberte.

Saw an American 20 dollar gold piece which is now valued at 8,100 francs, or nearly ten times its value. Went to Mac's[25] with Jeanne and also to the station with her with Yvonne and Fred. Poor kid, she was very badly upset about having to go away. Also went to Mde Whight's in Lillers and met a surprising number of people who speak good English.

Have not so far mentioned the scrap in Crete but it was a good one and our boys got blasted out of it by parachutists and dive-bombers. I'm glad I was not there, it was not a nice place to be in. And now we have started a picnic in Syria which is technically French. As the General de Gaulle is there it is now French soldiers against French soldiers. No real news as yet. Churchill spoke to the representatives of the Freer Soldiers, Poles, Danes, Norwegians, French, Belgians and so on and his speech was reported tonight. It was really good and one phrase stuck in my mind 'We will not finish until every blot and stain of the vile Nazi doctrine is wiped away, sponged away, if necessary blasted away from the face of the earth'. It is a big programme. One of our friends has offered yet again to write to England for us and get a reply. Arthur has had one reply but it took seven months to get here.

Sunday 15th June Had a letter from Jeanne, also wrote to her and Gilberte and Louisa. Have had Aimee in three times today and together we kept up a really disgusting conversation on paper. There

---

[25] Mackay MacLeod, Helene's father, at 12 Rue Wagner, St Pierre les Auchel

is a young woman who badly wants me to have a go at her and Aimee finds it highly amusing that we can't fix it up. She is also the most highly sensual girl I have ever met and that is really saying something in France. Haven't found my diary yet which is a bastard.

Friday 20th June Have got a rotten cold in my head and feel like something the cat left behind. Also two aching teeth. The news on the wireless is rather involved but encouraging, it looks as if Hitler is going to demand a good deal from Russia but I don't believe that any war will come from it. And if it did it would be a carve up, Germany would grab great stretches of Russia and then have a Peace Treaty that includes them keeping them and Stalin could not do a great deal about it. Nor could we because we could not get into Europe at all.

Had a young woman who is a school teacher come here the other day. This is Rennee Maquet, a girl of about twenty to whom I wrote a good many letters, more for practice in French than for any other reason as there was never anything between us. A very tall girl, dark and with simply enormous eyes of incredible depth, slim with beautiful hands, long smooth and white, the loveliest hands I have ever seen, she was a near being a lady as one of her age can be. She speaks quite passable English but she has dampened my hopes of ever learning French, there is too much of it and when one has learned the rules of a highly complicated grammar one has also to learn all the exceptions, which are multitudinous, and idiomatic French is about as easy as spherical geometrical mathematics or three dimensional chemical formulae.

Sunday 22nd June Before I start writing to my multitudinous lady friends in the Nord et Pas de Calais I must record that Germany is now at war with USSR or the URSS as they say here. The technique was the same as with all the other countries, a lot of rumours, the accusation that Russia was going to attack Germany, troop

manoeuvres, the finding of the inevitable 'papers' and at last the
invasion of the *frontiere* in the early morning, 3 o'clock this time.
And on a 1500 mile front. What good it will do us is not very clear
but it ought to do some although I have very little hope that Russia
can hold the Jerries for long. But I would give a good deal of my life
(perhaps all of it) to be over there with a Bren gun or preferably a
Spandau. The RAF have been doing some really heavy raiding over
Germany for the last ten nights and have also had a go very near
here, St Omer and Boulogne got it yesterday. We went on a little
visit yesterday, in a doctor's car to see another bloke in the same
racket, also his wife, who had *les Anglais debarqué*, and a very shy
but sweet young lady of about seventeen. Were invited to go
swimming with them on Wednesday but do not know if it can be
wangled as we can only go out now if the old man is out and does
not know.

Wednesday 25th June On Tuesday we went to [heavily crossed out]
by the bus. The service here is something special, one bus a day.
Spent quite a nice day and got back just before 9.00. Today the
doctor wallah came for us in his car and we went, two carloads of us
to the swimming pool at Lillers which is not a bad place at all. The
driver is roughly as mad as he could be and keep on the road, he
took risks that even Cyril[26] in his drunkest moods would never have
taken. But we got there after all and had quite a nice swim. It was
not too cold but I have nearly forgotten how to swim and have
forgotten all the little I did know about diving. While we were
having a drink afterwards a young lady whom we know quite well
came in and recognised me. Which reminds me that Gazelle Eyes
came to see me this morning, a tall graceful beautifully fresh
creature she is. I can't imagine her as a participaton [sic] in a

---

[26] Cyril Mant of Avon Road, East Molesey- a friend in England from before the
war

violently passionate love scene but should like to be the other half of it if she ever did. Then we had dinner at the sawbones and I had the worse dose of toothache I have ever had the misfortune to meet. *C'etait vraiment formidable.* I didn't lose it all day and when I went to see Arthur in the evening I nearly went mad. I have erroneously told everyone that it is a year today since I came here but although it was a Wednesday it was the 26th and I have had three bunches of flowers given to me, all roses. They are lovely.

Saturday 28th June Went to the *dentiste* for the second time and my God did he give me Jeep. He filled two bad teeth and took out the nerves: and I nearly went crackers, I have never felt such exquisite agony in all of my life. Afterwards I was in a bad way and came straight home. The dentist is a darn good bloke at his trade however. Also visited about half a dozen places and got nearly drunk. And won a new pair of trousers and a pair of braces.

Tuesday 1st July Another *visite* to the *dentiste* but he did not do a lot today. Also went to Peter's place but the reception was a little bit cold. He was not there and his wife was full of troubles. I believe that the real trouble is that he has not the time or strength to give her as much dick as a tart of her description requires. I should like to help him out but can't. Have heard that Jeanne's mother does not want her to come here again as she is getting too fond of me, which is probably true but a pity just the same. And it does not look as if I shall have a lot of chance with Gilberte as Yvonne is thoroughly putting the tin hat on my going over there again.

The Royal Air Force have been having daily sweeps over Northern France with varying success. They are a bit late as most of the Luftwaffe have gone away to Russia and they fly at a God's Almighty height, it is nearly impossible to see them The other day they dropped a lot of stuff on Hazebroucke, some bombs, a lot of machine-gun slugs, pamphlets, two ounces of Medium Navy Cut and two score copies of 'Every Boy a Practical Scout' written in bad Esperanto. They smashed up the station, a trainload of Jerries going on leave and in the rumpus someone rifled the slot machine and got away with 24 francs 17 centimes, four marks and a luggage disk for the town of Llijypskkchl-yttsk on the Trans Siberian railway. Seriously though there was an awful mess and a lot of people were killed and injured. One bloke with his arm broken said *'Shairy ann, she lesh anglis'* which is patois for 'It does not matter, it was the English'. One afternoon, after bombing the power station at Chocques a Blenheim bomber was shot down at Allouagne and its crew of three killed. The French people covered the graves with flowers for at least six weeks on end and photographs of the grave were sold by dozens of people.[27]

Wednesday 2nd July It was poor old Babe's 24th birthday yesterday, Flo is now nearly 28. Jeanne's mother does not want her to come here again as she believes that she is getting too fond of me and Louisa thinks the same about Gilberte which is gratifying but a bastard for all that, I am not a good 'great lover' really and do not get enough affection as it is now without warning anyone off of the grass.

Saw part of a big air fight today, a British fighter dived out of the clouds, a Messerschmitt fired a burst of cannon shells at it and the whole machine blew up in mid-air. The pilot came down at St Pierre and escaped on a bicycle.

We could see the pilot descend by parachute in the fields nearby where he was found by my French friends. Before the Germans could locate him he was whisked away in a brewer's truck to a safe hiding place. ... Shortly afterwards I was invited to meet the

---

[27] This is the Allouagne Communal Cemetery also visited by evader George Barclay ("Fighter Pilot" p165) A Blenheim IV from 110 Squadron had been bombing the Kuhlman factories at Chocques on 21st May 1941

escaped pilot. He was an American [sic] *of French extraction serving with the RAF, Robillard by name. (Arthur Fraser 1958)*

A German bailed out at above 15,000 ft and took nearly a quarter of an hour to land, coming down near Marles. The RAF raided Maireville and claimed at least 17 planes for 9 lost. The Russians and Germans make the most fantastic claims about tank, air and infantry losses and I don't believe either of them The only fact that emerges is that Jerry is advancing at a good rate.

Monday 7th July Saw a real air raid today, three four motor bombers came over at what seemed a ridiculous rate and with a fighter escort of about fifty. I believe they were American, either Liberators or even Boeing Flying Fortresses, at least they were immense. They flew straight on and about four minutes later I saw what looked like sparks from an electric battery in the air and the thump-thump of heavy AA fire. I have never seen actual fire in the air before, only balls of smoke, this must be new stuff of Jerry's. Well, the big planes went on, inexorable as fate itself and then came two heavy WUMP WUMPS, just like that and the wireless went off. They had unloaded their big eggs onto the power station at Chocques and witnesses swear that the place was blown to hell. Anyway we had no power for about four hours.

Had our big friend from Lillers come to see us, she is not in the least pleased at the way I learn French, with all of the slang and catch-phrases usual round here. But I am; although I do not doubt that Fred knows more French than I do at least my conversation is more interesting because I do not search after conjugations of verbs like he does *'je sais - je sus, je savoir, je savvy'* and if I don't find the French for it I use the pâtois which they all know.

Tuesday 8th July The planes came over again today and bombed Lille, the noise of them and of the AA guns was terrific. A big one shot down near Lillers, about six kilometres the other side of it.

Got up early and went over to the swimming pool with Yvonne and Fred. The day was as hot as hell and the water was lovely even if it was a bit thick. We knew about half of the people there but did not know a couple of Jerries as they had no swastika on their bathing drawers. Afterwards went to a friends where we had a good dinner and a good deal to drink and afterwards on to the English lady who had been expecting us for hours. Got back about 9.00. Had a long and rather pathetic letter from Gilberte, the poor kid is just about fed up what with one thing and another. I should very much like to see her.

Wednesday 9th July More air raids this morning. Yvonne and Fred have gone to Louisa's for the day and it is a bit peaceful here, especially as the old lady has been to bed most of the afternoon. Aimee says that she will bring her sister here this evening.

Yesterday the Americans landed troops in Iceland which is what Germany describes as 'another bestial rape of a small unprotected nation' which is only funny. On the Russian front things are very hectic but have not moved much for four or five days, it is an affair of attack and counter-attack with both sides claiming to have inflicted enormous losses on each other. I do not believe the Russian air figures however, they get worse and worse: they started by being 348:329 in Russia's favour then it got to 129:73 and later on 67:27 and yesterday it was 53:5 which is absurd. When the Luftwaffe comes up against the RAF it swaps more or less plane for plane, perhaps a bit in our favour because our boys have a longer training, and it is laughable to believe Soviet pilots however good are ten times as good as German ones who, after all, have had at least two years of actual war flying as well as really good machines and guns.

We have a lot of trouble with the water here now, it has to be all fetched from the pump about a hundred yards away and the pump only runs for about an hour, always changing, each day.

Saturday 12th July Yvonne and Fred have been over at Louisa's for three days each this week which is all right with me. Mathilde has come back here for good because her mother is too ill to carry on alone. She is very much bigger and taller than when she went away and finds it *'extraordinaire'* that I have learned so much French (and pâtois) since she left. Aimee's sister Alfreda has a weeks holiday also, a big bold strapping wench she is too, who is learning to be a mid-wife.

Sunday 13th July On the one o'clock news we were told to stand by at 2.00 and hear a special announcement. It was that Great Britain and Russia had concluded a Pact that they would aid each other in every way until the Germans were beaten and that neither would conclude any armistice without the others consent (which is a lesson that we have learned from France). In Libya the Vichy general Dentz asked for an armistice and so the fighting ended after four weeks. We have not yet heard the terms of the Armistice there.

The Russians are steadily losing ground but are doing a terrific amount of damage to the Germans and are also destroying everything that they leave behind. If they are doing this in the Ukraine they are burning the biggest harvest in Europe, what is rather poetically called Stalin's 'Parched Earth Policy'. The Germans are credibly reported to have lost a million men and about five thousand tanks but are still advancing. The Russians, either by accident or design, leave behind big bodies of troops who do not follow the classic but by no means heroic example of the Allies in France but engage in guerrilla warfare that is said to be very effective in the huge spaces of Russia. The German radio complains bitterly that the Russians do not know one of the elements of warfare, that if an army is surrounded it must surrender, but carry on happily trying to blast their way out in any old direction. The newspapers here have ghastly atrocity stories of the 'German deliverers' arriving too late and finding prisons full of dead men only. In one town alone 3,000 persons are said to have been murdered by submachine-guns and automatics. There are big pictures of hundreds of bodies laid out in rows. And other pictures of Germans, armed with Tommy guns, being welcomed by beautiful girls in Estonia and Latvia.

In four weeks of extensive bombing Mr Churchill claimed that half the weight of bombs dropped on us in 22 months had been poured onto Germany in four weeks. He also promises that "We can, and will continue in an ever-growing crescendo to bomb Germany until either Germany is beaten or better still, the people of Germany rise up and throw away the yoke of Nazidom". Incidentally the power station that the three bombers blew up will take a year to put into working order so it is only reasonable to suppose that all of the hundreds who go off every night do not really only hit an empty hospital and kill the caretaker's cat. Well Sunday Yvonne and Fred came back from Sains and Gilberte came over for the day. She was however told that she was not to stay the night.

Tuesday 15th July Fred has gone to Sains by himself and I am quite happy by myself here. Gilberte came over yesterday and as it rained a good deal she stayed the night. She slept with me for two or three hours but little lady got the wind up and kept coming in and making such a hell of a row that I was afraid that she would wake up the old lady. Still, it was very nice and in the morning I had some more love but not from the same person, it was in fact a bit of a surprise but I have waited long enough for it. And such is the kingdom of Heaven.

Sunday 20th July According to the wireless and papers the greatest battle in history is now raging in Russia, just over nine million men and practically every weapon known to science is being used by both sides, from revolver and grenade scrapping to the submarine and air war against shipping. The Russians are being driven back but seem to be giving a good account of themselves as they go. The RAF come over here nearly every day now and the marking of Vs and *Lorraine Crosses* on the walls and houses has just about reached its climax. They tap out the letter V in Morse now - like this - dot dot dot dash. Just what good it does is obscure to me but several of the local villages are *consigned* for several Sundays, that is the people are not allowed out on the streets at all that day. We both went to see Arthur the other day but he was not there, however he came to see us the next day.

Friday 25th July The Germans have now adopted the V for their own use, it now stands for the German word *Victoria*, which is all very puzzling as well as amusing, but there is not the slightest doubt but that it is a very clever move.

Airman George Barclay shot down near St Omer that summer commented in his own diary that the Germans started putting white V's on their vehicles with little swastikas under them and then larger ones on walls in towns, the whole device being surrounded with laurel leaves. The French retaliated by obliterating the swastikas and substituting a croix de Lorraine inside the V - France therefore was littered with two kinds of V's (see 'Fighter Pilot' p149)

Three days ago a tall man wandered in and said in English "I am a British Secret Service agent, do you want to come to Spain with me?" He said that he would take us to Free France himself in about two weeks. He was exactly my idea of the real article; was not in the least concerned as to whether we went or not "It's not my job to get you to go" referred to us as a "couple of squaddies" which must have hurt Fred's feelings a lot, and rushed off. Well I at least did not want to but we arranged to go if Arthur would go too. He jumped at the chance. Worse than that I am now fairly certain that Yvonne is pregnant, her mother is too. And no need to mention who the father is. Have had quite a good watch given me by a young man who came here.

On Thursday we went to a sort of pilgrimage to Amettes, the birthplace of Joseph Benoit Labre, a saint of some importance here. Went over the farm where he was born and went into the big, although dingy, church of Amettes. The day out was not a success at all and we got back tired and bad tempered.

Saturday 2nd August Have got my gun back as well as a new box of Browning cartridges for it. Have been over to Arthur's place and have had a great many people come here, including Louisa who slept here for the night. I got extremely bad tempered with her and she knew it. Gilberte writes that she will not be allowed to come here again, for which I have to thank Yvonne and Fred and their filth. Have drunk three bottles of cognac in ten days and do not feel much better for it. Have started kissing Mathilde now that it is too late, not that she minds at all but is absolutely indifferent.

The news is good at the moment, the Russians have almost halted the Germans and are doing some real damage. Unfortunately the RAF seem to have slackened off on Germany, she is not getting her fair share of H.E.

Sunday 3rd August Had both Gilberte and Louisa come, the latter got very little change from me and poor Gilberte was very ill and went to bed most of the afternoon. Louisa was annoyed that she stayed here to sleep but could do very little about it. Also had Aimee and Georgina but no other company.

Wednesday 6th August Well Gilberte was not so bad as she made out and about ten minutes after she had gone to bed she was in my bed, and she stayed until about 2 in the morning. It was very nice indeed as it was fairly cold and it was not too hot close together. She said that she would sleep there for the night and asked *'Vous ne fait* *pas de bêtises quand je dor, si vous plait?'* But she did not sleep there as Yvonne got the wind up again and she finished the night with her.

On Tuesday morning I went to Sains with her and stayed for dinner, got back here by 5.00. The old man raised Cain because I had taken his bike with his name on it. See Mathilde nearly every day now. It was the child's birthday [Yvonne's daughter Anne Marie] here yesterday so I gave Mathilde 100 francs to get her something and she bought a little woollen smock affair and a big money box. She collected 26 francs in two days.

Thursday 14th August Well, we have still not gone away, the day has been changed three times and now we do not know. Gilberte was here on Sunday. All three of us were over at Sains on Friday and a bloke came and told us that another bloke wanted to see us and so we borrowed bikes and rushed back. He was a real Englishman and had been arrested at the same time as poor old Teddy. He has been here for 23 years. On Saturday I took one of the bikes back and had a row with Louisa because she would not let Gilberte come back with me. However Gilberte managed to get a bike and caught me up at Floringhem. She stayed the night and slept with me until 5.00 in the morning which is the first time that I have ever actually slept with a girl. It was very nice in spite of the fact that she had *'les Anglais debarqué'*. She went back on Sunday, I went with her as far as Sains and stayed the night there. Slept like a log as I had very little sleep the night before. Came back on foot and in the Place of Pernes got copped by a bloke who had a bottle of Scotch which was thirty years old, which we sampled not wisely but too well. So I got home by car about 4.00. Amiee came and brought me a really good pair of shoes. Mathilde came too and the poor kid upset herself because we, or at least I, was going. Poor kid, she sat on the edge of the bed looking white and apprehensive and when I kissed her she put her arms round me in a truly maternal manner, she is a big girl now, weighs nearly as much as I do, and did not want me to see her eyes. I like Mathilde in a queer, almost platonic way, she does not appeal to me sexually but she is just good and honest right the way through. She is too good a girl to be the wife of some Pas de Calais miner, bearing children and scrubbing and working her heart out as her mother has. Her said mother came in and raised hell because she was there, she is cognisant of Yvonne's condition and does not want her in the same predicament. Arthur and Helene ['Eileen'] came with the news that the day had been changed again.

Gilberte came again for the week and she, Marcelle [Cruppe] and myself made a cycle tour of the battleground around Bethune. There were hundreds upon hundreds of graves roughly half German and half British but only a very few Frenchmen, less than ten anyway. In one huge grave were buried over a hundred Britishers. I spoke to one of the Frenchmen who lived a hundred yards away, he said that they were men who were taken prisoner and after being made to dig a huge hole were lined up and machine-gunned. This story appears to be vouched for by every person for miles around.[28]

Sunday 17th August Still here, very little news, have been flailing corn today, a very tiring job indeed. Louisa sent me a letter, demanding to know the truth about Yvonne. She knows it now. Gilberte is once more forbidden to come here. Fred was taken ill about 8.00 AM, don't yet know what it is.

Roosevelt and Churchill have had a meeting in the middle of the Atlantic but nothing new seems to have come of it. The radio has made a lot of it but to me it seems to be sheer melodrama, the President went off in his yacht *'Potomac'* and a few days later

---

[28] Men of the 2nd Royal Norfolks shot by Totenkopf SS after surrendering at Le Paradis in May 1940

Churchill came to meet him in the *'Prince of Wales'*, our newest
battle cruiser. They were unanimous in deciding about what to do
after the war is won but made no mention of how it is going to be
won, which to me seems to be a most important point. The Russians
are having their usual success, they withdraw at about eighty
kilometres a week. The radio announces that to conquer all of Russia
is impossible, which if not literally true is at least practically true but
my humble opinion is that if the *Wermacht* occupy all of the Ukraine
and all the land west of a line running from Archangelsk to Moscow
and from Moscow to the Sea of Azof they can leave the wastes of
Siberia and the largely useless lands of Central Asia to whoever
wants them. I say useless in the sense of useless at the moment, there
is not the slightest doubt in my mind that Central Asia south of the
meridian 50° or even 55° could be exploited in the same way as
Europe has been. I have had an idea in my mind for a very long time
that I would like to travel in Northern, especially North Eastern
Russia and see some of the life there, to see the gigantic rivers that
no-one in England knows the names of, the huge lakes and come out
on the shores of the Arctic Ocean. There must be things up there that
are worth while, something to shoot, something. But I shall never
see them, I'm afraid that there is not much of the explorer in me, as
well as the damning fact that I have no money. And my difficulty
with the French language does not encourage me to start on another
half a dozen or more.

Thursday 21ˢᵗ August Well on Tuesday Gilberte came but did not
have a lot to say, neither did we get a chance to be alone together.
The atmosphere has been very strained here for a long time and then
Louisa wrote and asked me to ask Madame if it was true or not that
Yvonne was in the pudding club. Well that started things up a bit
more until Wednesday morning I found that my gun, which had
been hidden pretty carefully, had been pinched so there was only
one thing to do, I insulted Fred until there was nothing else he could

do but fight which he would have done in any case, even if I had had to hit him into it. Still he was not in the least unwilling and we had a go which was unfortunately stopped by Yvonne. He was as peeved as I was about it: I have never seen anyone as frightened as she was, and she really did have cause to be because I had no intention of making it a boxing match but a real fight and that means all in. One of us would have got pretty well mauled about, and although he is a bit heavier than me I am fairly sure that it would have been him. Still it is only postponed until a better time and place turn up. Well of course then it came out about the gun and the old lady told him that he was to go and see a doctor at [sic] her daughter and to give him his due he went off to get one straight away. The old lady said that Y had pinched the gun because she was afraid that I would shoot Fred but that she believed that she wanted it to shoot herself if Fred went away. All of which is very melodramatic because if I had any intention of killing him I should use a knife, not a gun. Anyway I believe that he will suffer more if he lives. The ethics of murder do not enter into it, there is no law to protect or punish either of us here.

Well today they have gone to Lillers to see someone about an abortion. God only knows what will happen when her husband comes back because as sure as God made little apples he will hear about it from someone or other. The same applies to the old man here, there will be blood to mop up if and when he knows. So I've hidden the gun again as it was put back in my drawer last night, not too sure that I won't get the first slug out of it into ME. Still there is not much fear of that because no-one in this house has ever fired one before and I move bloody quick myself, the first slug will have to do the job.

Saturday 23rd August Jeanne came on holiday, do not know if she will spend much time here or not but hope so. She has lost a lot of weight as well as looks since she was here last. Have been getting on very well with Mathilde lately but nothing special has come of it. We had three lots of fat for making chips with given to us in two days and yesterday we had about ten pounds of good meat in the house. As I say to them here *Vive la Marche Noir*, because without it we should go bloody short of grub. Heard of two young Dutch officers who have just got to London after trying ever since the invasion. They got across in a small boat from Holland after trying to get through Spain and Portugal. So much for our chances. The bloody razor blades that we buy here are like shit, they are supposed to be Blue Gillette but after two shaves they are finished. And we have a Barbary duck and five little ones who amuse me no end. Every morning I say to her *'Bon jour Madame, ça va ti?'* and she always puts out her tongue and hisses at me.

Tuesday 26th August Well, Yvonne has not got rid of her bastard yet as far as I know, Jeanne is here on holiday but will not sleep here, poor Mathilde is going to be sent away again because her mother thinks that she is struck on me and altogether things are in a hell of a mess here. Gilberte came here this morning with very grudging permission from all concerned. By Christ I seem to have lost more by this filthy business to date than anyone else, neither of them appear to have the slightest intention of finishing it now and the old lady is too dense to realise that whatever wrong is being done, is done under her own roof. We have been warned to get out of here because things are going to blow up in two or three days but actually we have nowhere to go now and that is no exaggeration.

Yesterday I went with Jeanne and her mother to Mac's but left alone after about half an hour. Went into the café and got a real welcome from both of them. They seemed to have a sort of beanfeast on and after a bit we were all slightly drunk. Mathilde was mad because I went out with Jeanne but cheered up when I came back alone. She is still forbidden to come here but still comes. I am a lot better with her

now than ever before because I understand her better. She is
temperamentally very similar to Babe, but not exactly because she is
French. I am sure that she has an immense reserve of passion in her
somewhere and the man who taps that will be a lucky one indeed for
she is no shallow nature and what she gives will be with all her heart
and soul. I was alone with her for three hours the other day and
gained some idea of her will power and character. She has a row
every time she comes here but she still comes. I looked into her
quiet brown eyes and was sorry that she was not my girl, not just
something to play with but a real soul-mate, someone for whom I
could wait for and work for but no, I'm afraid that I am not of that
type.

Thursday 28th August Last night we heard on the wireless that a
young Frenchman named Collett or some such name had sent a
bullet into Laval and another jackal of the same calibre on the
parade ground of Versailles.[29] It was at a parade of volunteers to
fight against the Russians but as the young soldier said 'I keep my
bullets for the real enemies of France'. Well, Laval has had it
coming to him for a very long time, it is only what three people out
of five in France would like to do. The killing of Germans is getting
to be so common that they put up a notice in two languages this
morning in the papers that for every German so killed they would
shoot five hostages. Two officers got theirs at Lille and there is
going to be hell to pay if someone does not take the can back for it. I
do not altogether agree with this stabbing in the dark business but
what else can the people do? Any organised revolt is put down with
wholesale arrests and shootings.

---

[29] Right-wing Nationalist Paul Collette shot and injured collaborationists Pierre
Laval and Marcel Déat

Saw Jeanne off at Lillers station, she was rather upset, as usual, especially as we have had very little time alone this time. Yvonne is not yet clear of her trouble and is very ill today.

Sunday 31ˢᵗ August More trouble, we are now on our way to Free France again, much against my better judgement. We had arranged to sleep at Madame Whyght's [at 82 rue Savenoal, Lillers] but as we visited several friends on the way we did not arrive before eleven o'clock. Still can't be helped. Had only two days notice, said goodbye to no one and slept at - *left blank* . Yvonne is clear of her trouble but has been very ill indeed for four days. Have not said goodbye even to *Pauvre* Mathilde who is really upset about it all. I shall believe that we are going when we get there as I feel that somewhere or something is not quite all that it might be.

Pas de Calais area June 1940 to August 1941

On the Way Home

There are many things that I have missed out from this narrative, some of them that are best missed out, some that I just forgot, some that took place so very gradually that they seem to have been part of the accepted order of things. The abortive coal strike that started when I was at Sains, the visits of the young school mistress of Arras, the time when I had four thousand francs given me in one week by the shop keepers at Lillers, when we all went to the midnight Mass at the big church in Auchel, the amount of writing that I did, including two attempts at a novel, the time I nearly drank myself to death on good cognac and about all the utter misery that I suffered when I could see what was going to be the end of Wilkinson's affair with Yvonne and could do nothing to stop it; all of these formed part of the incredible story that was not complete and probably never will be.

We slept the night in Lillers, Wilkinson and I in one room and Yvonne and Madame and her daughter in the next door so that any farewell presents were not possible. Yvonne had her miscarriage the day before so it was just as well. We were up at 6.00 the next morning and after goodbyes all round went off to the station. There was no-one there so I went off towards Burbure to meet Arthur and Eileen, who came along just before 6.45. We then had a drink in a café and Dubois gave us our new passports then we got on to the train for Bethune. To my surprise the girls came too, although the train was full of Germans. We passed Chocques and saw some of the damage done by the RAF and then arrived at Bethune. One of the Germans on the platform had a Lee Enfield rifle on his shoulder. We then went to another café and were told that we had to wait another couple of hours so we went to see a friend in the centre of Bethune. It was market day and the sides of the streets near the Grande Place were crowded with boxes of fruit, mainly tomatoes and apples but bags of other stuff was there as well. We had a hard job to find this house and when we did the people were not yet up. They were very surprised to see such a crowd of us but asked us in and made us coffee. They had a Mills bomb on the mantle-piece but all of the explosive had been taken out of it. I took it to pieces and had a job to put it back together again. It has always been a disappointment to me that I carried more Mills bombs about than anyone else whom I ever met (when captured I had fourteen) and yet have never yet seen one go off.

Well at ten o'clock we were back at the café and met again the officer[30] who had been to see us, a young Frenchman called Roland and another fellow like Dubois. They had only two guns with them and I rather regretted that mine had been left behind. We asked him by which route we were going and when he said Abbeville it rather upset me because that place has always been a bit of a hoodoo with me. I've been there three times before and never had any luck at all connected with it.

Cole was in charge but in my mind did not inspire much confidence. He was tall and thin with reddish hair and small moustache. His whole appearance was the continentals' idea of a typical Englishman. His French was deplorable and spoken in an accent unmistakably British. He was loud-mouthed, perhaps to cover his nervousness, although while I knew him, he showed no fear. (Arthur Fraser 1958)

Well on the train we were introduced to four other fellows, Crowley-Milling an English pilot-officer, 'John Love' a Czechoslovakian sergeant-pilot and 'George Brown' and 'Archie' both Poles. We had to say goodbye to Yvonne and Eileen on the platform, Yvonne was crying but Eileen was all right and then we got away.

---

[30] The "officer" was Sgt Harold 'Paul' Cole - a British Army deserter - see historic notes for more details of him, Roland Lepers and other people mentioned as working on the escape line

On the Way Home

We were all a bit diffident at first but long before we got to Colonne Ricouart we were all pretty good friends except Crowley-Milling who never during the whole trip forgot that he was an officer and we were not. When we went past the Mairie of Colonne I felt that I was losing something that meant a lot to me, I don't know what the other two felt. It was not a particularly long journey to Abbeville and at the time (1st September) there did not appear to be many Germans there.

We went from the station in pairs and were to follow the party in front at a distance of about a hundred yards, by no means an easy job in a busy city. We got to a house [next to the church on rue du Cimitiere Saint-Gilles] and gave up one of our photographs which were then put into genuine identity cards and stamped with stamps that even an expert would have had a great deal of trouble to identify as fake.

We were led to the house of Abbe Carpentier, a brave man, later to be betrayed by Cole and executed by the Germans. Head of the local organisation, he had collected identity cards and passes from his townspeople. Their photographs were detached and ours, which had previously been taken, were fixed in their places and counter-stamp faked over. (Arthur Fraser 1958)

It was a bit of a rush as we had to catch the four o'clock train to Paris. The purpose of these cards was to allow us to pass over the Somme which forms the barrier between *La France Occupé* and *La Zone Interdite*, in which of course we lived.

To get over the river we went up to the bridge one by one and handed an enormous sentry the two cards, one the ordinary identity card for occupied France, for which incidentally I used my own that I'd had for a year and not the new one, and the *laissez passé* which is printed in both German and French, bears the Nazi eagle and the signature of the town *Kommandant*. It was only then that I found out that I was supposed to be a clergyman, which of course I did not in the least resemble.

Be that as it may we all got across without a question asked but on the train both of them ejected cartridges from their automatics. We each bought tickets to Paris separately, the place was absolutely full of Germans who seemed to be going to Paris, unlike the town in which there was not a great number. We reached the Gar du Nord at Paris about seven o'clock and very nearly lost ourselves in the Metro, which is the underground railway, every bit as noisy and full of people as the Inner Circle of London. Each and every one of us was jammed in between German soldiers but we were about used to them by now and took no notice of them. We stayed the night in a hotel that was in reality nothing else but a brothel, each bed for instance was surrounded by huge mirrors so that as Roland quaintly put it "You can lay and see yourself fucked in forty-one different positions". We had just put our gear in the rooms, I had one to myself, when they called us to go out to dinner. We had quite a decent dinner which cost about fifty francs each, say about six shillings, but had to surrender quite a lot of ration tickets for it. The wine was very good, it seemed a pity to drink beer with it. The *Parisiens* and *Parisiennes* did not impress us much in that particular place although it was very far from being a dive. On the way back to the hotel we had three women stop us and say *"Fait d'amour mes enfants"* but we did not like the looks of them and passed on. John found a nice one and took her to bed but found that he could not do anything with her and asked for his money back.[31]

---

[31] According to Murphy (109) 'John' had been sharing a room with Crowley-Milling but this arrangement resulted in C-M moving down the hall to share Cole's room - see Brendan Murphy "Turncoat" (1980) Macdonald & Co (Publishers) Ltd

Monday 1ˢᵗ September Am writing this in a hotel in Paris which is farther than I expected to get, having crossed one line at Abbeville very easily. The whole of the north of France is packed with Germans, thousands of them. Yvonne and Eileen came as far as Bethune with us and we went with a real mixed bunch of lads, all airmen bar us three. Had quite a nice supper in Paris but it cost me 165 francs for four of us, say five bob each. Went to bed early.

That was the last entry in the diaries - the remainder of this story comes from the notes and resume written at Gibraltar

We had a good night and set out early the next morning before it was light. There were huge piles of cabbage stacked on one side of the street, more cabbage than I've ever seen before in my life and vans unloading it every minute. We had coffee and rolls at a small café where they seemed to know all about us and fixed us up with real coffee, which has been a rarity in France ever since the New Order cast its influence over Europe. Then on to the train again, this time for Tours, a big town very near the demarcation line between *La France Occupé* and *La France Libre*.

We got there about two o'clock and there saw for the first time the German version of the ATS, a big strapping wench wearing a fine looking uniform with the trappings of an Oberleutnant particularly took my eye, she seemed to be the very personification of German womanhood militarised. She was a girl of about twenty-five, tall, say five foot ten and weighed perhaps twelve stone, of which not much was fat. With her were two full corporals and five or six other girls, one or two of whom seemed a bit scared of their surroundings. So would our ATS be if they were suddenly dumped in Magdeburg or Essen among people whose only thoughts are hatred for the people who have conquered them. The station was however packed tight with German troops of all sorts, the usual Army of Occupation but also Gestapo and Death's Head men as well as dozens of Military

Police and a good few Luftwaffe men. There were also sailors, some of them from submarines though what on earth they were doing here was and still is a puzzle to me.

We had some food in a hotel near the station and then the officer left us and went to make arrangements to take us over the border. About 5.00 we got on a local train but about five minutes before it started got off again because there were too many Germans on it. Again at seven we boarded the train, each one in a different carriage, with our instructions as to which station to get off at and what to do. The first three stations that we passed I failed to see the names and so was forced to ask which station was mine. A woman who was in the carriage and who had evidently been shopping said "But St Martin le Beau that is my station also, get off where I do". Whether or not she knew I was English, she certainly suspected that my objective was to cross the border. Well at the station it must have looked suspicious to anyone watching to see nine fellows, all between twenty and thirty and all carrying suitcases, dive off the train and, studiously avoiding each other, make straight for a little pathway. It was worse still when we got to the road because we were strung out but all plainly visible to each other. A man approached me and asked me something in an unintelligible patois so I just shook my head and walked on. We all hid behind a big barn at the corner of a field, the people who were working at the other side must have seen us. After about half an hour a gendarme came round to see us, he seemed to guess what we were for, he asked if we were all prisoners to which we all said yes although only Arthur and myself had ever been prisoners. We had to wait until well after dark before we could move, Roland and Paul [Cole] were nervous because a man who used to help them and incidentally earn a good deal of money by it came nearly to our hiding place and then went away again. They had not used him for some time because they were afraid that he was planning to sell us out at the first chance. At last however it was dark enough to move but the moon was full and in places it was as bright as day. We moved in single file across the fields and came to a partly completed bridge over a fast river. Getting across this without being seen was not easy as we walked on a single plank about a foot wide - and the river was nearly sixty feet below us if we lost our footing. However we did it and successfully located our guide who was to take us across.

All went well for about five miles when, after moving across fields we came to a big road. I was two from the last and the guide had just got in the middle of the road when he turned and ran and the others followed him. Five or six men went past me in a mad rush and so I also joined in. Then a voice hailed us from the road *'Eh bah, tu es malade ou qu'est que c'est?'* and rather shamefaced we made our way back; it turned out to be only two men on cycles who were probably engaged in a little *marche noir* business. About half an hour later we crossed the actual line and then after a swig of cognac that I had brought along we sent the guide[32] back and set off.

On the way we tried some of the grapes that were growing in the fields but they were so bitter (they were wine grapes) that it was impossible to eat them. We walked fast all night, about four o'clock we knocked up a farmhouse and tried to get some food but all that we could get was some milk. Then soon afterwards, because we found that we should get into Loches earlier than was convenient we lay down and tried to sleep for half an hour. I myself slept but the others could not because it was too cold. Towards seven o'clock it was a job to keep going, we had been walking for ten hours and had done thirty miles and three of us had trouble with our feet and one of the Poles said that he could go no farther. At last however we

---

[32] Notes suggest this guide was Portuguese - Pte Charles Knight travelling in a party guided by James Smith in July 41 also mentions having a Portuguese guide at this point (see WO208 3309-798)

staggered into the station and dropped wearily into the train for Chateauroux. It was not a long journey but most of us were asleep by the time we arrived.

We had another meal and sent off cards to our families and then got on to yet another train for Toulouse. Again we slept for most of the journey but also talked a good deal; by now we had got each other roughly summed up. John, the big Czech pilot was the life and soul of our party but Roland was a bit of a comic too, although he made us a bit nervous at first by speaking in English wherever we happened to be. Crowley-Milling was still reserving the benefit of his wisdom for more intelligent company and the two Poles kept very much to themselves. Paul, who was in charge of the job told us a good deal about his life in England but very little of what he had done in France. Well at last we got to Toulouse quite late in the day and almost at once got still another train for Marseilles.

This did not leave until midnight but as it was crowded with passengers we had to get our seats at about 10.00. When it did eventually move every available inch of space had been filled up, the corridors and lavatories included. Paul slept in the luggage rack and seemed to be quite comfortable while we tried to fit ourselves in as best we could. We slept on and off but a French train has not much to recommend it as a substitute for a bedroom. Just as it got light we got into Marseille, that port that had been the Mecca of so many of our boys and which, even at that moment held three hundred of our boys in the prison at St Hippolyte.[33]

---

[33] St Hippolyte du Fort is situated about 40 kms north-west of Nimes. The old military school was used as an internment camp for what the French called 'Détachement W' from January 1941 until March 1942 when the inmates were transferred to Fort de la Rivere, La Turbie, in the hills overlooking Nice. Today a road runs through what used to be the exercise yard and the building houses the town's Tourist Office.

On the Way Home

We had to show our *cartes d'identité* at the barrier but it was only a superficial glance. I was very much impressed by the city, the second greatest in France I believe, although I did not see much of it. We went down a long flight of stone stairs and along to a café where we had chocolate and long hard bread rolls. There was not enough sugar in the chocolate but it went down very well after our journey. Then we went to a barber and had ourselves made a little more respectable, in fact when he had finished with me I owed him thirty francs, which is a lot of money in *La France*. We had to spend the rest of the day somehow by ourselves and went to three cinemas as well as doing a bit of shopping as our suitcases containing the spare kit of Arthur, Wilkinson and myself had been lost at Tours. I had a long conversation with John Brown, one of the Poles and got very friendly with him. Then about nine o'clock we found that we had lost another of the suitcases and Arthur and George went back to get it. When they came back Paul told us that it contained not only enough papers to get us all ten years but also his Mauser automatic and a hundred rounds and about eighteen thousand francs. Luckily it had not been searched or our gang would have lost at least two of it numbers.

As we were going along the harbour Paul said "Be careful now, there is a man who has been following us for four hours and I want to lose him". I laughed and said "If you lot walk on I'll lose him for you - in the harbour". My intention being to knife him and push him into the water but Paul would not have it, saying that he would fix him the next day when we were well on our way to the Spanish border. So we lost him and then found that we had also lost ourselves and had to get a taxi.

Arthur, John and George came with me to a hotel where we met a very charming gentleman who showed us to our rooms and gave us

167

our instructions for the morning. The others were off at a big private house and appear to have had a very good time.

The 'very charming gentleman' was Louis Nouveau and my father, Arthur Fraser, Rudolf Ptacek ('John') and Henryk Stachura ('George') all stayed in his apartment. My father is mentioned in Helen Long's 'Safe Houses are Dangerous' and his name appears in Louis' records of the time. It was Louis that kept dad's diaries safe and posted them back to him after the war which is probably why he was able to record my father's name and (spell it correctly) whilst the rest of party are not mentioned. The envelope they were sent in has Louis' name and return address stamped on the back. Denis Crowling-Milling, Fred Wilkinson and Adolph Pietrasiak ('Archie') stayed with Dr Georges and Fanny Rodocanachi.

From the manuscript by Louis Nouveau - "Of the list of airmen who spent a few days, varying from one or two to fifteen, in our flat in Marseilles between May 1941 and November 1942. I wrote down their names in the inner margins of separate pages of Volume 44 of a Complete Edition of Voltaire's works, in 70 volumes ... Unfortunately, I only began to do this after a certain number of them, perhaps 25 or 30, had stayed with us, having at first omitted to do so; so that the names of our earliest guests are missing, except the very first one of all those names I remember perfectly, as he stayed in the flat a fairly long while."

Page 1 - Sergeant Philip HERBERT - 15 days.
Page 5 - No names given, roughly about thirty.
Page 24 - Peter SCOTT JANES[34]

---

[34] Actually in Louis Nouveau's book *Des Capitaines Par Milliers* it is spelt Jones but Helen Long took her details direct from the Volume 44 of Voltaire held at the Imperial War Museum where it is spelt correctly

Page 25 - LOCKHART ? Sergeant pilot.

(Helen Long Appendices)

NB. My neighbour W/C Leslie Pearman tells me that many of the later entries were written by the servicemen themselves

We spent a good but very short night and were up at five the next morning. The man told us that he had a son in the concentration camp in Spain and that we would all have to pass through it as well. This was the first intimation that we had of what was going to happen in Spain, up to now it had been all a nebulous uncertainty, even now we felt that we should have rotten luck if we did wind up in a prison of any sort. Perhaps had we known what the future held we should not have been so jubilant.

It was still dark as we made our way to the station, about the last thing our friend said was "When you get to Miranda ask for Peter Bedard".[35] Then off again, this time to Perpignan. The train was terribly slow and we gave up our role as deaf mutes and talked away cheerfully in our respective languages, that is to say English for most of us, French for most of us, Polish for three of them, German for five of them, Czech for four of them and a little Hungarian by way of a diversion.

There were four men talking in English in our carriage who were also going to Spain, from their conversation I took them to be journalists, either American or English. At about two o'clock we arrived at Perpignan and after being carefully scrutinised by the police we went down into the town and into a garage. Here we were received by a man who spoke not only every language that we did, viz six, but also four more, he also told us that he spoke eleven more

---

[35] He actually wrote Peter Bider in the diary but Louis' son Jean-Pierre had left Marseille for Spain travelling as a French Canadian using the name J P Bedard (see WO 208/3303 284-290 App C)

but not so well. A most remarkable linguist. We gave up our cards and also most of our money, I had nearly three thousand francs, which was more than any two of the others put together. He then gave us the rather startling advice to give ourselves up to the police as soon as we got to Spain. He then gave us twelve hundred pesetas in exchange for our money and took us by car to a dirty little café in Banyuls, a village about two miles from the foot of the Pyrenees.[36] It was the sort of place that one sees on the pictures, a sort of hiding place for doubtful characters, in which nomenclature we doubtlessly figured at the time.

Well after waiting in a back room for about two hours we met the man whom we had to contact. At first, speaking very bad French he said he knew nothing about getting us over the hills but at last admitted that he did and then said that we should have to wait several days as all the guides were away at the time. We told him that that was impossible and so he went out muttering to himself to return about four hours later with the news that he had found a man, a smuggler, who would take us across the next evening. So we had to spend the night in the café. Luckily the beds were good and we got some coffee in the morning which was very bad indeed. John then asked the woman to send out for some tomatoes and we also drank a good deal of wine. This wine was some of the best that I tasted in France.

We waited all day until seven o'clock in the evening and then went out of the place two by two and made our way to the rendezvous

---

[36] This account (but not the notes) specifies Banyuls [sur-Mer] but Crowley-Milling says they crossed from La Rocque in the only E&E report that gives a place name. That makes more sense as this account makes no mention of the sea, nor does Arthur remember seeing it, which is clearly visible all the way up the mountain from Banyuls. Also the crossing from Laroque-des-Alberes is a fair bit tougher and at least 300 metres higher - a crossing from Banyuls by the obvious route should not have caused them so many problems.

which was a wood by the side of a vineyard. In about an hour
everyone was there except the guide and we were all eating huge
clusters of purple grapes as fast as we could eat them, I suppose we
ate about two pounds each, all one had to do was pick them.

Just as it was getting dark our guide turned up and then we had an
argument because he said that he was only paid to take us to the
frontier, which is in the middle of the mountains. At last by giving
him a thousand pesetas extra, that is about twenty-five pounds, we
induced him to take us another ten kilometres. It was getting dark
when we got to the foot of the mountains, the way was through
hundreds of cork trees and the slope was very steep. Within twenty
minutes we were all panting for breath and Arthur and Crowley-
Milling were in a bad way. We had very little luggage with us and
what we did have was passed from hand to hand. We had left one of
the Poles, Archy [Pietrasiak] behind in Marseilles because when he
had jumped from his plane he had hurt his ankle and the long march
at Tours had made it worse. The way was by now all rock, rock such
as I have never imagined before in my life, huge single rocks sixty
feet high lying loose on the side of the mountain as well as smaller
ones, with not a scrap of vegetation growing except small grey
leafless bushes with innumerable thorns on them.

It was now quite dark and the pace was of necessity slower but it
was still quite severe on most of us. Towards eleven o'clock I was
taken ill with violent cramp in my stomach, in addition I found a lot
of difficulty in breathing. All at once I collapsed and everything
went black. At first my place had been at the end of the column but
for some reason I had slipped up one, otherwise I should have been
left behind. Four times I collapsed, getting weaker and weaker
because each time I had to be sick before my breath would come
again. Then it started to rain and in ten minutes we were soaked to
the skin, it simply poured down with the wind driving great gusts

into our faces which stung like so much rice. Towards midnight I felt that I was finished, my breath simply would not come but kept staggering on as best I could. In all we crossed five mountains and my condition was all right in the lower parts, it was on the high parts that it was worse. None of the others were ill but they told me afterwards that they were glad of the rest afforded by my halts. At ten to one we crossed into Spain and the worst of the night's journey lay in front of us. All the time the rain did not let up for a single minute. On the high plateau, covered with coarse short grass we were surprised to find a lot of cows, each one with a bell round its neck, also several bulls. About four o'clock the guide left us and the rain changed to a steady drizzle. We soon saw ahead of us some lights and as they were in the right direction made for them.

At first they looked to be about three miles away but after two hours solid slogging they seemed to be even further away than ever. The ground here was covered with huge rocks and small, incredibly thorny bushes which tore our hands, legs and faces to ribbons. The scratches on my legs were visible four weeks later and two slashes on my right hand were not healed three months later. The ground was more or less flat but cut by innumerable small water courses, each one of which was of course full of water.

By six o'clock we were about all in but still kept plugging away to the south. The lights had disappeared by now and the rain had almost stopped. The mountains seemed to be very close to us still, we could not have been making much progress. Then we found a rough track that led nowhere, then another and still another, losing more and more time and energy. Then we came to another vineyard and knew that houses could not be very far away. Just after dawn, about half past seven, after ploughing through acres of mud and water we saw a building in front of us. It was just a square affair with a door that we could not open but as it got lighter we saw another about fifty yards away. We managed to get a door open and get inside, it was an earth floor and a low rough affair, also someone else had had a fire in one corner of it although there was no chimney hole. In about four minutes I had a fire going using a small book of Shelley and a couple of five franc notes for paper and the few charred sticks of the previous fire. After a quick look round we found several small sticks which kept the fire going until John and I had broken up the door into enough small pieces to put on. For the rest of the day the place was like a nudist camp for not one of us had a dry rag on us. George the Pole had a dry shirt in his bag but all the rest of us had their stuff round the fire, crouching down because all the smoke was collected on the ceiling and it was impossible to stand up without getting half blinded by the smoke. Some of us tried to sleep but it was a hard job on the iron-hard floor. About one o'clock the rain stopped and Wilkinson, having dried his clothes decided to go to the nearest house and find out if we could get any food and what were our chances of getting to Barcelona.

While he was gone I went outside, as naked as the day I was born, to have a look around. The building had obviously once been a water mill but had not been used for some years. It had a huge stone mill pond because these streams flow only for a few days at a time when there is rain or snow on the mountains. The stream was about forty feet wide but not more than four feet deep at any point, the whole bed being of solid rock which was worn to the smoothness of glass. Near to the mill was a garden, in which to my delight were growing tomatoes and peaches, both of them ripe. It did not take me long to get a good few of them and carry some back to the mill for the others.

The beauty of the mountains with the sun on them was striking, enhanced by the clear blue sky and pure white clouds. The Pyrenees at this point are not very high, I think that the highest mountain was not much more than three thousand feet but the very mass of them was a grand sight to anyone who like myself had never seen a mountain before. Then there were hundreds of olive trees with the tiny green olives on them and also huge brakes of canes or bamboos, some of them very tall.

At about two o'clock a man came down to do some fishing and immediately saw us. We could speak no Spanish and he no French but after a bit we managed to tell him our yarn, we were all British airmen who had escaped from a German prison camp at Cologne.[37] He was as excited as a schoolboy and rushed off, to come back later with wine and potatoes and salt. He said that he could get no bread as it was strictly rationed. About six o'clock he came back yet again on his bike and told us to get going as the Civil Guard knew that we were there and were going to arrest us. As this was what we wanted we stayed where we were and just before seven o'clock we saw the first of them and I went out to him. He held his rifle at the ready and called out to me to put up my hands, which I would not do but called out for the others. I then saw that there were six of them and that they had the mill surrounded.

They seemed surprised to find so many of us, that is six, as they had only been told to pinch three of us. They searched us and took away our knives and afterwards marched us down to the village which was about three miles away. It was dark when we got there and John (the big Czech pilot) asked the policeman if we could have a drink and to our surprise they agreed and we all went in and had a quick one. Then they took us to the local police station and searched us again, this time taking our razor blades and all of our money, a matter of 300 pesetas (£7/10/0). Then, to our great surprise they took us to a

---

[37] In international law, evaders (in this case most of the party) who entered neutral territory were supposed to be interned for the duration whilst escapers should be allowed to contact their relevant military attache

café and we had a good meal, rabbit, a sort of salad with stuffed green peppers, bags of bread and as much wine as we could drink. We finished up with as huge a slice of melon as I have ever seen and grapes by galore. Then they took us to a really filthy hole of a place and locked us in for the night. Never, before or since, have I passed a worse night than that one. But I have missed out the best part of this crazy day.

They took us to a dance hall. It was the sort of dive that one sees in cowboy films, a big room with a well supplied bar, a raucous band playing quick staccato music of the tango variety and dozens of onlookers who clapped and sang in time with the music. Some of the girls were real beauties, dark and white skinned with big flashing eyes and wonderful teeth. John wanted to dance but they did refuse him that. No-one seemed to find anything incongruous in seeing us as prisoners drinking like fish, we really did mop up an awful amount of wallop.

Well, then we went to our bedroom, phew it stank awfully, there were only four iron bedsteads with no mattress or blankets and the moment we lay down we were eaten alive by bugs. Now I had never seen a bug before but these were really bad and there were thousands of them. If any one of us slept for more than a couple of hours it would surprise me a lot.

In the morning we were woken by the policeman, had a wash at the pump and then taken to wait for the bus. The place that we were in had had a bit of a bashing in the war and many of the houses were badly battered. The bus was full of people the moment it stopped but people continued to pile into it with the utmost unconcern. We were shepherded up to the top where we sat down holding onto the single rail, about four inches from the roof, which was to stop us from falling onto the road. Some of the roads down which we had to go seemed to be impossible but the driver took it all with the utmost unconcern, taking corners with a clearance of an inch at times. It stopped several times and still more people got on, no-one ever seemed to get off. At one place a man climbed on and then proceeded to haul up basket after basket of fruit. Sardines in a tin had a definite advantage over us in the matter of space because it was not possible to put any olive oil between us.

The villages that we passed through were picturesque in the extreme but pathetically poor, the people were in the same nomenclature. At last we arrived in the town of Figueras and conducted to a small office where we were formally charged with entering the country without passport or papers.

We had arranged names and addresses for the Czech pilot and the Polish fellow. At this and subsequent interviews we used the French language exclusively, even when an interpreter was present who could speak English. From there we were taken to a sort of military headquarters and were put amongst a big crowd of men, many of whom were men who had fought against Franco in the Civil War and had afterwards escaped into France. We were sorted out and after a lot of waiting were shown into a large room, bare of anything at all. We immediately chose a corner to get down into and tried our best to get our two small tins of salmon open. It was John who eventually succeeded, using a safety razor and a shaving brush. Then two fellows were shown in who turned out to be English. Both of them had had their heads shaved and looked pretty awful, which was not surprising when we heard their story.

They had spent a year in the French prison of St Hippolyte and after crossing the mountains, which took them five days, they had been whammed into the jug at Gerona. Well of course they came over to our corner and for the first time I heard some of the news of this now famous prison. It appears that most of the inmates escape at one time or another but that it is not easy to keep escaped.

On the Way Home

The whole of that day we did not get any food and it was only with the utmost difficulty that I was able to get a drop of water, which I had to drink out of a dirty salmon tin. That night, in company with one hundred and twelve others we slept on a stone floor without a thing except what we stood up in. Not one of us had an overcoat and it was damned cold. The next day we were fed pretty well and in the evening had four small loaves given to us which were to last us for three days. They were about one hundred grammes each. Also that day we were questioned several times and we stuck to our story that we had all escaped from the prison camp at Cologne, which we gave as Stalag 17, and made our way as far as Spain without any help from anyone.

I must say that most of the interrogators were very sympathetic to us and congratulated us on a good job well done. Early the next morning, long before dawn, we were taken to the station and put on a train which at length got to Barcelona. This Spanish train was a good example of the others, slow and uncomfortable, stopping for long periods for no reason at all and burning what smelt like a mixture of old Army socks and camel's dung. Incidentally Spanish soldiers do not, in common with many other European soldiers, wear socks.

The scenery for the best part of the way was of rock and still more rock, in fact my impression of Spain as far as Madrid is of nothing but arid rocky country with great ranges of bare mountains. Barcelona seemed to be a pretty enough city in spite of the bashing that it is reported to have had in the Civil war. The train service however was primitive in the extreme and because, as prisoners we did not pay, we had to stand out on the platform. Then we had a long walk and came at last to the prison, which was a good modern type of place, at least from the outside. The gates are very strongly guarded with soldiers with fixed bayonets but as we wanted to go in and not out we were allowed to go in.

Some of the prisoners were busy plastering and painting. We found afterwards that the whole of the work, including altering the place, was done by prisoners without any supervision by officials, in fact we only saw about six officials during our stay there which lasted nearly four days. We were searched again and then our fountain pens and various other articles were taken away and marked with our names and then we were put in the strangers gallery where we found a whole batch of pals of all sorts, Poles, Belgians, French, Dutch and a few British. The cells were about fourteen by ten and perhaps ten feet high and ten men had to get in there somehow. There was a water tap and a lavatory in one corner and a small heavily barred window high up and that was all of the furniture of our home from home.

The food was awful, a sort of horrible watery cabbage soup with small pieces of potato in it. We were also given a hundred gram loaf in the morning and a half a pint of a sort of broth. Prisoners, who numbered seven thousand, many of them serving thirty years sentence, were allowed out in a sort of exercise yard twice a day, one gallery at a time for half an hour. In this yard were several sellers of fruit and other articles, the fruit was reasonably priced but most of the other stuff was exorbitantly priced. We had no money whatever so we had nothing to worry about. The main trouble with Barcelona was that we had no blankets to sleep in and it was damned cold at night. We had to sleep close to each other and cover ourselves with our jackets and hope for the best. During our stay here we were twice given a bath, a cold shower and our clothes sterilised by steam. Now a cold shower is all very well but when one has no towel it is not much of a joke, especially as our clothes came back damp and sticky. And in one hour we were again infested with lice and bugs because the walls of the cell were alive with them.

In the gallery above us were five young men condemned to death for offences committed during the Civil War, they were visited every day by a sister in white clothes, a rather coarse looking woman, not at all the type of woman one would expect to be a nun.

Still on the whole the life in the prison was much more congenial than one would expect under the circumstances, most of the prisoners were a cheerful lot. I was told by one man who was incidentally a fine linguist, that in Spain there were three million men in prison and the majority of the rest of the male population were in some sort of military organisation. Small wonder that Spain is one of the poorest countries in Europe and the standard of living is about the worst.

The prisoners had a fair amount of organised games such as football, basket ball, racing and boxing, any man taking part in any of these receiving double rations, still very poor nourishment. On the second day in this place we all had our hair cut off, right down to the scalp, some of them raised Cain about it but it made no difference. I gave the barber my comb and bottle of hair cream, as it would not be needed for some time. We looked a proper gang of criminals then, I think Arthur looked the worst, while John looked exactly like the photographs of General Ludendorff. On the third day we were taken to another cell which was absolutely alive with bugs, they literally dropped on us from the ceiling. Also we went upstairs to an office four times to have our fingerprints taken but according to Spanish law a representative of the police must be present and the result was that only two of them had their prints actually taken, and they both did their best to muck them up.

Very early on the morning of the fourth day we were marched off and put on a train for Saragossa or as the Spaniards say *Zaragoza.*

On the Way Home

We were handcuffed together with steel chains, one man's left wrist to another's right and the bloody things cut slices out of our skin. On the station we looked round for the British Consul whom we expected to come and see us but it was not until five minutes before the train moved off that he came along. He brought cigarettes and some English illustrated papers and gave Crowley-Milling six hundred pesetas (£15) for the six of us. Now the two lads who had come from Gerona had already drawn money and the intention would seem to be that we had a hundred pesetas each.

Well, it was a very uncomfortable journey and a long one too. Fortunately the guards were quite decent and not only took off our handcuffs but allowed us to buy food from the various stations at which we stopped. All of the passengers knew who we were and at two halts some of the soldiers got off the train and pinched grapes for us from the vines on the side of the tracks. The journey took all day and when at last we reached Zaragoza just after nine o'clock at night we were not sorry. The guards had been changed three times, each set of men handing us over as we reached the limits of the various administrative boundaries. At Zaragoza we had to wait for about half an hour and then a big lorry came from the prison and took us back, tearing along through the beautiful wide streets at a terrific pace. To feel the wind on one's face after so long in a stuffy train was a real pleasure.

It seemed to be a really well laid out city, with fine buildings and plenty of trees along wide streets. The prison also was, like Barcelona, a modern affair and we had hopes of rather better accommodation. In fact the accommodation, if it can be called that, was even worse.

We were kept waiting for about an hour in the entrance hall while a big tough looking bruiser type of fellow searched us, and then taken, one by one into the glass-sided office that seems to be part of the

Spanish prison system. The man who appeared to be in charge was the type that one associates with Spain in her more happy days, a startling good-looking fellow with moustaches and flashing teeth and a quick nervous way of moving very quickly, a proper bloody Wop. We told him in French that we had had no food and he told us that we should have some that evening but we did not put much faith in his word, having by now got somewhat used to Spanish methods. He asked us all the usual questions and one of them is 'What is your religion?' to which most of us answered 'Church of England' which he found very amusing as he thought that we had said 'Churchill' and so to this day there are Spanish records with a strange religion marked down for five fellows.

The prison was a bit of a shock, it is three stories high and every inch of floor space, passages and all, was occupied by men sleeping or trying to sleep. We had to walk on their beds to get up the stairs. Our cell was set aside for us, marked *'Transidos'* which appears to mean that we were not inmates of the prison but only in transit to our destination, the promised land of Miranda.

By this time we had heard so much about Miranda that it had assumed a sort of Paradisial aspect, sort of promised land where all our troubles would be over. We were put into a small cell, ten of us because we had two French gypsies with us now, heaven only knows why. When we had been in the cell about five minutes the guards brought us a pail of water and a big pan of rice. The water was very welcome, in spite of having to drink it out of our plates but the rice was uneatable, hungry as we were. The next day was Sunday and we had therefore to spend an extra day in this place.

Early in the morning a man came round with a heavy iron bar and banged on the four bars of the window to make sure that we had not sawed them through. We could hear him smashing and banging at the bars all along the passages. Much against the advice of the other

On the Way Home

two who had been in Gerona, I climbed up and looked out of the window, they assured me that to do so was to get shot for certain. All of the prisoners seemed to spend the whole of the day in the yard and it seemed as if the main object was to make more noise than the next man, who had the same ambition, the net result being hellish. It was a long day and we slept through most of it, between swapping happy reminiscences and lies. Then early on Monday morning we were taken and put on the train for that last time because this time our destination was Miranda. This time the journey was not long and we got to the station at Miranda soon after four o'clock in the afternoon.[38]

The prison, it is really a concentration camp, is about a mile from the station and we walked along the permanent way to get to it. Our impression of the place was a good one, the entrance was through an ornamental archway and on the right was a very modern swimming pool while the buildings all looked clean and well looked after. The *Commandant* of the place made us laugh by asking if we had 'any revolvers, automatic pistols or grenades' when to have got a safety razor blade as far as this would have been darned clever. At the gate several fellows asked if we were British and on receiving an affirmative lost interest in us. We had a good deal of formalities to go through before we were at last shown to our new home, hut No 23.

As soon as the two Gerona boys got inside they were greeted by the shout "Fucking hell, I know those two cunts" from chaps whom they had known in the Fort St Hippolyte. We were issued with two blankets, a plate and spoon and left to find ourselves a home. There were at the time about thirty Britishers there of whom roughly two thirds were military figures which did not vary a lot during our stay. I got a place next to a civilian whose name was George Merrit and

---

[38] This was Monday 15th of September 1941

with whom I got on reasonably well. There were several others in the same hut, Doolan and Candelier[39] whose nationalities I do not know to this day but they both seemed to have served in the French Army, Mr Marshall, Mr Oakley, both of whom came to Gibraltar later on.

At first it was a relief to get to this place, the weather was very warm during the day but cold at night which can be explained by the fact that the Campo is high up in the mountains and surrounded by them. We soon collected extra blankets and plates but got a shock of an unpleasant nature on the second day when we were drafted into a potato peeling squad which worked seven hours a day. About 30 or 40 men sat in a hut with a long heap of potatoes in front of them and peeled them with a very crude instrument which consisted of a piece of zinc nailed to a short stick. It was heart-breaking work and raised blisters on our hands and in return we were allowed the privilege of buying a sandwich of bread and fish for one peseta (6d). The food was not bad, one could have lived on it but it was very monotonous, a watery sort of potato soup most days, at 12 and 6 and a cup of quite good coffee in the morning. We also got a bread ration of about 125 grammes (about four ounces). Also about twice a week we got fish and once a week a ration of wine, which was of quite good quality. Also every week or so a representative of the Military Attaché in Madrid brought us food and money (50 pesetas, about 24/-) and clothes, and while we were there we had good blankets issued out to us.

There were representatives of every nation there, including a number of Germans who, in spite of the fact that they had no income always seemed to have plenty of money. Among what we called the Consul's rations was tea, sugar and milk, a good deal of tea but not

---

[39] Note in resume: Gilbert Candelier c/o Mrs Collins, 53 Lower Henley Road, Caversham, Reading, Berks

much of the other two, milk in particular often being only one tin for four men for a week. Bully beef and tinned herrings were usually a tin each and two tins of Maconochies and four packets of biscuits completed the ration.

From the first I took on making tea as my job, sometimes over someone else's fire, sometimes making one of my own and often going over and bribing the carpenter to let me use some of his as it was going always. It ran to about two cups each day but the last couple of days we had to drink it 'sans sucre ou lait'.

Each morning we got up at about eight and lined up for a tin of coffee, which surprisingly was real coffee and of good quality and then had to form up for the ceremony of saluting the flag. Everyone had to stand in his company and face the flagstaff and then the band struck up and each man had to raise his right hand in the Fascist salute. Failure to do it meant getting a bashing up in the calabozo [solitary confinement]. Then each man received a small pink ticket with which to get his bread, any of them that worked were called out and lastly any whom they wanted to inoculate. This business of filling us up with needles was a bad one, most of the prisoners got from five to eight in the first month and some of them were really painful. There was only one water tap for two thousand men and the result was an enormous amount of skin disease of all sorts. There was also a lot of venereal disease, especially syphilis but most of the known cases were in a separate place. There were about forty-five to fifty nationalities in the camp, every European nation was represented except Ireland, for some obscure reason these were absent. Most of the Poles and Czechs who wanted to get out put themselves down as Canadians, the number of Canadians was phenomenal. In all there was an average of thirty Britishers all the time I was there, they came in in batches of five or six and went out in tens or so every fortnight. One day we had two lads come in who said that they were British and we found out that they came from the Kings Regiment at Gibraltar and were in fact deserters. Both spoke good Spanish and we found out later that they had served in the Spanish War but not on which side they were. There were a lot of birds who had been in that mucky affair, most of them on the Government's side.

There was a canteen in the grounds at which we could buy many things, all of them dear but not really excessively so. Good Malaga wine could be had for eight pesetas (4/-) a litre, red wine 3ps (1/6) and apples at 2ps a lb., onions the same and tins of fruit, peaches, apricots and pears (3.5 - 4ps = 1/9 - 2/-). There was also tins of tunny fish and octopus and sometimes sardines but not often. We could also get cognac and anisette from various people in the place at about 25ps (12/6) a bottle. Personally I was drunk about every ten days but some of the lads made it twice a week, while others like Arthur and Wilkinson never did get drunk. The cognac was real bad but it did have the desired effect, that is to say it made us forget our troubles and most other things as well.[40]

At first I was put onto potato peeling but soon got myself transferred to 'stones' which was really a variety of jobs, sometimes carrying stones, sometimes sweeping the parade ground, once it was carrying tiles up to the top of the roof, a job at which I excelled but nearly broke my neck at all the same. One day we were taken down to the river for a swim. The river is not a very big one at this time of the year and the bed is full of huge rocks, also all of the sewage from the camp drained into it, which discouraged most of them from going into it. But I had a good swim above the discharge pipe and felt a good deal better for it. It was also possible to have a shower bath

---

[40] Note that in these pre-decimal days the English pound was made up of 240 pennies with 12 pennies to the shilling hence 12/6 was 12 shillings and 6d (pence) - the equivalent of 62.5 new pence

some days, one had to get a little ticket from the doctor for it and almost the only regular visitors were the British and Poles, rarely if ever did we see a Spaniard there although they were the predominating race in view of numbers.

Behind the barracks was a huge pile of wood which we took to make our fires. One day I pinched a big pail and knocked holes in it and made a very good brazier of it. It roared like a furnace and gave out a phenomenal amount of heat. Sometimes five fellows would be working round it at one time and we burned wood as thick as our legs in it. As the weather got colder we had it in the barrack more and more, often burning piles of wood to make a bucket-full of ashes. We made tea and toast, soup and omelettes, boiled eggs and Lord knows what over that stove. There were others but none of comparable size to mine. Another stunt was to heat up litres of wine to go to bed with. Towards the end of my stay we had a gang of interesting people come in, the most interesting being the Newton Brothers who I believe act on the stage under the name of the Bourne Brothers.[41] They were full of stories, dozens of them, some very good. They appear to be tap dancers and acrobatic dancers but I would not swear to their nationalities or even if they are brothers. The amount of stories that we told each other at this place would make half a dozen good novels. The Battles of Belgium and Sedan, Abbeville, Dieppe, Calais, Dunkerque, the Somme and St Valery were fought and re-fought, especially St Valery en Caux because nearly all of us had been in it. We wrote home but no-one ever got any answers so after a time we lost interest.[42] Life was not too bad at

---

[41] The Newton Brothers [Henry & Alfred] were well known on the continent as the *"Boorn Brothers"*, travelling acrobats in a variety troupe (see "SOE in France" (1966) MRD Foot p203 and *"No Banners"* (1955) Jack Thomas) - and notes

[42] Three letters written at weekly intervals to his mother were carefully preserved by her in their original envelopes. The first one was sent about the 18th Sept and

this place, mainly because we all expected to soon be out of it. There were a lot of Germans there, most of them really nice fellows and one day the Gestapo came and asked if any of them would like to be repatriated. Only eight out of a hundred volunteered, so about five days later they took away by armed guard all those who were not Jews. Gardner and Merrit raised a laugh by going up as volunteers and asking to be sent back to England which made the Gestapo boys mad. It was all the guards could do to stop us from stoning the bastards out of the gates.

On Thursday morning [23rd October 1941] I heard for the first time that I was to be released for certain although I had known it for more or less certain for four days, together with Fraser, Wilkinson, Gardner, Williamson, McLaren, John Love and George Brown (Henryk Stachura) and the two Gibraltar boys Handly and Williamson and the little bomber pilot Herbert. We had drawn rations and money on Tuesday and so I sold all of my spare rations to the Germans in 23. Waited all day Saturday but no news came but we did not bother because we did not expect to go before Monday anyway. I was *imaginero*, that is to say night watchman for Saturday night and could not get drunk but promised myself that I would on Sunday night. The two boys who deserted for Gibraltar have adopted one of the camp's several dogs, a splendid young Alsation of about five months and they lift him up to the top staging about five or six times in the night. One of them is a real black sheep but it is hard not to like him because he is so full of life. I have been practising making a distinctive signature much after the style of the few Spaniards who can write and it took about five hundred repetitions to get it more or less uniform.

---

arrived on the 21 Oct but her return letter dated 22 Oct did not reach Burgos until 5 Dec and was returned to her marked 'Gone Away'

On the Way Home

Marshall kept us interested practically all of Friday night by telling of his travels in Europe. It appears that he is a gentleman's servant of some description and although he speaks no language but his own has travelled over most of Europe. He told me of getting stranded at Basle and not knowing a word of French, German or any other useful language and he was walking the platform cursing and blinding in fluent Anglo Saxon when a small ragged boy of fifteen or sixteen came up and asked him in precise English "Excuse me sir, but may I be of assistance to you". This lad, who despite his poverty spoke three languages perfectly was eventually successful in saving Marshall 830 marks in Customs duties. When Marshall asked him if he was hungry he insisted upon going home and changing his suit before he went into a restaurant with him. When he went away he said "I hope sir that, should it happen that I have been of assistance to you that you will utilise my services again should you or your friends do us the honour of visiting Basle again". Then the station master asked him to dinner and introduced him to his wife who was a Sheffield girl. It appears that the SM was a German prisoner of war and while in a prison camp at Sheffield he met this girl and falling in love with her came back again after his repatriation and married her. The story of M then went about how he was with his employer in South of France when the war was on and they stayed on until after the invasion of the Low Countries when his boss died and Marshall was unsuccessful in getting place on what became known as Somerset Maugham's boat and stayed on. He explained that each Englishman drew ten pounds a month from the American Consulate and they lived a good life of frugal but none the less real luxury. They had good hotels at very low prices at first, some of them lived on some of the many luxury yachts that lay off the coast and nearly every one had his own special girl because money was so scarce among the French people. This is understandable because the tourist traffic has always been a very considerable help to the people of the French Riviera. Then after trying hard to get his papers put right enough to get home, and after that trying to get false ones, he came over the mountains and was caught after spending several weeks as the guest of the British Consul in Barcelona. He was told that he would be fined four hundred pesetas, about eight pounds, and released but at the time of speaking he had been in various prisons for ten weeks.

Well I did my night as watchman during which I put down a folded blanket to sit on and when I left it for ten minutes I found the dog which has already been mentioned fast asleep on it. Later on however he woke up for just enough time to eat up my day's bread ration before getting down again.

On Sunday I began systematically to get drunk to such an extent that by *bandero* in the evening I had to be held up to avoid falling down.

On Monday forty-eight pesetas went for the purchase of booze ranging from bad cognac to good Malaga. This is slightly more than a pound in English currency. I borrowed five hundred pesetas from a fellow to be repaid by £7 in England. He sold a good few French francs for pesetas and had nearly two thousand which he hoped to be able to change. Well by Monday night not only myself but nearly all the released men were in a very bad state of intoxication. The two Gibraltar boys who are listed as deserters got to fighting and I got out of bed with a champagne bottle in my hand and offered to put the pair of them to bed. When the *Silencio* sounded, that is to say time at which everyone had to be in bed, we all stood up, faced the tiny Union Jack and sang 'God Save the King'. Our efforts to sing the *'Marseillaise'* were foiled by the arrival of an officer and two sentries who threatened to shoot the first man who sang another note of it so we sang *'Madelon'* instead.

In the morning my head was like nothing on God's earth, but fixed up everything that I could remember, gave the carpenter ten pesetas

and the old cabbo a new bottle of red wine. Then the mattress and
the cupboard were sold for five each and at long last after handing in
plates, spoons and blankets we set off to the gate. John was with us,
that is the Czechoslovakian pilot but Brown the Polish one was not
there. It was not until we were in the ambulance that we learned that
he also was on the list. That meant that with the exception of
Crowley-Milling who was in a hospital in Madrid with typhus, and
the other Polish pilot who is in the Embassy, all of us were together
just as we came from Bethune station.[43]

As soon as we got into the town of Miranda the driver stopped at a
café and bought us each a cup of bad coffee and a raw bacon
sandwich. Then we found we could buy cognac and the driver had a
bad half an hour getting us into the ambulance. He was as bad a
driver as he was a psychologist and we had to tell him that every
single one of us could drive and that it was a matter of complete
indifference as to whether we went to Madrid with him or without
him. He would not go at more than forty kilometres an hour and we
got fed up with him. We got stopped once by Guardia Civile and it
was long after dark when we got to Madrid.

On the way we stopped and had our first civilised meal for many
weeks and again he raised objections because we wanted to buy
extra wine or spirits. The boys razzed me a lot because as we had
half an hour to kill before our dinner was ready I spent it chopping
wood. Then we went on to Madrid, dozing most of the way. It was
just after nine o'clock when we got to the British Embassy and the

---

[43] While the rest of the party went on to Spain, 'Archie' stayed in Marseille and
had his ankle treated by Dr Rodocanichi. He eventually joined another party
which included F/Lt Winskill, Sgt McKee, Dvr Strachan & Pte Clarke and crossed
into Andorra. He was taken to the British Consulate in Barcelona and then on to
Madrid by car where he rejoined the original group.

car had to be driven right into the yard because although we had been released we could have been arrested for being without papers and probably sent back to prison for several weeks while the lethargic Spanish government sorted out the case.

Once inside we were taken and all our clothes taken away from us and we all stepped into a huge bath together under a hot water shower, which was more in the nature of a deluge than a shower. We had the bath of our lives, laughing and shouting like children as we lathered ourselves and let the gloriously hot water course over ourselves. While I was sorting out my lot I discovered that one of the chaps who was in the Embassy already came from Lillers, he knew Auchel, George [Pearson] - everyone and everything. Then we had an enormous meal of M & V and hot tea by galore, and then we asked the Military Attaché's secretary if he would change some of our pesetas for us which he did at the rate of ninety to the pound or rather under half of their price. But we knew we should not be able to get a better price for them and so I changed 450 and McLaren changed 800. Then, tired out and full up we went by car to the Hotel Moro and found that we had another meal laid out ready for us. We were three of us in my room, Fraser, Gardner and myself. I took good care not to get into the same room as Wilkinson. And then we ate our dinner and went to bed between sheets at last. And so our period of discomfort was ended for a bit at least.

We were at the hotel for four days. During which time we nearly ate ourselves to death. The food was good and we had half a litre of wine each for each meal which was more than ample. And most of us spent the time in between meals drinking cognac and Benedictines, Dubonnets and Picons at the bar. The prices of the boozes were awful, practically everything was three pesetas (1/6) but as long as we had any we spent it. I was drunk most of the time.

On the Way Home

One morning we went to the Embassy and had to sign a paper that we would not give any newspaper interviews or write any articles for publication. The same evening we went to a cinema show at the Embassy and before, we had a good many drinks at a sort of private bar that the employees ran.. There was a queer sort of crowd there, the Embassy staff, some of them obviously cultured people and some of them very flashy types, especially some of the girls. One girl particularly struck me as being a good personification of a bright young thing, full of wisecracks, covered with brilliant cosmetics and showing an exorbitant expanse of sheer silk stocking. Still she was pretty good company and certainly gave us a few laughs. Colonel Drummond, the Military Attaché was there, a big man with a good air of fine personality about him. We had a large number of brandy and sodas with big cubes of ice in them. There were a number of fellows staying at the Embassy who had come direct to Madrid or the Consulate at Barcelona without being caught by the Spanish police, hence they had all of their hair left, a point that made us slightly contemptuous of them. There were a good number of Germans at the hotel and we were told not to pick any rows with them because one lot had slung a Jerry through the hotel window and caused a lot of trouble. There was a lovely young woman at the hotel whom we thought was attached to the German Embassy, she was a beauty with creamy skin, very dark hair and a charming smile. John (the Czech pilot) said that she was a Hungarian but she spoke several languages very well but not English as far as we knew. I said to the others "I hope that she is a Gestapo agent and offers to sleep with me to get information".

We had trouble with bread at the hotel and the Embassy sent us each along a big white loaf of it and it caused a bit of a bother with the other guests because they only had the day's rations of about three ounces for three meals. But the other food was good and plentiful and the only flaw being that we had far too many olives and none of us ate them. The page boy amused us a lot, a young fellow of about sixteen with a lot of dark hair like a girl, he spoke a few phrases of English and French and German but hardly understood a word of either language. We used to call him the 'five peseta boy' and say that he was a *'gonga wallah'*. Then we got the news that we would move off the next morning and at a trifle before nine the Embassy bus drew up and we all piled in. It was a tight job as there were a number of men from the Embassy there as well as a Spanish detective, seventeen of us in a bus made for ten. We went up past the hotel to get petrol and when we got back to the entrance Colonel Drummond, the Military Attaché was there and Clarke one of the Embassy boys whom we did not particularly like, had to get off and go back as it had not been possible to get a new pass for him.[44] On the journey we bought drinks by galore and towards the evening the great majority of us were drunk, including myself. One fellow, Strachan, opened the car door to be sick and very nearly fell out while the car was doing just over sixty. Then someone slung my shoes out of the window and after that I remembered nothing else until we reached the hotel at Cordoba, when I woke up in bed with a young Spanish girl asking me if I wanted anything to eat. Well, I had my meal and drank all of the bottle of wine to make sure that I would sleep. We were all up and in the car by seven o'clock but then one of the Air Force fellows found that he had left his watch behind and wasted about twenty minutes looking for it. It was just dawn when we did move off through a strangely beautiful city. About ten miles out the driver remembered that he had left all the spare petrol behind and back we had to go.

---

[44] Pte J T Clarke had escaped from St Hippolyte and then travelled with Strachan from Nimes as far as Madrid. He was kept at the Embassy until 8 Dec due to "some confusion about his name" (WO208 3307-655)

On the Way Home

This petrol business in Spain is awful, the petrol pumps are about fifty miles apart and they are not allowed to sell any to put into cans, which with a high powered car like ours are a necessity. We had a Spanish detective with us who wore a huge coloured metal badge behind the lapel of his jacket. This he flashed at regular intervals and police, soldiers and customs men sprang aside at the mere sight of it. That and the magic words *'El Consuelo Brittanica'* cleared the way a treat. Well at one garage the badge and words had no effect on the petrol pump attendant who was solidly chewing tiger nuts, the law was the law, he would put petrol into our tank but not in the cans. At length we borrowed a long rubber tube, drove twenty yards up the road and siphoned twenty odd gallons of spirit into five gallon tins. Then we drove back and solemnly saluted the man *'Buenes tardes senor, el Consuelo Brittanica'* and he filled up the now empty tank.

On both days we stopped at roadside cafes and opened dozens of tins and cut up big two kilo loaves of white bread, a rarity in Spain. There were seventeen of us altogether, a mixed bag which consisted of the driver, who is a Gibaltarian, the Spanish detective, a Polish flying officer, a Polish *'officier éleve'*, one Czechoslovakian sergeant pilot, an English pilot officer, a Belgian flying officer and a Belgian airman and seven British soldiers of all sorts and two sergeant pilots of the RAF.

The Polish flying officer was 'Archie' - Sgt Pilot Adolf Pietrasiak - the Polish officier éleve (cadet) was Henryk Stachura aka 'George Brown', the Czech was Sergeant Pilot Rudolf Ptacek aka 'John Love' and the English pilot was F/Lt Archibald L Winskill. I have no information on the two Belgians but the soldiers were Driver J Strachan, Pte J McLaren, Pte T Williamson, Cpl W F Gardner along with Arthur Fraser and Fred Wilkinson. The two RAF sergeants were Sgt Pilot L M McKee and "the little bomber pilot" Sgt Philip R Herbert.

On the Way Home

Our food consisted of tinned sausages and corned beef, margarine and bread washed down by plenty of quite good wine. How the pair of us got drunk was simple, we were drinking 'Cognac Domeques' in threes, that is to say three good brandies in one glass so that each of us drank roughly thirty or thirty-six glasses of good brandy each. It was a wonder we did not have the DTs let alone a drunk.

The second day was very like the first except that we kept reasonably sober. We stopped at Sevilla for breakfast at the Hotel Ingleterra, and a queer crew we must have been with our ragged clothes and shorn hair and I with no shoes. One thing that struck me as we went along was the number of fires, the Spanish seem to take an almost childish delight in building fires. Well the driver was a good one and bowled along at a good speed, ranging from 60 to 120 kilometres an hour although in actual ground covered we only did about sixty or seventy an hour. About forty odd miles from Gibraltar was passed a huge sea salt recovery farm, miles and miles of pools and huge stacks of dirty white salt. Then we had our last stop and ate all we could of our rations but found that we could only drink four litres of wine between us. Half an hour later, towards three o'clock in the afternoon we caught our first glimpse of the Rock of Gibraltar.

However it took us a very long time to reach it as the roads not only wind round and round and ascend about two thousand feet but also go right round the bay. However we got to La Linea and after waiting about for about an hour in a dirty little office during which we cursed the Spanish and Spain and British Vice Consuls in Spain with gusto. It appeared that the other party from Miranda should have come down with us but that in Spain, owing to the gradients, the scarcity of coal and the locomotives themselves it is not rare for a train to stop for a couple of hours while the crew and any passengers who are so inclined to cut down trees and put them into the furnace. I am assured that this is not a joke but true.

The first soldier we saw was a lance corporal of the Kings Regiment and he had a Tommy gun under his arm. Then, trying to avoid the anti-tank obstacle the driver had his first accident, smashed up the sentry box and broke a man's leg as well as scattering papers all over the road. However a sergeant got us out of the car and took us into a canteen where for about the thirtieth time we had our names and numbers taken again and after that they took us on to what they called the Spanish Pavilion.

At Spanish Pavilion we were given cigarettes, a thorough medical examination and afterwards a good feed of hot stew. Afterwards we were issued with blankets, bedding, razor, towels, gas mask and cape, soap and then battle dress and ammo boots as well as underclothing. We had become soldiers again at last. Still another ride and we were in Alemeda, a group of huts near the fire station where we made our beds and met the boys who had left Miranda a month before, Kett, Sarda[45], Brown, Doullen and one or two more, all of them civilians.

The next morning we found that we could have a hot shower, really bloody hot, and then went down to breakfast. The only drawback to the place is that all the water is sea water, there is no fresh water on the rock, it all has to be brought from Algeciras by sea. The bay was full of ships of all kinds including three capital ships and two aircraft carriers. One of these, if one is to judge from the sailors caps, is the much sunk but still floating *Ark Royal*. Well might Dr Goebells ask "Where is the *Ark Royal*?" anyone in Gib. would tell him for the price of a pint but there is very little that he can do about it.

---

[45] Note in resume: Peter Sarda of Wavre Brabant, Belgium

Diary Gibraltar 1941

Each of the huts has a radio set and we hear the news on the short wave bands. It is not really a set at all but a speaker as it is connected by wires to a master set somewhere and all that it will get is Station Gibraltar. The food is good and the quantity fair but we have all been on short rations for a long time and a little extra would be very welcome. However we have so far drawn two pounds and can buy all sorts of stuff but it is not cheap. The third day that we were here I went up the rock as far as I wanted to climb but did not get anywhere near the top. The whole rock is full of tunnels but I do not believe that we are allowed in them. I saw a big family of rock apes, the last wild monkeys in Europe. The largest weighed about fifty odd pounds and the smallest about two pounds. They are very tame and have no tails. The view from half way up is marvellous, the big rocks of Ceuta in Africa can be seen very plainly.

I have bought most of the odd things that I need, tooth-paste, chocolate, boot polish, paper and ink and a big bottle of Phosphorine tablets. Not that I have a lot wrong with me but I have had a rather a lot of booze lately and it's a habit I don't particularly want to take to England with me and the best way to forget it is to get into really good health. I have been to the pictures several times and went out on one boozing party when I met two Canadians who were billeted in the Thatched House, Broom Close up in Esher which is a terrific coincidence. I have met several people here who know Claygate very well but so far no-one who lives there.

The other night a soldier knocked on our door and said "Does this belong to you?" and two of his mates carried in one of our gang. He was blind drunk but when we took off his boots and put him to bed he just got out again and went to sleep. A quarter of an hour later two more soldiers brought in another one who was also straight out and we did the same with him, when he went quietly like a lamb. Then a trio of Canadian civilians brought us in a third one and he

2

8

8

was not so easy. He kept shouting and yelling and saying "I can speak any fucking language you want, any fucking language you like". I carried him outside to have a piss twice and moved my bed because I was afraid that he was going to be sick. Eventually however we got him quiet and then two more came in under their own power but very pissy all the same. Of such is the Kingdom of Heaven.

Well there is a lot to see here but when it is all seen it is a very small rock and I can quite understand the chaps getting browned off. Have had our first real news of the war for ten weeks: the Germans have not yet taken Leningrad and Moscow although four months ago the road to Moscow was supposed to be open. They also claim to have put out of action between ten and eleven million Russians, which is rather more than the whole of her three fighting services complete. The Americans have launched a new flying boat that is the biggest thing that flies, it carries a bomb load of nearly twenty tons and can fly from New York to Berlin and back with it. They also claim to have a still bigger one already in progress which will carry forty odd tons, which is some weight. On the 7th November we made the biggest raid on Germany ever and lost 37 machines but some of them are supposed to have been wrecked by the really bad weather. Well I'm glad to hear that we really do mean business but 37 planes is one hell of a lot to lose.

Tuesday 11th November This morning we were lugged out of bed by a sergeant who told us that we had to see General Gort in forty minutes. We all rushed round shaving and dolling ourselves up but I made sure that I got my breakfast first. Nothing short of a Field Marshall is going to do me out of my breakfast. We were marched through the town and taken to what I took to be garrison headquarters. We were sent in one by one and had what Franklin Delano Roosevelt would call a fireside chat. Gort is a big man, very heavily built and completely bald. He speaks rather softly and laughs easily. He seemed genuinely pleased that we had got as far as here and also seemed to be very interested in the opinion of the French people of the air raids.

The same afternoon, that is to say Tuesday, I was walking past a four gun 3.1 battery when without the slightest warning at all, all four fired three rounds each. The detonation of these guns close up (I was within thirty yards) is terrific and really painful to ones eardrums. Saw a good boxing match on Wednesday. Have sent two telegrams home but so far have had no reply which bothers me a bit naturally. We expect to go any day now as a convoy is piling up in the bay. I have been to the pictures nearly every day up to now, it only costs about six pence. Have not yet changed my £5 cheque which I got from the Consul.

Saturday 15th November Yesterday the enemy, I don't yet know if it was the Germans or the Italians, sunk the *Ark Royal* about forty miles east of here. She was hit by three torpedoes and sunk while she was being towed in. The escorting destroyers dropped over five hundred depth charges but did not see any sign of the submarine. In spite of the three hits however they say that only one man was killed which is pretty good. The *Ark Royal's* men came into town last night wearing all sorts of weird and wonderful dress. Then about five o'clock three of our lads came in in a state of hilarious intoxication and just to keep the pot boiling three others of us got in as well. We drank seven bottles of Johnny Walker whisky and by seven o'clock I was down on the boards as blind paralytic drunk as I have ever seen anyone. The whole place was a Bedlam until one by one we were laid out and then one by one we arose and created more hell. My last recollection was of laying down to sleep in the lavatory and being rooted out of it by the others whose need was more urgent than mine. A big fellow with a most interesting history then came in, straight out of hospital, carrying a bottle of White Horse. They kicked me awake enough to drink a good deal of it and the next thing I remember is that at three in the morning three of the lads wearing nothing but ammunition boots started off in search of water to drink. The taps being empty they woke up the corporal and a sergeant and then proceeded to pump up the water from the well. As we sleep on the third floor, one of them turned on the tap while the other two took turns at pumping, all three shouting at the top of their voices. As the weary occupants of the barrack turned in to try and sleep a private named Janes insisted that he would render *'J'allendrai'* as a solo from the main landing. Also an indecent amount of perverted instinct appears to have been rife, one fellow being discovered wanking off another one, two more indulging in a little sodomy while another tried to get in bed with a Maritime Ack Ack gunner. What a night it must have been. Oh and when I did wake up someone had pinched my boots again.

Saturday 15th November Spent a couple of hours in a café while the crew of the *Ark Royal* and a few other boats made merry. About half a dozen fights broke out and then one bloke went from table to table smashing glasses with a pint bottle. It took four MPs and five civil police to clear the café in the end and the floor was littered with broken glass. No wonder beer costs 1/10 a pint here.

Sunday 16th November Received my first news from home for over seventeen months, a telegram from Mother I believe [RECEIVED YOUR NEWS ALL WELL HERE ALSO DOREEN HOPE TO SEE YOU SOON ROLLY ALRIGHT LOVE - JANES] anyway it says that all of the family, including Roland are alive and well, also Doreen. Spent a quiet day, haven't had any booze since our big piss up, neither has anyone else as far as I know. But the buggers will sit up half the night playing cards, it was gone 1.30 before they got down last night.

Sunday 23rd November We are still here and getting a little fed up with both each other and ourselves. We find, as do most of the folk here that there is not a lot to do on this rock apart from going to the pictures and getting drunk. And the last occupation is not very popular as the booze is a terrible price and we draw only a pound a week. I have lent most of my £5 out and have only about five bob of it left but as all the people concerned have sent home for money I have hopes of getting some at least of it back in the near future.

Saw some newsreel pictures of the war in Russia yesterday at the Royal Naval Cinema, they were taken by German cameramen and show very realistically what war is really like. I expect that most of the people who see them think that people die nicely and cleanly, with neat bullet holes in them, they do not realise what a man, or woman for that matter, look like when they are killed by a bomb or shell or machine-gun fire, have never seen anyone with the whole of their guts blown to dripping ribbons, their faces ghastly ruins of smashed bone and oozing brains. Well for them the picture will be a revelation of what war is but even then they will not realise the sights that lined roads and fields from Ghent to Abbeville and beyond when German planes roared slowly down on to the congested masses of starving refugees fleeing from their land to the slow misery of begging from people who had nothing, for scraps of bread and water from stagnant ditches. They will not know the mental sufferings of a proud people who believed in their fighting forces when they, believing that the German invader was being held a hundred miles away, awoke one grey June morning to find the market squares full of grey vehicles, grey guns, grey tanks, and the silent grey figures, hideous with grime and mud and steel helmets to whom their land now belonged, to do what they would with it. This they will not know, if - and only if - they work and fight as never they worked and fought before.

Friday 28th November Still in Gib. We are most of us fed up with the place now, there is so very little to do. We have had several more very bad drunks including one night when we were up until 3.00 trying to stop four Scotsmen from, as they picturesquely called it 'kicking the cunt in' and 'bashing the piss out of' another Scotsman because of something that he had said about the French. This business of arguing about the French people and especially the women causes more rows than anything else here, some of the lads here have not the most elementary knowledge of their subject. The unfortunate part of it is that they will be looked upon as experts when they get home and so their half-baked notions will become incontrovertible fact, because 'I was there'.

We have had a bit of a laugh about one of the fellows here, Gardner. At Madrid he gave us several 'straight from the heart' lectures on how beautiful a thing is courtship between a decent man (himself) and a decent girl (his girl) about how much they understood each other and that a formal engagement was not necessary because of the depthless understanding between them. One evening we were discussing French girls and he was leading forth on his girl, the gist of it being that there could be no comparison between an alliance so obviously made in Heaven as his and a loose alliance with a French girl (Gilberte and myself). Just about an hour later a telegram came from his girl announcing her engagement to some other herb. We laughed and he blew up but after a while made the amazing remark "I know very well that her feelings for me are exactly the same now as they have always been, its just that some rotten fucker has, in a mad moment, put her in the family way and has to marry her". It does not seem feasible to him that she prefers someone else and that that is all there is to it.

Monday 1st December Still in Gibraltar but expecting to go in a couple of days. We have all of us got into lazy habits here now, lying in bed until 10.00 while someone else brings up the tea, not shaving until the afternoon and only leaving the flat for meals. I get on with nearly everyone here, which is more than a good few of them do, I am especially all right with the Scotsmen who are a very clanny lot as a rule, one reason being that I am genuinely proud to have served with a Scottish Division, the Fifty First, the only mob to put up a real show in France. We have a queer card here, we call him Big Mac, he was at one time in the Metropolitan Police, got into some sort of trouble and joined the French Foreign Legion. He was fighting in France at the time of its collapse and taken prisoner but managed to escape somehow. He is afraid of getting into trouble when he lands but hopes to get out of it, don't know how though.

Friday 5th December Have got into the habit of serving out the meals for two good reasons, one that I can eat all I want and get tea at almost any time and another that it passes away the time which is beginning to hang on our hands a bit now. Today also I got into a row through wearing a Balmoral hat with battle dress on a Pay Parade, a privilege which belongs exclusively to Highland regiments. There is an immense convoy out in the Bay but although we have had enough and to spare of rumours as to when we shall go, we are still here.

Sunday 7th December America came into the war, declaring war on Japan. Now we <u>are</u> off.

Thursday 11th December Well the Japs have hit hard and often, bombed Hawaii and Guam, bombed the Philippines, attacked Hong Kong, Shanghai and Malaya, had a go at the Singapore district, sunk the *Repulse* and our newest battle cruiser *Prince of Wales* and had a shot at the *Barham*, all in three days. So far neither we nor the Yanks have done a thing. And a good deal of the Yankee fleet has been bombed, bashed and buggered. And the little yellow-faced bastards calmly announce that they can go on with this war for a hundred years. And if we don't wake up a bit they won't have to. Had a letter from Babe full of love and delight at my being alive.

Sunday 21st December Have had no more news from home and have given up hope of getting home for Xmas. Have had a touch of my old trouble, athletes foot, and after trying to cure it myself with Milton I went sick. They sent me by car to the Zymotic hospital where I saw a doctor who took a scraping from my feet and put it under a microscope. To my surprise the Major who saw me made me a hospital patient and a bed patient at that. So all of my gear except toilet stuff and gas mask had to go into the stores and off I went. I was given a white shirt, a blue suit, a cup, plate, bowl, knife, fork and spoon and bedding including sheets, which is a welcome change from blankets. The treatment was simple enough, iodine foot-bath and Whitfields paint but it was very effective.

The ward in the hospital was nice enough and when I came in they were putting up decorations for Xmas. There were a variety of lads in there, boys who had been at Narvik, Dunkirk and Greece, one who was at the sinking of the *Bismarck*, fellows who had been torpedoed, bombed, mined, machine-gunned; and they had a variety of complaints from acne to syphilis. One fellow who was in the BEF recognised one of the fellows and his girl from Locon, which is a coincidence if you like.

Some of them were really bad, one fellow had the whole of one leg a mass of diseased tissue, another had a splinter from a pom-pom shell under his eye but on the whole we were a cheerful enough lot. The beds were good and the food was a lot better than in any other part of the Rock, in fact on the whole we had a really pleasant time, only marred by the thought that we would not be out for Xmas and in my own case, anxiety as to whether the big ship in the harbour would sail without me.

Diary Gibraltar 1941

The three Scotsmen who were with us at Spanish Pavilion have been blind paralytic drunk for the last forty-eight hours, Farrell for instance has had to be carried upstairs three times but as soon as they can walk again they go out and buy whisky and away they go again. Fortunately no-one in authority takes any notice of them.

Heard a good story the other day, when Lord Gort was appointed the Governor of Gibraltar one lad wrote home to his mother 'We shall not be here very long now, our new chief is the great Evacuation Expert, Gort'. And he got six months for it too. I don't consider it a bit fair on Gort because if by the evacuation of Dunkirk he lost a certain amount of face, he also saved three hundred and eighty thousand men who would otherwise now be dead or prisoners.

Tuesday 23rd Still here, feet a good deal better. Have been in bed most of the time. Some of the boys are in a bad way here, it is a hospital for skin diseases and some of the cases are not very pretty. The amount of skin disease here is alarming, due probably to the lack of clean water and to the prevalence of tinned food in the rations.

Friday 26th December Well yesterday was my birthday therefore I am now twenty-four, which is getting on. Probably the biggest item of news yesterday was that the garrison of Hong Kong surrendered to the Japanese; a bloody lousy Xmas present for a good many of the lads and their families. We took Benghazi for the second time and the Russians are advancing steadily.

As far as I can make out it was hell on earth in town yesterday, one big café at least was wrecked and most of the others closed, some of the Canadians tried to break into the WRNS barracks and had to be dispersed with bayonets and batons and generally the whole of the rock went mad.

Diary Gibraltar 1941

We had a very good Xmas dinner, turkey, cauliflower, roast
potatoes, cabbage, apple sauce, Xmas pudding and custard, oranges
and raisins and two bottles of beer each as well as plenty of
cigarettes on the table for those who wanted them. And we were
waited on at table by the officers, which was very nice. There was an
alarming quantity of alcohol brought into the wards and I made my
first acquaintance with *Merry Merry* which appears to be a sort of
thin port laced up with methylated spirit. Most of us were well under
the influence and although there was not a lot of damage done it
surprised me at least. Got a pay-day today but could only get 8/6
which is rather a pity as I've just about enough in credit now. Had a
cablegram from Babe but no news.

With another fellow, who was in the Army Dental Corps, I went on
a tour of the tunnels of which there are miles in Gib. We went along
about a mile of tunnel fitted out as a hospital reception bay and came
to a huge power station in the rock itself. To make a map of Gib,
with its hundreds of different levels and tunnels would defy the
genius of any but a master spy. By the Sunday after Xmas my feet
were about cured and I was sweating that the troopship would sail
before my discharge and asked to be discharged. That same evening
about eleven o'clock a corporal came up from Spanish Pavilion and
called for me and it did not take me long to get my kit sorted out.

The boys had already had their notice and were very despondent
because they had had a lousy Xmas and were most of them
recovering from a booze-up the night before. The next morning I
had to pay 1/6 because someone had pinched my mug and plate
while I was in hospital. Then we were put into a lorry together with
about a hundred Allies of various sorts and taken down to the docks.
There we had to wait for about three hours and each received a huge
sandwich of bully beef. Then we were put onto a ferry boat and
taken out to the ship, a big converted Polish passenger boat of about

18,000 tons named *MS Batory*.[46] We had to wait another two hours alongside her and they reared up a lot of the lads by shouting repeatedly 'Allies first'. At last however we got onto the boat and were shown into a sort of passageway where we were to sleep. Altogether there were 17 ex-POWs, six Maritime AA gunners and eight odds and sods, thirty-one in all. The beds were so close together that it was nearly impossible to get out without waking half the room. We were on the boat for two days before she sailed and when she did clear harbour it was at six in the evening, that is to say broad daylight.

---

[46] SOE agent Peter Churchill had sailed out in *SS Batory* just a few days earlier and he described her as a medium sized liner that had been brought out of Gydnia during the German occupation. She was converted to work as a troopship and armed with Bofors, Oerlikons, Pom-Poms and a four-inch gun at the stern. (Peter Churchill (1952) "Of Their Own Choice" Hodder & Stoughton). In June 1940 she and *Sobieski* had evacuated 4,000 Polish troops and 500 civilians from the Bayonne and St Jean de Luz area of France (Brooks Richards (1996) "Secret Flotillas HMSO p349) and in July she was one of three former liners engaged in secretly transporting Britain's gold reserves to Canada in convoy with the battleship *Revenge* and cruiser *Bonaventure*. (Leland Stowe "How Britain's Wealth Went West" from "Secrets and Stories of the War Vol 1" (1963) Reader's Digest)

At first we did not go very fast and we set a course due west which we kept to for thirty-six hours. The courses after that were so many and so varied that it was impossible to follow them. The second day out I was seasick, not really badly but uncomfortably so, it was alright when I lay down. One of our various duties was feeding the German prisoners, mainly U-Boat men. The food given to these men was better in some cases than our own, the officers had the first class passengers food. I was given the job of NAAFI duties, a very light job as it consisted of about a quarter of an hours carrying every day. The NAAFI man was quite a decent old fellow who had been on the ship since she had been carrying troops, that is to say two years. Well, in short we raised the Holy Ghost for the whole time that we were on the boat. I got very pally with some of the fellows on the anti-aircraft guns and was present at the try-out with the Lewis and Hotchkiss guns when I should have been below decks.

On the morning of Friday [2nd Jan 1942] we sighted land for the first time, the Old Head of Kinsale they said that it was. It was not until twenty hours later however that we saw Scotland, this time it was Ailsa Craig, a huge bare boulder sticking up from an unfriendly looking sea. Arthur told me that it was a bird sanctuary and that it was impossible to land on it most times of the year. About six o'clock at night we went up the Clyde as far as Greenock, a cold bare little place it looked to me and all of the hills around had snow on them. We lay in the middle of the river for all of the night with several other big boats.

The next morning all was bustle and excitement, the Customs officers came on board but did not worry us, which was as well because the seventeen of us had something like thirty thousand cigarettes between us. Then the emigration people turned us out of our room and Tim [Williamson] got drunk and started shouting "You're worth fuck all - the whole fucking bunch of you, Joe Stalin, that's the man we want, Joe Stalin, that's the man we want" and various other far from complimentary things. Still no-one took a lot of notice of him and we got our kit together and waited to get away. All of the boys had to have a medical inspection but I was down at the bottom of the boat and did not know anything about it until it was all over. One of the gunners told me that we had had a torpedo fired at us but that the destroyers had not been able to find out where it was from.

I did not like the sea voyage at all, I don't like the sea and had been very sick for a couple of days. Seasickness is an unpleasant malady and the more one is sick the worse it gets because heaving on an empty stomach is horrible.

Well, about four o'clock that afternoon we got off the boat on to a big tug and were taken to Greenock, only about a quarter of an hours journey. To our surprise there was no Customs search and so all our thousands of cigarettes went ashore without question. We were on a troop-train for London and within half an hour were off. We were five in one carriage and in order to sleep I got up in the luggage rack, but it was not particularly comfortable and I ended up on the floor. At one station the little officer who was in charge of us got out and we had some tea and sandwiches which went down very well. We arrived in London just after half past seven and raised hell on the platform, dancing around and shouting 'We are the last of the B.E.F.'. Little Farrell lost his steel helmet which rolled under the train so I jumped under it and struck matches until I found it. A porter told me I was mad and I answered 'Maybe mate, but it takes a lot to shake us boys'.

From Victoria we went to the Transit Depot at the Great Central Hotel, a lovely place it was too. They found us rooms and then we had a really good slap up breakfast, porridge, mashed potatoes, bacon, bread and marmalade galore, in fact some of us could hardly stagger when we had finished eating it. Then we went back upstairs to wait for dinner. This also was a really good meal and when I had finished I had a lovely hot bath that almost made me glad that I had come back.

We could not be interrogated that day but we filled up huge forms of questions which took about four hours each to finish. Most of the facts, dates, figures etc. came out of my book, this one, so that they must have made queer reading.

That evening we were allowed out and as I went to check out the Regimental Copper pulled me up for not having cleaned the buttons on my overcoat. To my surprise he said "Come in and borrow my cleaning kit" and we sat telling yarns for about an hour and cleaned the buttons between us. Then I went off to the pictures and saw Deanna Durbin in 'It Started with Love' but she was not nearly as good as she used to be. Then back to bed, I did not make any attempt to go home or write to them as I wanted it to be a surprise.

The next morning we were interrogated by a Captain. A very clever man to my way of thinking, there was also a Naval Officer there but he hardly said a word the whole of the time.[47] Then we had to wait for our railway passes and found that we had each to go to different Depots, mine was Canterbury. Just before I got away a high ranking Naval Officer asked me some questions, not all of which I could answer but he seemed quite satisfied with the answers. Then we had all to say goodbye, rather a pity in some cases, I had got to like Tim and Mack [McLaren] and Farrell a great deal, as well as Arthur. Even Wilkinson seemed unhappy at parting, for one thing his wife was ill in hospital so he would not be able to do quite all he had planned to do. And so off we all went down to the Tube station

---

[47] F/Lt Barclay, who was interviewed there on 11th Dec 41 indentified his 'interrogators' as F/Lt Grey, Capt Langley [James Langley of MI9] and Captain Le Brimier ("Fighter Pilot" 177)

where we all went our different ways. Our big adventure was ended finally.

I had to go to the depot that night so there was not much chance of getting home, anyway I did not want to as it would have meant leaving almost immediately. The journey to Canterbury was a long one, full of stops and changes but at last I reached the station. Was lucky enough to fall in with a fellow who was also quartered there so the blackout did not bother me as much as it might have done, the depot is well over a mile from the station. They issued me blankets and mattress for the night and it was a relief to get down to it.

Next morning it was all rush and tear, a visit to the Medical Inspection room to be graded, which was a farce, the MO simply said 'What grade were you before' and I said 'A1' and down it went. Might have been concealing syphilis, tuberculosis and flat feet, he would have known no better. Then a visit to the CO, who was a Major, who asked the usual inane questions that I was beginning to get used to and to which I gave the usual evasive answers. He then gave me fourteen days leave and told the SM to get me off that afternoon. Then a visit to the stores where I drew practically a full kit, including another gas cape, two pairs of long pants, an overcoat and new battle-dress, all of which I had already drawn. The whole lot took up a terrific amount of space and as I intended taking all the 'buckshee' stuff home with me it was a pretty full kit-bag that I had. Then a visit to the Paymaster who gave me £5 and when I said that it was not enough he gave me another £10 to avoid changing his books. And then off for home.

When I got to Waterloo was surprised to learn that the trains no longer ran to Claygate direct but that I had to change at Surbiton. It was nearly ten o'clock when at last Vale Road was reached.

It was with a feeling of unreality that I went into my gate, often in France the same thing has happened in a sort of trance. To my surprise they were not surprised to see me. Mr Finch had told them that I had landed that same day. The Jeep dog had died[48] and in his place was a smaller, although still big, lady dog whose name was Leodride Demoiselle but whom I immediately christened Miss Tails. Dad and I went down to Mr Finch who seemed very pleased to see me and brought out a bottle of Scotch to have a drink all round. Then back home where I learnt that they had had various news of me at different times,[49] that Captain Thomson was in England, and that Babe had been a good girl and was waiting for me to come back to her.

---

[48] Jeep died in his sleep on the night of 1 May 1941

[49] Three letters from France had come via Geneva, one arriving September 1940 and stamped Bethune which read: "My dear mother. I am alive and in very good health. Also very much free. I hope to see you all before very long but can't promise that. Sorry I have no address but that cannot be helped in the circumstances. Please tell Babe I have written and my very best wishes to all at home, especially that black faced Jeep. Can't write more. Love to all of you and plenty for Babe. Yours very sincerely, Peter Scott Janes" and two more in December 1940 plus one letter in his own hand, apparently sent by 'a Frenchman'. They also received news of him from 4969510 Sgt A Barson who left Auchel in November 1940 and wrote to them from his home in Swansea in April 1941

Historic Notes

Peter Scott Janes was tranferred to the Suffolks in February 1942, then to the Beds and Hants Regiment. In the August he moved to the RUR and then in March 1943 to the Royal Inniskillin Rifles where he stayed until his demob in 1946 after serving in Italy.

Rowland Janes married Miss Doris Gibbons on 8 February 1941 and they had three children: my cousins Bob, Barbara and John. Rowland died in 1992.

Donald Harry Janes joined the Royal Signals towards the end of the war and served in the Far East and Australia. He never married. Although he never met them, Donald kept in contact with the Francoise family for many years, the last communication I have is a Christmas card from Yvonne and Albert together with their new address in Rimbert-les-Auchel postmarked 1975.

Gladys Doreen (Babe) Cooper and my father were married at Kingston Registry Office 19 December 1942. My mother passed away in May 1999.

Wynne (Kitten) Eggleton died in hospital after a long illness on 24 October 1944. In a later diary my father described her death as like "throwing acid on a butterfly".

Alex 'Alec' Thomson was badly wounded on the right arm by a shell burst on 8 June towards the end of what became known as the Battle of Aumale. He was evacuated by French troops and embarked on the hospital ship Shropshire from St Nazaire on 14 June 1940. After a long convalescence, Alec joined the Queen's Own Royal West Kent Regiment and commanded 'B' Company on the advance north from Rome to Florence. On 28 July 1944 in an attack against German positions on Monte Scalari, he was again wounded in action. For his *"personal example of gallantry and leadership"* Major T A Thomson was awarded the Military Cross. Alec Thomson died on 4 June 2000.

Historic Notes

John Redfern was also wounded on 8 June, suffering with shrapnel wounds to the leg from a hand grenade. Rescued next morning by men of 12th Chasseurs, he was also evacuated on the hospital ship Shropshire. He met up with Alec Thomson again at Hill End Hospital, St Albans. For his actions in France he was awarded the Military Cross. He later served in Burma. John Redfern (Major) is Branch Secretary of the 2/6 East Surrey St Valery Association.

John Naylor took over command of the Company after Alec Thomson was wounded and led a small group of men safely away from the battle, eventually reaching Le Mans before being evacuated back to the UK from St Malo.

6142323 Pte J W Morris was captured at St Valery but on 21 June escaped with two other men from the line of march near Bethune. They "hid up in a Frenchman's house" near Calais for 7 months. Finally heading south, Morris reached Marseille in February 1941 where he was immediately sent to Fort du St Hippolyte prison. On 15 May the Military Medical Commission (which included Dr Georges Rodochanachi) certified him as being unfit for military service by due to "bad eyes" and he was passed for repatriation, reaching the UK on 6 October 41 (WO208 3306-546)

2879108 Pte A F D Harper his cousin **2879107 Pte R Dunbar** and **2879102 Pte Stanley Westland** - all Gordon Highlanders - were captured at St Valery but escaped the line of march together on 22 June near Bethune.

Harper left Auchel on 12 November and made his way to Marseille where he was interned at Fort St Jean. In late February he left Marseille as part of an organised party of 12 servicemen and crossed the Pyrenees only to be arrested in Madrid. He was finally released and sent to Gibraltar on 15 April 41 and reached the UK on 18 May (3303-302)

Historic Notes

Dunbar was denounced by a Polish girl in September 1940 and sent to a prison camp in Stuttgart. He escaped from there in February 1941 and made his way back to Auchel. In April he left the area with a guide who took him to Paris and Montlucon where he was arrested and sent to St Hippolyte. He escaped from there with others and went to Perpignan. From there a party crossed the Pyrenees only for him to be arrested yet again and sent to Figueras and Miranda. He was released for repatriation 14 October and reached the UK 26 October 1941 (3307-581)

Westland left Auchel 19 November and made his way to Perpignan. He crossed the Pyrenees into Spain in early December but was arrested and sent to a series of prison camps before being repatriated back to the UK on 13 July 1941 (3305-429)

1859826 Spr A Cook & **1863093 Spr W G James** were captured at St Valery but escaped the line of march near Lille on 22 June and were sheltered for nine months in the Pas de Calais district. In March 41 they made their way to Marseille where they were arrested and sent to St Hipplyte but later passed for repatriation by the MMB, arriving back in the UK 6 October 1941 (3306-540/541)

812356 Driver R M Rodgers & **777195 Signaller A Rodiguez** both from 23 Field Regiment RA escaped the line of march on 25 June near Carvin. They stayed in Auchel until 25 March 1941 when they left for Marseille. They were interned at St Hippolyte but left next day and crossed the Pyrenees from Banyuls. They were arrested at Rabos and sent to a series of prison camps which ended at Miranda. They were repatriated from there on 28 May and finally reached the UK 13 July 1941 (3304 357/358)

Yvonne Francois was betrayed and arrested by the Germans in 1942. After the war she was reunited with her husband Albert and my parents went out to France to visit them.

Historic Notes

Albert [**George Pearson**] *had made no attempt to escape and was eventually caught by the Germans. His lady friend had been taken ill in hospital and called out for him. When asked by a nurse about him she said he was her English boyfriend. The nurse said nothing but the conversation was overheard by a woman in a neighbouring bed who was the mistress of a German officer. Albert broke down under interrogation, and probably torture, and betrayed many of those who had looked after him. The MacLeods were amongst those arrested.* (Arthur Fraser 1958)

Had a letter from mum, it was a translation of one from France. It appears that the root of the whole trouble with the family was a yellow bastard by the name of **George Pearson**. *If he had gone off at the same time as we did there would never have been any link between the various people involved. Still, the only hope is that a quick victory will soon get my people free although they will have been in over two years now. And shall look forward to meeting George.* (Peter Janes 1 March 1945)

Arthur Fraser was subsequently commissioned into the Seaforth Highlanders and served in West Africa, India and Burma and in his own words "was fortunate to have survived, unlike many of my friends and comrades". In 1946 he returned to France to visit the MacLeods. The following year Hélène visited Arthur in Scotland and they were married that July. Arthur died in March 2004.

Hélène MacLeod is the daughter of a Scottish father and French mother and their home at St Pierre became a temporary refuge for many allied evaders. Being obviously older than Hélène, Arthur stayed at the house as an illegitimate son with Fernande's maiden name of Bossuge, a story that the whole neighbourhood adopted with some amusement. Hélène was arrested along with her parents and sent to prison for a year. She served her sentence in France before returning to work with the Resistance.

Historic Notes

Mackay and Fernande MacLeod were arrested in May 1942 and condemned to death, later commuted to life in prison. Mackay died in Diez-Lahn concentration camp near Frankfurt in July 1944. Fernande spent the rest of the war in prison until liberated by the Americans in May 1945. In 1960 Mackay was posthumously awarded the Médaille Militaire and the Croix de Guerre. Fernande was also awarded the Medaille Militaire and made Chevalier de la Légion D'Honneur.

Gilberte Guilbert married a M Bouquillon and they had three children before her death in 1958. On 1 March 1945 my father wrote in his diary: *"Had a letter from mum ... Gilberte is now married and has a daughter. ... It is a lucky man indeed who has married Gilberte. I hope they are happy."*

Louisa Gournay married Jules Duhem and now lives in a retirement home in Bethune.

Marcelle Domarle (nee Cruppe) now lives in a retirement home at Barlin. She is known as *Tantante* by her niece Marie-Helene Gournay who wrote to me in March 2001 to tell me her aunt well remembered Peter and Fredy (sic) well. It was Marcelle and Marie-Helene who were able to identify the the Gournay family farm at Locon as the site of some of the photographs.

R.54188 Sgt Pilot J G L (Larry) Robillard RCAF was involved in a dogfight with several Messerschmitts that day, shooting down two Me 109s before his own Spitfire exploded. RASC escapers H C D Simmons and J A Mowat also watched the action and both were able to confirm Robillard's kills. They later met up with him and escaped to Barcelona together with F Rowe RASC (3305-528,529 & 535) and fighter pilots H P Duval and D B Crabtree.

We could see the pilot descend by parachute in the fields nearby where he was found by my French friends. Before the Germans

*could locate him he was whisked away in a brewer's truck to a safe
hiding place. ... Shortly afterwards I was invited to meet the
escaped pilot. He was an American [sic] of French extraction
serving with the RAF, Robillard by name. Like other pilots engaged
in operations over the north of France, he had to memorise an
address in Roubaix, which, if shot down, he should endeavour to
reach, and from where he would take instructions. His information
delighted the patriots, for this contact with a genuine organisation
working in liason with the British was what they had searched for
so long. But how tragic it was to turn out, for the agent in Roubaix
was none other than Paul Cole, the traitor who later was
responsible for so many of their deaths.* (Fraser 1958)

Robillard survived the war and I spoke to him on the phone in April
2001 when a chance meeting in London with fellow Canadian
evader Al Day put us in contact.

Auchel in particular and the St Omer area generally was something
of a hotbed of resistance with many escapers and evaders living in
or being routed through that small town. Interviewed 19 March
1941 Private Rankin reported to MI9 that "There is an active
organisation known to Capt Murchie RASC (at Marseille) at St
Omer helping British personnel escape to unoccupied France ...
Agents should be sent with money around farms in and near
Cauchy, Auchy and Auchel." (3302-229)

Drotais Dubois was a coal miner from Burbure and one of Cole's
principle helpers in the Lillers region. Believed to have been
betrayed by Cole, and arrested 9 December 1941, he was executed
30 June 1943 at Dortmund with the Abbé Carpentier and others.

1877989 Sgt Harold 'Paul' Cole (1906-1946) was the
Organisation's man in Lille and his job was to collect escapers and
evaders and bring them down to Marseille. Cole was a petty
criminal and British Army deserter who later became a traitor and

(reputed) double agent. He was confronted by Pat O'Leary, Francois Duprez, Mario Prassinos, Bruce Dowding and Andre Postel-Vinet in the Rodocanachi appartment on 2 November 1941 accused of stealing funds. He escaped from the flat and went first to Paris and then back to Mde Deram's home at La Madeleine where he and Mde Deram were arrested by Cornelius Verloop, a Dutch penetration agent working with the Abwehr, on 6 December. Cole's arrest was witnessed by Roland Lepers who promptly left Lille and made his way down the line to England where he joined the French air force.

Two days later Alfred Lanselle, Pierre Carpentier, Désiré Didry, Bruce Dowding, Maurice Dechaumont and Drotais Dubois were all arrested by the German *Geheime Feldpolitzei* (GFP) and in at least two cases, Cole accompanied them. On 11 December Cole again accompanied GFP men to arrest Vladimir de Fligue and Fernand Holweck in Paris and on 14 December it was the turn of Andre Postal-Vinay. Cole then got away from the Germans for a while and on 10 April 1942 he married Suzanne Warenghem in Paris. However this union did not last long as on 9 June Harold Cole and Suzanne Warenghem are arrested by Louis Triffe of the Vichy police DST in Lyons. They were charged with espionage and brought to trial on 21 July 1942. Cole was sentenced to death but Suzanne was acquitted. She went to Marseille where she gave birth to Alain Patrick in October but despite the best efforts of Dr Rodocanachi, he died in January the following year. In November 1942 Cole was saved from execution when the Germans took over Vichy France and eventually he was recruited by SS Major Hans Keiffer to work for them.

Cole survived the war but in June 1945 he was arrested in Saulgau, Germany by Peter Hope of MI5 and sent to a prison in Paris. He escaped the Paris Detention Barracks in November and was finally shot dead in January 1946 by Paris gendarmes looking for deserters.

I shall never fully understand how, why and when Paul Cole defected to the enemy, but in so far as it concerned my British friends and me, he served us well. (Arthur Fraser 1958)

Roland Hector Lepers, believing he had been betrayed by Cole, was evacuated to England via Gibraltar and later joined the Free French forces. Lepers became a pilot and (I believe) served with the French 342 Squadron. In June 1945 he was called to Paris to identify Cole after his arrest by MI5. His girlfriend and fellow courier, Madeleine Damerment was also sent out down the line. She later joined SOE and was parachuted back into France 29 February 1944 but was arrested on landing in an SD trap and executed at Dachau that September.

78274 Denis Crowley-Milling was a Flight Lieutenant at 610 Squadron and on his second mission of the day, escorting Stirling bombers to Lille, when his Spitfire was shot down on 21 August 1941 south-west of St Omer. Rescued by French civilians he was taken first to Hucqueliers and then to Renty where he stayed with Norbert Fillerin and put in touch with "the Organisation" before being driven to St Omer by Desiré Didry and taking the train to Lille. He stayed either at Madeleine Deram's house or the flat of Jeannine Voglimacci where he first met Ptacek until 1 September (3307-604).

When the rest of the party went on to Gibraltar, Crowley-Milling was in hospital in Madrid with typhus. He was later repatriated via Gibraltar and flown home by Sunderland on 2 Dec 1941. On his return to the UK C-M resumed command of E Flight of 610 Squadron and in September 1942 received his first squadron command flying Typhoons for ground attack. He became Wing Commander the following summer until eyesight problems took him off flying. That autumn he joined the USAAF HQ to co-ordinate fighters with B-17 bombers on their daylight missions. He retired from the RAF in 1975 as Air Marshall Sir Denis Crowley-Milling, KCB,CBE, DSO, DFC and Vice President of the RAF Escaping Society. He was appointed Controller of the RAF Benevolent Fund and also took over the Bader Foundation after Bader's death in 1982. C-M died in 1996 aged 77.

'John Love' was **787437 Sgt Rudolf Ptacek** RAFVR of 222 Czech Squadron RAF, whose Spitfire IIA was shot down during a fighter sweep the evening of 19 August 1941 north-east St Omer by the Me109 of Oberleutnant Johannes Schmid, one of the 'Abbeville boys' of Adolf Galland's JG 26 claiming his 24th victory. Ptacek force-landed wheels up in a field and made a run for it. He was rescued by French civilians and taken to St Omer. From there he went alone to an address he had been given in England, a safehouse shop in Lille, where he stayed until 31 October when a member of "the Organisation" arrived (3307-643).

On 28 March 1942 Sgt Ptacek was flying a Spitfire VB from 602 Squadron on a RODEO fighter sweep over enemy territory when he was reported missing, presumed shot down near Calais. His name is inscribed on Panel 73 of the Runnymeade Memorial.

The address Ptacek was given was No 1 rue de Turenne, La Madeleine, a hairdressing salon owned by Jeannine Voglimacci with a flat over it that was used by Cole as a safehouse. This was the same address that Robillard had when he was shot down 2 July 1941. Squadron Leader EPP Gibbs concluded his September 1941 debrief *"Sgt Phillips, RAF, who gave a lecture at Tangmere in Jun 41 told his audience* [they] *should apply for help to No 1 Rue Tourraine, Lille. I was told in France that this info got across to the Germans who promptly rounded up the inhabitants at this address and took them away."*

Historic Notes

'Archie' was **784763 Sgt Pilot Adolf Pietrasiak** of 308 Squadron RAF. On 19 August 1941 his Spitfire IIB was scheduled for CIRCUS 82 as escort cover for Blenheims attacking Lille. When the bombers failed to make a rendezvous, fighters from 306, 308 and 315 Polish Squadrons went on a SWEEP mission instead and Pietrasiak was shot down by AA fire after claiming a 109F destroyed south of Dunkirk. Rescued by French civilians he was then driven to St Omer by "the Organisation" before being taken by train to Lille where he stayed until 1 September. When the rest of the party went on to Spain, Archie stayed in Marseille and was treated by Dr Rodocanichi. He eventually joined another party and crossed into Andorra. He was taken to the British Consulate in Barcelona and then on to Madrid by car where he rejoined the original group (3307-642)

'Archie' returned to 308 Squadron 10 September 1943 but on 29 November Pilot Officer Pietrasiak DFC, with eight kills to his name, was brought down during operation RAMROD 339 over Dunkirk and ditched in the sea - his body was not recovered. This was just twelve days after his twenty-sixth birthday.

'**George Brown**' was Polish Cadet **Henryk Stachura** who, according to Pietrasiak, had escaped from Germany. Although he had Stachura's home address in his diary my dad seems to have assumed that he was an airman when in fact he was a soldier.

Henryk Stachura survived the war and met up with Arthur Fraser at Dundee in 1946. I have been unable to obtain any more details on Henryk's career since there does not seem to be any record at the PRO of his being debriefed by MI9 and so I cannot get his service number.

The **Abbé Pierre Carpentier** (1912-1943) was a key agent of the Pat O'Leary Line and he prepared identity cards using his own printing press at his home at 13 place du Cimitiere Saint-Gilles. Arrested at his home on 8 December 1941, he was beheaded at

Historic Notes

Dortmund on 30 June 1943 along with four other Pat Line personnel. Today the Place Abbe Pierre Carpentier in front of his church at St Gilles is dedicated to his memory.

Known historically as the Pat O'Leary escape line and founded by Capt Charles Murchie and Sgt A K Clayton, Capt Leslie Wilkins, Capt Ian Garrow, Tom Kenny and others, this was the first organised escape network of its kind. Running from Lille to Marseille and then over the Spanish border. It was taken over by Belgian Army Doctor Albert-Marie Guerisse aka 'Lt Commander Patrick Albert O'Leary RN' after Garrow's arrest in October 1941.

Louis Nouveau (1894-1966) began helping Murchie and Garrow by raising and collecting funds for the Organisation before he and his wife Renée allowed their flat at 28a Quai de Rive Neuve to be used as a safe house. They sheltered more than 150 people in their flat between Herbert's arrival on 13 June 1941 and November 1942 when indications that Louis' name was known to the Germans forced them to leave their beautiful apartment. In January 1943 Louis was betrayed by French double agent Roger le Neveu (as was Pat O'Leary that March) and arrested whilst working as a courier. He was eventually sent to Buchenwald but survived the war and was awarded the George Medal. After Louis' arrest, Renée escaped to Spain in April 1943.

Dr Georges Rodocanachi (1876-1944) was a British born, naturalised Frenchman of Greek descent who allowed his home to be used as a safe house that soon became headquarters of the Pat Line at 21 rue Roux de Brignoles. The Rodocanachis simply could not accept the collapse of France which left the British in such a desperate situation. George, a medical practitioner in Marseille with the Legion of Honneur from WW1, and his wife Fanny, born in Paris to Greek parents, decided that they should now become involved in hiding the remnants of the Dunkirk evacuation and

223

subsequently any allied airmen who were on the run in enemy occupied territory. Georges was arrested on 26 February 1943 and interned in St Pierre prison in Marseille. In January 1944 he was transferred to Buchenwald where he died the following month. Fanny was not arrested, she survived the war and in 1948 she reluctantly accepted an OBE for her and her husband's work whilst Georges was awarded a Certificate of Commendation, the highest recognition for bravery that could be awarded posthumously to a foreign national. Fanny died of cancer at St Mary's Hospital, London in 1959 (Courtesy of their niece Helen Long)

2818481 Pte T Williamson and **2818441 Pte J McLaren**, both Seaforth Highlanders, were captured at St Valery-en-Caux but escaped from the column of march at Renaix. Rescued by French civilians they eventually stayed five months at a house in Tilques, just west of St Omer, along with two other soldiers, Pte Harry Cowan and Pte John Syme. In October Cowan was arrested and Williamson and McLaren were moved to Roubaix where they remained for another month. From there they and Syme joined a guided party of eight Frenchmen to Paris where the group of eleven were greeted with "Toujours le Football" by their contact. From Paris they took the train to Tours and crossed the demarcation line near Loches by boat. Two more trains saw them in Marseille where the three Englishmen were taken first to Donald Caskie's Seamen's Mission at 46 rue de Forbin and then St Hippolyte where they met Gardner (3307-646 & 647) John Syme was later POW in Italy.

5567722 Cpl W F Gardner (2 Wiltshires) was captured at Arras 23 May 1940. He escaped from the column of march in Luxembourg but was recaptured three days later. He escaped again on 30 June from a prison camp at Hirson and spent the next few months in northern France. He was contacted by "the Organisation" in December and at the end of January was driven to Auchel. From there he was driven via Abbeville and Paris to cross the demarcation line at Vierzon. He was arrested in Chateauroux and sent to St Hippolyte at the end of March where he met Williamson and McLaren. They escaped from there in June and walked to Nimes. After making their way to Perpignan they were driven to the Spanish border which they crossed on foot to Figueras. They then walked to Gerona and jumped a goods train to Barcelona. Despite emergency identification cards from the British Consulate they were arrested in Barcelona and sent to an series of prisons which ended at Miranda (3307-648)

T.110158 Dvr J Strachan RASC was captured at St Valery-en-Caux but escaped with Gnr Fryer (660) and L/Bdr Heather (659) from the line of march near Fournes. All three stayed in hiding in and around St Omer until August 1941 when they moved to Lillers. On 22 September, Strachan joined a party that included F/Lt Winskill and Sgt Pilot McKee and travelled to Marseille in much the same way as my father's party. From Marseille they went to Canet Plage and then Ax-les-Thermes before a six day crossing of the Pyrenees and on to Barcelona and Madrid (3307-661) From Canet Plage the party also included 'Archie' (Pietrasiak)

2819021 Pte J Farrell of 2 Seaforth Highlanders was captured at St Valery-sur-Somme on 12 June 1940. Two weeks later, he escaped from the line of march near Renaix with Pte F Butters and Pte I Temperley. He made his own way south, eventually arriving at Marseille in October where he was arrested and interned at Fort St Jean. Farrell was transferred from there to St Hippolyte in January 1941 and in September, at the fourth time of trying, finally escaped with Pte A McRae of the Camerons and went to Gaston Negre's house in Nimes, the address of which they had been given in the camp. Joined next day by Pte Clarke they were guided to Canet-Plage. On the way McRae was arrested (later POW in Italy) whilst

Historic Notes

changing trains at Narbonne. Farrell and Clarke crossed the Pyrenees from Prats de Mollo and arrived at the British Embassy in Barcelona on 18 September from where they were driven to Madrid on 5 October (3307-654)

959970 Sgt Philip Herbert 15 Squadron RAF was second pilot of a Wellington bomber which crashed into the sea south of Malaga after running out of fuel. The surviving crew were picked up by a Vichy French ship some days later and taken to Marseille. Soon after escaping from Fort St Marthe he made contact with "the Organisation" in Marseille. He joined a party which crossed the Pyrenees in a similar way to my dad and got as far as Barcelona before being arrested and eventually sent to Miranda (WO208 3307-629) Herbert was the very first 'guest' at Louis Nouveau's home where he stayed for about a fortnight. Nouveau escorted him to the station and according to Brome (39) it was the newly arrived O'Leary that took him to the border.

The Newton Brothers [Henry & Alfred] were topping the bill with their comedy act at the Casino in St Jean de Luz when war broke out. After sending their family on to Lisbon for repatriation back to Britain the brothers set about establishing a resistance network in south-western France. Eventually they were compelled to escape themselves, making their own way across the Pyrenees only to be arrested by the Spanish authorities and sent to Miranda.

Notes at the back of my father's résumé give their contact address as Ernest Newton and family c/o Thomas Cook & Sons, London. What they did not know at the time and what the brothers only found out when they got to the British Embassy in Madrid that Christmas, was that their whole family - parents, wives and children - had been killed that September when their ship the Avoceta taking them home from Gibraltar was torpedoed in the Atlantic.

Historic Notes

On their return to England the Newton "twins" trained as SOE agents with the code names Hubert and Arthur and parachuted back into France in July 1942 where they operated until their capture in Lyon in April 1943 just as they were about to make their second escape from the country. They were eventually sent to Buchenwald from where they, along with Christopher Burney and Maurice Southgate were the only four surviving British agents in the camp when it was liberated in April 1945. They were each awarded the MBE (Jack Thomas "No Banners", MRD Foot "SOE in France")

Information for the notes on people who worked the Pat Line comes mainly from the literature while information on the airmen and other escaping and evading servicemen comes mostly from the MI9 debriefing reports held at the Public Record Office at Kew in the WO208 series. Additional information on airmen, especially Pietrasiak and Ptacek comes from the RAF Air Historic Branch, Squadron Leader Chris Goss, Jaroslav Popelka in the Czech Republic and the Polish Institute, London.

* * * * *

Historic Notes

Bibliography

Barclay, George (1994) *Fighter Pilot* Crecy (originally 1976 William Kimber)
Brome, Vincent (1957) *The Way Back* Cassell
Churchill, Peter (1952) *Of Their Own Choice* Hodder & Stoughton
Darling, Donald (1975) *Secret Sunday* William Kimber
David, Saul (1994) *Churchill's Sacrifice of the Highland Division* Brassy's
Edgar, Donald *The Day of Reckoning* John Clare Books
Foot MRD (1966) *SOE in France* HMSO
Foot MRD & Langley JM (1979) *MI9 Escape and Evasion 1939-45* Bodley Head
Hargest, James (1945) *Farewell Campo 12* Michael Joseph
Hart, B H Liddel (1970) *History of the Second World War* Cassell & Company
Long, Helen (1985) *Safe Houses are Dangerous* William Kimber
Murphy, Brendan (1987) *Turncoat* Harcourt Brace Jovanovich, Orlando, Fla.
Neave, Airey (1969) *Saturday at MI9* Hodder & Stoughton
Richards, Brooks (1996) *Secret Flotillas* HMSO
Thomas, Jack (1955) *No Banners* W H Allen
Young, Gordon (1959) *In Trust and Treason* Studio Vista

Information also from Arthur Fraser's 1958 personal memoir which was partly reproduced in the *Inverness Courier* of 12 June 1990 and from research by Derek Richardson for his forthcoming book *Detachment W*